ANTHOLOGY
OF
VICTORIAN POETRY

AN
ANTHOLOGY
OF
VICTORIAN POETRY

EDITED BY THE RIGHT HON.
SIR MOUNTSTUART E. GRANT DUFF

Granger Index Reprint Series

BOOKS FOR LIBRARIES PRESS
FREEPORT, NEW YORK

First Published 1902
Reprinted 1970

INTERNATIONAL STANDARD BOOK NUMBER:
0-8369-6200-1

LIBRARY OF CONGRESS CATALOG CARD NUMBER:
72-133070

PRINTED IN THE UNITED STATES OF AMERICA

PREFACE

In the beginning of last May I delivered at the Mansion House, in connection with the University Extension Movement, an address upon Victorian poetry, to which I had from early days given much attention. Presently afterwards it was suggested to me that I should make a Victorian Anthology, and I agreed to do so, in the hope that I might bring together, for the benefit of my readers, a good many old friends, and enable them to form a good many new acquaintances. In forming the earlier portion of the selection, I have been much assisted by a manuscript Anthology made by me for my own use in the early sixties.

I have not the slightest desire to sustain, by the present publication, any critical theory, or to enable my readers to study the general development of poetry during the Victorian Age. There are abundant helps to doing that, as, for instance, the large and very useful book of Mr. Miles, entitled *The Poets of the Century.* My purpose is a far humbler one; I wish to collect a number of Victorian poems, very varied indeed in character, but all of which happen to give me pleasure, because I think the chances are that they will give pleasure to not a few other people who have similar likes and dislikes, though I am perfectly certain that my choice will be in many instances entirely disapproved by those whose likes and dislikes are different. That is inevitable ; but if the ayes to the right exceed the noes to the left sufficiently to give one what we used to call in the House of Commons " a good division," I shall be perfectly satisfied.¹

It was said of the Address out of which this volume arose, that " the personal equation was very much to the front " in it, and the same criticism will be made, with perfect justice, about the collection I am now publishing. I maintain, however, that in such a book as this " the personal equation *ought* to be very much to the front." If the choice of poems is not thoroughly individual, the result will be good for very little.   It is idle to dream of meeting the tastes of readers who belong to a dozen different schools.   The collector must consider himself, and himself alone, to be responsible for what is taken or omitted, save in so far as his selection may be modified by copyright difficulties or other *force majeure*.

I have arranged the authors of whom I have to speak in three classes :—

1. Poets who, born in the eighteenth century, lived on into the reign of Queen Victoria and did work during it.

2. Poets born in 1801 or later, who lived far into the reign of Queen Victoria, or even outlived it, but who are now dead.

3. Poets who wrote during the reign of Queen Victoria and are happily still with us.¹

To each of these classes I have prefixed some brief introductory notes.

I trust that I have succeeded in presenting to the reader a large number of the best poems produced in

¹ Sir Franklin Lushington, who heads this class, died, alas, whilst these sheets were passing through the press.

the age which it is intended to illustrate, but really the production of that age was so large that any one could put together a very respectable second volume of the same size as this, without drawing on the stores of any of the writers from whom I have quoted.

Some editors of Anthologies—Archbishop Trench, for example—have constrained themselves to give only complete poems, not extracts from poems. This self-denying ordinance seems to me unkind alike to the poet and to the reader, for it involves the sacrifice of a great deal that is very valuable. To leave out the extracts which I make from St. Stephen's, for example, because I cannot reprint the whole poem, would surely be absurd.

It remains to express my gratitude to many friends, and to many whom I have not the honour to know personally, for the assistance I have received in a piece of work which has given me much agreeable employment.

Almost every one to whom my publishers or I applied for permission to print some of their poems were kindness and courtesy itself. Only in a very few cases were difficulties made which have prevented my including two or three pieces.

I have great pleasure in thanking the following ladies and gentlemen for permission to print their poems which appear in this volume :—

Lady Currie (Violet Fane), Mrs. Meynell, Mrs. Earl, Miss E. M. P. Hickey, Miss May Probyn.

Messrs. George Meredith, William Watson, E. C. Pember, K.C., Austin Dobson, Algernon Swinburne, Edmund Gosse, A. Johnstone, Aubrey de Vere, C. K. Paul, Herman Merivale, J. W. Courthope, A. Simcox, F. Bourdillon, W. B. Yeats, A. P. Graves, H. Newbolt,

S. Waddington, Rudyard Kipling, Richard Le Gallienne, Stephen Phillips, Arthur E. Legge, Walter W. Greg, Laurence Binyon, Douglas Ainslie, Sir Edwin Arnold, K.C.I.E., C.S.I., Sir Lewis Morris, Sir Alfred Lyall, G.C.I.E., K.C.B., the late Sir Franklin Lushington, the Most Rev. W. Alexander, D.D., Primate of all Ireland, the Right Hon. W. H. Lecky, M.P., the President of Magdalen, Dr. Richard Garnett, C.B., the Rev. Father Ryder, the Earl of Crewe, Sir F. Pollock, Bart.

I am also indebted to the following for permission to use the poems of which they have the control :—

The Countess of Lytton for those of the late Earl of Lytton.

The Marquess of Dufferin for that of the late Lady Dufferin.

Sir Herbert Stephen, Bart., for that of the late J. K. Stephen.

The Hon. and Rev. E. Bowen for that of the late Lord Bowen.

Miss Emily Jolly for that of the late Sydney Dobell.

Mrs. Alice Greathart for that of the late Mrs. Archer Clive.

Miss Laura Monkhouse for that of the late Cosmo Monkhouse.

Mr. Horatio F. Brown for that of the late J. Addington Symonds.

Mr. Lloyd Osbourne for that of the late R. L. Stevenson.

Mr. S. C. Cockerell for those of the late W. Morris.

Mr. Thomas Webster for that of the late Mrs. Augusta Webster.

Mr. B. Dobell for that of the late James Thomson.

Mr. Craik for that of the late Mrs. Craik.

The *Spectator* for a poem by Sir F. Pollock, Bart.

Messrs. Longmans & Co. for those of the late E. E. Bowen.

Messrs. Longmans & Co. for those of the late Cardinal Newman.

Messrs. Longmans & Co. for that of the late Jean Ingelow.

Messrs. Macmillan & Co. for those of the late Professor Shairp.

Messrs. Macmillan & Co. for those of the late A. H. Clough.

Messrs. Macmillan & Co. for those of the late C. Kingsley.

Messrs. Macmillan & Co. for those of the late Christina Rossetti.

Messrs. Macmillan & Co. for that of the late Frederick Myers.

Messrs. Macmillan & Co. for that of the late Hon. Mrs. Norton.

Messrs. Macmillan & Co. for those of Aubrey de Vere.

Messrs. W. Blackwood & Sons for that of Moira O'Neill.

Messrs. Burns & Oates (Ltd.) for those of the late Father Faber.

Messrs. George Allen for that of the late J. Ruskin.

Messrs. Smith & Elder for those of the late Robert Browning.

Messrs. Ellis & Elvey for that of the late D. G. Rossetti.

Mr. John Murray for that of the late Lord Bowen.

Messrs. G. Bell & Sons for that of the late Adelaide Procter.

If I have forgotten any one, I make my apologies *d'avance.*

CONTENTS

PART I

	PAGE
INTRODUCTORY NOTES	3–12

SAMUEL ROGERS—
| The Sasso di Dante . . . . . . | 13 |
| The Night and Day . . . . . . | 13 |

CAROLINA, LADY NAIRNE—
| Would you be Young Again? . . . . . | 15 |

WILLIAM WORDSWORTH—
| The View from Fox How . . . . . | 16 |
| The Pillar of Trajan . . . . . . | 16 |

WALTER SAVAGE LANDOR—
| The Hamadryad . . . . | 19 |
| On his Seventy-fifth Birthday . . . . | 24 |

THOMAS CAMPBELL—
| The Parrot . . . . | 25 |

THE REV. GEORGE CROLY—
| Pericles . . . . | 26 |

JAMES HENRY LEIGH HUNT—
| Captain Sword . . . . | 28 |

THOMAS LOVE PEACOCK—
| Love and Age . . . . | 30 |

xi

THE REV. RICHARD HARRIS BARHAM—

PAGE

As I lay a-thynkynge 32

DEAN MILMAN—

The Nativity 34

THE REV. JOHN KEBLE—

Third Sunday in Advent 36
Twentieth Sunday after Trinity 38
Christmas Day 39
First Sunday after Epiphany 41
Second Sunday after Easter 42
First Sunday after Trinity 45
Second Sunday after Trinity 46
Saint Matthew 49
Twenty-first Sunday after Trinity 51
The Gathering of the Church 53

THE REV. GEORGE CORNISH—

To the Redbreast 54

J. GIBSON LOCKHART—

Lines 55

GEORGE DARLEY—

" It is not Beauty I Demand " 56

THOMAS CARLYLE—

Speech of the Erdgeist in " Faust " . . . 58
To-day 58

THOMAS HOOD—

From " The Haunted House " 59
The Deathbed 60

LORD MACAULAY—

The Armada 61
Naseby 65
The Muster (From the " Lays of Ancient Rome ") . 68
Lines Written in August 1847 70
Epitaph on a Jacobite 73

PART II

PAGE

INTRODUCTORY NOTES 77–100

JOHN HENRY, CARDINAL NEWMAN—
Knowledge 101
Rest 102
From " The Dream of Gerontius " . . . 102

MRS. ARCHER CLIVE—
From " The Queen's Ball " 104

WINTHROP MACKWORTH PRAED—
Verses on seeing the Speaker asleep in his Chair . . 107
The Dying Girl to her Lover 108

L. E. MACLEAN (L. E. L.)—
Felicia Hemans 109

LORD LYTTON—
St. James's Street on a Summer Morning (From the
" New Timon ") 111
Lord John Russell 112
Consequences of the Reformation 113
Sir Robert Walpole 115
Fox 116
Pitt 118
Lord Melbourne 119
O'Connell 120
The Orator 121
The Successful Politician 122

SIR EDMUND HEAD—
Translation from Propertius 123

FRANCIS MAHONY (" FATHER PROUT ")—
The Shandon Bells 127

MRS. BROWNING—
Sleep 129
From A Vision of Poets 131

MRS. BROWNING (*continued*)—

PAGE

A Musical Instrument 131
To L. E. L. on the Death of Felicia Hemans . . 132

E. FITZGERALD—

From the "Rubáiyát of Omar Khayyám" . . . 135

LORD TENNYSON—

Circumstance 137
Morte d'Arthur 137
Love and Duty 145
Ulysses 148
Eve of St. Agnes 150
From "In Memoriam" 152
Oh, that 'twere possible 156
From "Elaine" 159

LADY DUFFERIN—

To my dear Son 161

MRS. NORTON—

From "The Lady of La Garaye" 163

R. M. MILNES (LORD HOUGHTON)—

The Greek at Constantinople 165
On the Death of —— 169
Moments 170

FRANCES ANNE KEMBLE—

Evening 173
Art thou already Weary? 173

HENRY ALFORD—

Lady Mary 174
Filiolæ Dulcissimæ 175

HENRY NUTCOMBE OXENHAM—

"The Earth, with its Bright and Glorious Things" . 178

W. BELL SCOTT—

Below the Old House 180

ALFRED DOMETT—

                                     PAGE

   The Nativity 181

ROBERT BROWNING—

   My Last Duchess 183
   Incident of the French Camp 184
   Home Thoughts from Abroad 186
   " De Gustibus " 187
   Evelyn Hope 188
   A Grammarian's Funeral 190
   " How they brought the good news from Ghent to Aix " 195
   The Lost Leader 197
   Meeting at Night 198
   Parting at Morning 198
   The Bishop orders his Tomb at Saint Praxed's Church . 198
   From " Holy Cross Day " 202
   A Toccata of Galuppi's 204

W. M. THACKERAY—

   From " The Chronicle of the Drum " 208
   At the Church Gate 209

THOMAS DAVIS—

   The Battle-Eve of the Brigade 211

F. W. FABER—

   Preface 212
   Past Friends 212
   Written in Conway Castle 213
   Genoa 213
   To a Lake Party 215
   Therapia 217
   Aged Cities 219
   From " Bamberg " 219
   The Shadow of the Rock 222
   The Flight of the Wild Swans 225

DR. CHARLES MACKAY—

   From " Sisyphus " 227

PRINCIPAL J. C. SHAIRP—

   A Remembrance 229
   The Bush aboon Traquair 237

THE REV. THOMAS WHYTEHEAD—

                                             PAGE

    The Second Day of Creation 239
    To a Spider 241

EMILY BRONTË—

    Remembrance 243

G. SMYTHE (later VISCOUNT STRANGFORD)—

    From " The Aristocracy of France " . . . 245
    From " The Merchants of Old England " . . 247

A. H. CLOUGH—

    Easter Day, Naples, 1849 250
    Claude to Eustace 256
    Come, Poet, Come ! 258
    Quâ Cursum Ventus 259
    Some Future Day 260
    Where lies the Land ? 260
    Say not the Struggle nought Availeth . . . 261
    The Hidden Love 262

J. W. BURGON—

    Petra 264

CHARLES KINGSLEY—

    The Sands of Dee 265
    From " Hypatia " 266
    A Farewell 266

JOHN RUSKIN—

    The Madonna dell' Acqua 267

MENELLA SMEDLEY—

    Bishop Patteson 268

W. E. AYTOUN—

    James IV. at Flodden 269

LOCKER-LAMPSON—

    To my Grandmother 271
    The Rose and the Ring 273

MATTHEW ARNOLD—

	PAGE
The Tomb in the Church of Brou	275
Stanzas in Memory of the Author of "Obermann" .	276
Requiescat	283
Stanzas from the Grand Chartreuse . . .	284
Tristram and Iseult	291
Cadmus and Harmonia	313
Dover Beach	314
A Summer Night	316
Lines Written in Kensington Gardens . . .	319
Memorial Verses	320
The Scholar-Gipsy	323
The Forsaken Merman	331

JOHN O'HAGAN—

The Old Story 336

SYDNEY DOBELL—

The Ballad of Keith of Ravelston 339

W. CORY (formerly JOHNSON)—

From "Callimachus" 341

ADELAIDE PROCTER—

A Lost Chord 342

CANON BRIGHT—

Crowned and Discrowned 344

MRS. CRAIK (née DINAH MARIA MULOCK)—

Four Years 349

MORTIMER COLLINS—

Shirley Chase 350

DANTE GABRIEL ROSSETTI—

The Blessed Damozel 352

ELLEN MARY DOWNING (known as "MARY OF THE NATION")—

The Old Church at Lismore 357

b

CONTENTS

CHRISTINA GEORGINA ROSSETTI—

PAGE

Uphill 360
Too Late 360

JEAN INGELOW—

The High Tide on the Coast of Lincolnshire . . . 363

THE FIRST EARL OF LYTTON—

From " The Wanderer " 369
From " Good-night in the Porch " . . . 369
Aux Italiens 371
From " Lucile " (The Parting before Sebastopol) . . 374

C. S. CALVERLEY—

Shelter 377

A. LINDSAY GORDON—

From " The Sick Stockrider " 378

HON. RODEN NOEL—

Byron's Grave 379

JAMES THOMSON—

E. B. B., 1861 381

WILLIAM MORRIS—

The Eve of Creçy 382
From " The Earthly Paradise " . . . 384
Riding Together 385

LORD DE TABLEY—

At the Council 388
Nuptial Song 391
A Hymn to Aphrodite 392
Misrepresentation 394

CHARLES, LORD BOWEN—

Good-Night, Good-Morning 395

AUGUSTA WEBSTER—

The Brook Rhine 396

CONTENTS

FREDERICK MYERS—
    PAGE

    From " Saint Paul " 397

JOHN ADDINGTON SYMONDS—

    The Jews' Cemetery on the Lido 398

EDWARD BOWEN—

    Forty Years On 399
    Shemuel 400

COSMO MONKHOUSE—

    The Night Express 402

R. L. STEVENSON—

    A Requiem 405

JAMES KENNETH STEPHEN—

    Elegy on De Marsay 406

PART III

INTRODUCTORY NOTES 411–418

SIR FRANKLIN LUSHINGTON—

    The Fleet under Sail, 1854 419
    Alma 421

HENRY LUSHINGTON—

    The Morn of Inkerman 424
    Inkerman 425
    The Road to the Trenches 437
    To the Memory of Pietro d'Alessandro . . . 439

EDWIN ARNOLD—

    From " The Light of Asia " 442
    Adelaide Anne Procter 443
    Berlin—the Sixteenth of March 445

SIR LEWIS MORRIS—

    The Epic of Hades (Aphrodite) 447
    On a Birthday (Lord Aberdare's) 450

E. C. PEMBER, K.C.—

PAGE

Per gl' Occh' almeno non v'è Claùsura 452

AUSTIN DOBSON—

Before Sedan 456
The Ballad of " Beau Brocade " 457
A Fancy from Fontenelle 465
" Good-night, Babette ! " 466
To Lord de Tabley 468
" In After Days ". 469

DR. RICHARD GARNETT—

The Ballad of the Boat 470

WILLIAM ALEXANDER, D.D., Primate of all Ireland—

Oxford and her Chancellor 472
Oxford in 1845 475
Epitaph in Fahan Churchyard 476
Epitaph in the Cathedral of Derry . . . 477
Preface to " The Finding of the Book and other Poems " 477

REV. FATHER RYDER—

On a Photographic Album 479

EDMUND GOSSE—

The Charcoal-Burner 480

MR. JOHNSTONE—

The Gardener's Burial 482

SAMUEL WADDINGTON

Beata Beatrix 484

W. H. LECKY—

On an Old Song 485

GEORGE MEREDITH—

Dirge in Woods 488

AUBREY DE VERE—

Sad is our Youth 489
Le Récit d'une Sœur 489

SIR FREDERICK POLLOCK—

    The Sin of Sir Pertab Singh 491

C. K. PAUL—

    Lines 493

HERMAN MERIVALE—

    From " The White Pilgrim " 494
    From " Old and New Rome " 496

J. W. COURTHOPE—

    The Chancellor's Garden 498

ANONYMOUS—

    A Night in the Mediterranean (1877) . . . 501
    From the *Eton Magazine*, 1848 504

MR. SIMCOX—

    In the Jacquerie 505

SIR A. LYALL—

    Theology *in extremis* 507
    A Night in the Red Sea 511
    Meditations of a Hindu Prince . . . 513
    After the Skirmish 516

MRS. EARL—

    On the Death of Mrs. Holland 518

W. WATSON—

    In Laleham Churchyard 521

T. HERBERT WARREN—

    In Memoriam—Alfred, Lord Tennyson . . . 524

EMILY M. P. HICKEY—

    " Emperor Evermore " 526
    Harebells 527

MRS. MEYNELL—

    The Shepherdess 529

PAGE

MISS MAY PROBYN—

    Christmas Carol 530

VIOLET FANE (LADY CURRIE)—

    Afterward 532

F. BOURDILLON—

    The Night has a Thousand Eyes 533
    Where Runs the River 533

ANONYMOUS—

    Once 534

W. B. YEATS—

    The Stolen Child 536

ALFRED PERCEVAL GRAVES—

    The Wreck of the *Aideen* 538

MOIRA O'NEILL—

    Lookin' Back 540

H. NEWBOLT—

    The *Fighting Téméraire* 541

RUDYARD KIPLING—

    "What Happened" 543
    Mandalay 545

RICHARD LE GALLIENNE—

    To my Wife, Mildred 548

STEPHEN PHILLIPS—

    From "Marpessa" 549
    From "Paolo and Francesca" 550
    From "Herod" 551

ALGERNON CHARLES SWINBURNE—

    From "The Casquettes" 553
    The Garden of Proserpine 556
    The Making of Man 559

THE EARL OF CREWE—

PAGE

"Millet and Zola" 561

ARTHUR E. J. LEGGE—

The Losing Side 563

WALTER WILSON GREG—

On the Tomb of Guidarello Guidarelli at Ravenna . 565

LAURENCE BINYON—

Trafalgar Square 566

DOUGLAS AINSLIE—

Lines Prefixed to "St. John of Damascus" . . . 569

PART I

INTRODUCTORY NOTES

The poetry of the Victorian age has hardly received its due meed of appreciation. This need not surprise us when we consider the achievements of the forty years which immediately preceded it—years to which the genius of Byron, the greatest elemental force since Shakespeare, as he has been truly called, gave an overwhelming advantage. It has nevertheless some merits of its own which are not surpassed by those of any other period. In addition to its greater poets—those whose names are in all men's mouths,—it produced an altogether exceptional number of writers whom it would be ridiculous to describe as " minor poets," unless that phrase is used, as it so seldom is, in its true sense, to designate poets who have given to the world little in point of quantity, although the quality may entitle them to rank with the very greatest.

Distinguished as was the time of which I am speaking by the presence of a large number of poets, it would have been, had it begun even a very few years earlier, much more distinguished. Wordsworth's beautiful lines, written in 1835, are there to remind us how many stars set just before its commencement :—

" *When first descending from the moorlands,*
   I saw the Stream of Yarrow glide
Along a bare and open valley,
   The Ettrick Shepherd was my guide.

When last along its banks I wandered,
   Through groves that had begun to shed
Their golden leaves upon the pathways,
   My steps the Border-minstrel led.

The mighty Minstrel breathes no longer,
   'Mid mouldering ruins low he lies;
And death upon the braes of Yarrow,
   Has closed the Shepherd-poet's eyes.

Nor has the rolling year twice measured,
   From sign to sign, its steadfast course,
Since every mortal power of Coleridge
   Was frozen at its marvellous source;

The rapt one, of the godlike forehead,
   The heaven-eyed creature sleeps in earth:
And Lamb, the frolic and the gentle,
   Has vanished from his lonely hearth.

Like clouds that rake the mountain summits,
   Or waves that own no curbing hand,
How fast has brother followed brother,
   From sunshine to the sunless land.

Yet I, whose lids from infant slumber
   Were earlier raised, remain to hear
A timid voice, that asks in whispers,
   ' Who next will drop and disappear?'

Our haughty life is crowned with darkness,
   Like London with its own black wreath,
On which with thee, O Crabbe! forth looking,
   I gazed from Hampstead's breezy heath.

As if but yesterday departed,
Thou, too, art gone before ; but why,
O'er ripe fruit, seasonably gathered,
Should frail survivors heave a sigh ?

Mourn rather for that holy [1] Spirit,
Sweet as the Spring, as Ocean deep ;
For Her who, ere her summer faded,
Has sunk into a breathless sleep.

No more of old romantic sorrows,
For slaughtered Youth or love-lorn Maid !
With sharper grief is Yarrow smitten,
And Ettrick mourns with her their Poet dead."

If Lord Byron *had attained the sum of years which, as he tells us, the " Psalmist numbered out," he would have been long a subject of Queen Victoria. So would both Keats and Shelley, if they had passed middle life. A good many poets famous in the first part of the century actually did survive the year 1837. Southey died in 1843, Moore in 1852. The lamp in the case of both of these had begun to burn with a very feeble light before the death of William IV.; but we may claim as being alive and active after the accession of the late Queen, a large number of poets whose fame had been won earlier.*

Samuel Rogers (1763–1855), *though he lived through the first eighteen years of the reign of Queen Victoria, was a survival from a remote past; but the great editions of his " Italy " and of his " Poems," which put the seal upon his fame, were only published*

[1] Mrs. Hemans.

in 1830 *and* 1,834 *respectively, and he was an admitted arbiter of poetry no less than of taste as late as the earlier years of the last half-century.   He cannot accordingly be quite left out of the list of Victorian poets.*

LADY NAIRNE (1766–1845), *who will be long famous as the authoress of the "Land o' the Leal," was born before any one else save Rogers, of whose work I have given specimens in this book.   She died on the verge of eighty in* 1845, *and the very beautiful poem which I have quoted under her name was written near the end of her life.*

WILLIAM WORDSWORTH (1770–1850) *had done much of his best work a whole generation before the accession of Queen Victoria.   He survived that event, however, about thirteen years, and it was only after it that he began to receive the general recognition which had been denied to him so long.   In* 1839 *he was made D.C.L.; in* 1843 *he was appointed Poet Laureate, and in* 1844 *Keble dedicated to him his Latin lectures on Poetry.*

I have not thought myself justified in transferring to these pages any of his more important poems. They belong to another period.   The verses which I have quoted from him, in the body of this work, were products of the Victorian age.   They do not compare at all favourably with some of his earlier pieces, but no one should expect the setting sun to equal its meridian splendour.   The years from 1798 *to* 1808 *were Wordsworth's* Anni Mirabiles.

WALTER SAVAGE LANDOR (1775–1864) *came only a little later. I would fain have taken some of his earlier verses, such as those to Ianthe :*

> " *Well I remember how you smiled*
>> *To see me write your name upon*
> *The soft sea sand,—' O ! what a child !*
>> *You think you're writing upon stone !'*
> *I have since written what no tide*
>> *Shall ever wash away, what men*
> *Unborn shall read o'er ocean wide*
> *And find Ianthe's name again.*"

He wrote, however, some things during the reign of Queen Victoria which, although not equal to those, are nevertheless too good to be put on one side. I have chosen accordingly an extract which has the additional advantage of not being much known.

THOMAS CAMPBELL (1774–1844), *one of the most unequal of our poets, sometimes rising very high indeed, but not seldom sinking to or below mediocrity, lived to* 1844, *and published a volume not long before he died, which contains, however, nothing likely to be remembered save the graceful and well-known lines on the Parrot from the Spanish Main, which I have given below. They are strangely unlike his* " Battle of the Baltic," " Hohenlinden," *or* " Ye Mariners of England," *but very good in their own kind nevertheless.*

The Rev. GEORGE CROLY (1780–1860), *a London clergyman, long connected with St. Stephen's, Walbrook, considered by many to be the best of*

Wren's churches, was a very prolific writer, and widely known in his lifetime, though now nearly forgotten. He ought, however, not to be quite left out of a book like this, and I have included in it his fine poem on Pericles.

JAMES HENRY LEIGH HUNT (1784–1859) *lived for more than twenty years into the Victorian age, and evidently cherished at one time the hope of becoming Poet Laureate, for which office, indeed, some of his contemporaries, as, for instance, Lord Macaulay, thought him not unfitted.   Most of his best writing, however, in the latter part of his life, was in prose, and it would be difficult to find in his verse, of that period, anything at all worthy of the man who at an earlier date wrote one of the best sonnets in the language :*

THE NILE

It flows through old hushed Egypt and its sands,
  Like some grave mighty thought threading a dream,
  And times and things, as in that vision, seem
Keeping along it their eternal stands,—
Caves, pillars, pyramids, the shepherd bands
  That roamed through the young world, the glory extreme
  Of high Sesostris, and that southern beam,
The laughing queen that caught the world's great hands.

Then comes a mightier silence, stern and strong,
  As of a world left empty of its throng,
And the void weighs on us ; and then we wake,
  And hear the fruitful stream lapsing along
'Twixt villages, and think how we shall take
Our own calm journey on for human sake.

I have accordingly selected a portion of a poem

written only two years before the reign of Queen Victoria began, and which shows his very considerable power of versification at its best. It would be difficult to find any passage in which sound and sense are more closely knit together than in the description of the passing of the cavalry in that piece.

THOMAS LOVE PEACOCK (1785–1866) *is particularly interesting as forming a link between the poetry of the eighteenth and nineteenth centuries. Long known to his contemporaries as a most able official in the service of the Great Company, the immediate superior of John Stuart Mill, he will chiefly be remembered by his unique series of novels. In these pages I have only room for one specimen of his often quite admirable verse. It is taken from* " Gryll Grange," *which he published when a very old man. I doubt, nevertheless, whether at any period of his long and honoured life he did anything better.*

RICHARD HARRIS BARHAM (1788–1845) *was a London clergyman, the rector of St. Faith's. He is best known by his amusing* " Ingoldsby Legends," *but I have not attempted to place, in this collection, verse of a comic character, though the Victorian era produced a good deal which might well form the subject of a separate work. The piece by which I have commemorated Mr. Barham is in a different tone.*

The next place falls to DEAN MILMAN (1791– 1868), *who having become famous at Oxford by his Newdigate on the Apollo Belvidere, remained for many years faithful to his earliest pursuit.*

Far from unsuccessful as a poet, he deserved to gain, and before his long life ended actually did gain, recognition from the most intelligent men in England as having been the first to let in through his "History of the Jews" and "History of Christianity" some light into the chaos of illusions which was all that this country had to boast of in the way of theology and Biblical criticism till he began to write. He would perhaps have been recognised sooner if the authors of the "Tracts for the Times," belonging to a school diametrically opposed to Milman, had not inaugurated a movement which turned men's thoughts into a new direction, with results partly good and partly evil.

I have made many extracts from the "Christian Year" of the Rev. JOHN KEBLE (1792–1866), *because although that book was published as early as 1827, and some of the poems contained in it were written at a considerably earlier period, it is one of the most thoroughly Victorian of works. Keble's importance outside of Oriel may be said to have begun in 1833 when he preached the Assize Sermon from which Newman dated the commencement of the Oxford Movem nt, but up to 1845 he was only a secondary figure, the larger share of public attention falling to the remarkable man who was lost to the Church of England in that year. From 1845 onwards to his death in 1866, it would be difficult to exaggerate the influence exerted by Keble over a large portion of English society. The "Lyra Innocentium" was published in the reign of Queen Victoria, but it never attained anything like the position of its predecessor, although some persons whose judgment I respect, the late Lord Coleridge for example, considered that the poetry it contains was superior to that of the earlier publication, an opinion with which I have never been able to agree.*

The poem by JOHN GIBSON LOCKHART (1794– 1854) *which I have given was rescued from oblivion by Mrs. Norton, who sent a copy of it to the " Scotsman," where it appeared many years ago. I do not know when it was first published.*

GEORGE DARLEY'S (1795–1846) *beautiful lines imitated so well the diction and sentiment of the seventeenth century as to deceive even so accomplished a critic as the late Professor Palgrave, who assigned them to that period in the first edition of his delightful " Golden Treasury." Mr. Darley wrote, however, a great many other things, among them a song——*

" I've been roaming, I've been roaming "——

which was extremely popular in his own time. Its popularity was more or less revived by its being connected with some of the drawings of Mr. Miles, which became so well known in the seventies.

THOMAS CARLYLE (1795–1881) *wrote but little verse, but the lines cited under his name do no discredit to his powers.*

THOMAS HOOD (1798–1845), *not always most*

praised for his best work, but a very genuine poet as well as a humourist, might very properly have filled more room than he does.

LORD MACAULAY (1800 – 1859), *perhaps too much lauded in his lifetime, and certainly far too hardly criticised later, is now settling into the place, a very high one, which he will henceforward occupy in English literature. The* " Armada," *originally contributed to Knight's short-lived magazine, was made accessible to the general public by being added to the* 1848 *edition of the* "Lays of Ancient Rome," *which appeared first in* 1842. " Naseby," *an early work, became generally known in* 1860, *along with the fine poem which was the result of its author's defeat at Edinburgh in* 1847, *and with the* " Epitaph on a Jacobite," *perhaps the best thing he ever wrote.*

PART I

SAMUEL ROGERS. 1763–1855

THE SASSO DI DANTE

On that ancient seat,
The seat of stone that runs along the wall,
South of the church, east of the belfry-tower,
(Thou canst not miss it) in the sultry time
Would Dante sit conversing, and with those
Who little thought that in his hand he held
The balance and assigned at his good pleasure
To each his place in the invisible world,
To some an upper region, some a lower;
Many a transgressor sent to his account,
Long ere in Florence numbered with the dead.

. . . . . .

THE NIGHT AND DAY

Nor then forget that Chamber of the Dead
Where the gigantic shapes of Night and Day,
Turned into stone, rest everlastingly;
Yet still are breathing, and shed round at noon

A twofold influence—only to be felt—
A light, a darkness, mingling each with each ;
Both and yet neither.   There, from age to age,
Two Ghosts are sitting on their sepulchres.
That is the Duke Lorenzo—mark him well.
He meditates, his head upon his hand.
What from beneath his helm-like bonnet scowls ?
Is it a face, or but an eyeless skull ?
'Tis lost in shade ; yet, like the basilisk,
It fascinates, and is intolerable.

CAROLINA, LADY NAIRNE. 1766–1845

WOULD YOU BE YOUNG AGAIN?

Would you be young again?
    So would not I—
One tear to memory giv'n,
    Onward I'd hie,
Life's dark flood forded o'er,
All but at rest on shore,
Say, would you plunge once more,
    With home so nigh?

If you might, would you now
    Retrace your way?
Wander through thorny wilds,
    Faint and astray?
Night's gloomy watches fled,
Morning all beaming red,
Hope's smiles around us shed,
    Heavenward—away.

Where are they gone, of yore
    My best delight?
Dear and more dear, tho' now
    Hidden from sight.
Where they rejoice to be,
There is the land for me;
Fly, time, fly speedily;
    Come life and light.

WILLIAM WORDSWORTH. 1770–1850

THE VIEW FROM FOX HOW

Wansfell! this Household has a favoured lot,
Living with liberty on thee to gaze,
To watch while Morn first crowns thee with her rays,
Or when along thy breast serenely float
Evening's Angelic clouds.   Yet ne'er a note
Hath sounded (shame upon the Bard!) thy praise
For all that thou, as if from heaven, hast brought
Of glory lavished on our quiet days.
Bountiful son of Earth! when we are gone
From every object dear to mortal sight,
As soon we shall be, may these words attest
How oft, to elevate our spirits, shone
Thy visionary majesties of light,
How in thy pensive glooms our hearts found rest.

THE PILLAR OF TRAJAN

Where towers are crushed, and unforbidden weeds
O'er mutilated arches shed their seeds,
And temples, doomed to milder change, unfold
A new magnificence that vies with old;
Firm in its pristine majesty hath stood
A votive column, spared by fire and flood:—
And, though the passions of man's fretful race
Have never ceased to eddy round its base,
Not injured more by touch of meddling hands
Than a lone obelisk, 'mid Nubian sands,

Or aught in Syrian deserts left to save
From death the memory of the good and brave
Historic figures round the shaft embost
Ascend, with lineaments in air not lost :
Still as he turns, the charmed spectator sees,
Group winding after group with dream-like ease ;
Triumphs in sunbright gratitude displayed,
Or softly stealing into modest shade.
—So, pleased with purple clusters to entwine
Some lofty elm-tree, mounts the daring vine ;
The woodbine so, with spiral grace, and breathes
Wide-spreading odours from her flowery wreaths.
Borne by the Muse from rills in shepherd's ears
Murmuring but one smooth story for all years,
I gladly commune with the mind and heart
Of him who thus survives by classic art,
His actions witness, venerate his mien,
And study Trajan as by Pliny seen ;
Behold how fought the chief whose conquering
    sword
Stretched far as earth might own a single lord ;
In the delight of moral prudence schooled,
How feelingly at home the Sovereign ruled ;
Best of the good—in pagan faith allied
To more than Man, by virtue deified.
Memorial Pillar ! 'mid the wrecks of Time
Preserve thy charge with confidence sublime—
The exultations, pomps, and cares of Rome,
Whence half the breathing world received its doom ;
Things that recoil from language ; that if shown
By after pencil, from the light had flown.
A Pontiff, Trajan *here* the Gods implores,
There greets an Embassy from Indian shores ;
Lo ! he harangues his cohorts—there the storm
Of battle meets him in authentic form !

B

Unharnessed, naked, troops of Moorish horse
Sweep to the charge; more high, the Dacian force,
To hoof and finger mailed;—yet, high or low,
None bleed, and none lie prostrate but the foe;
In every Roman, through all turns of fate,
Is Roman dignity inviolate;
Spirit in him pre-eminent, who guides,
Supports, adorns, and over all presides;
Distinguished only by inherent state
From honoured Instruments that round him wait;
Rise as he may, his grandeur scorns the test
Of outward symbol, nor will deign to rest
On aught by which another is deprest.
—Alas! that one thus disciplined could toil
To enslave whole nations on their native soil;
So emulous of Macedonian fame,
That, when his age was measured with his aim,
He drooped, 'mid else unclouded victories,
And turned his eagles back with deep-drawn sighs;
O weakness of the Great! O folly of the Wise!
Where now the haughty Empire that was spread
With such fond hope? her very speech is dead;
Yet glorious Art the power of Time defies,
And Trajan still, through various enterprise,
Mounts, in this fine illusion, towards the skies:
Still are we present with the imperial Chief,
Nor cease to gaze upon the bold Relief
Till Rome, to silent marble unconfined,
Becomes with all her years a vision of the Mind.

WALTER SAVAGE LANDOR. 1775–1864

THE HAMADRYAD

Rhaicos was born amid the hills wherefrom
Cnidos, the light of Caria, is discern'd,
And small are the white-crested that play near,
And smaller onward are the purple waves.
Thence festal choirs were visible, all crown'd
With rose and myrtle if they were inborn;
If from Pandion sprang they, on the coast
Where stern Athene rais'd her citadel,
Then olive was entwined with violets
Cluster'd in bosses, regular and large;
For various men wore various coronals,
But one was their devotion; 'twas to her
Whose laws all follow, her whose smile withdraws
The sword from Ares, thunderbolt from Zeus,
And whom in his chill caves the mutable
Of mind, Poseidon, the sea-king, reveres,
And whom his brother, stubborn Dis, hath pray'd
To turn in pity the averted cheek
Of her he bore away, with promises,
Nay, with loud oath before dread Styx itself,
To give her daily more and sweeter flowers,
Than he made drop from her on Enna's dell.
Rhaicos was looking from his father's door
At the long trains that hastened to the town
From all the valleys, like bright rivulets
Gurgling with gladness, wave outrunning wave,
And thought it hard he might not also go
And offer up one prayer, and press one hand,
He knew not whose. The father call'd him in,
And said, "Son Rhaicos! those are idle games;

Long enough I have lived to find them so."
And ere he ended, sighed; as old men do
Always, to think how idle such games are.
"I have not yet," thought Rhaicos in his heart,
And wanted proof.

           "Suppose thou go and help
Echion at the hill, to bark yon oak,
And lop its branches off, before we delve
About the trunk and ply the root with axe:
This we may do in winter."

                Rhaicos went;
For thence he could see farther, and see more
Of those who hurried to the city gate.
Echion he found there, with naked arm,
Swart-hair'd, strong-sinew'd, and his eyes intent
Upon the place where first the axe should fall:
He held it upright. "There are bees about,
Or wasps, or hornets," said the cautious eld:
"Look sharp, O Son of Thallinos!" The youth
Inclined his ear, afar and warily,
And caverned in his hand. He heard a buzz
At first, and then the sound grew soft and clear,
And then divided into what seem'd tune,
And there were words upon it, plaintive words.
He turn'd and said, "Echion! do not strike
That tree, it must be hollow; for some god
Speaks from within. Come thyself near." Again
Both turn'd toward it: and behold there sat
Upon the moss below, with her two palms
Pressing it, on each side, a maid in form.
Downcast were her long eyelashes, and pale
Her cheek, but never mountain-ash display'd
Berries of colour like her lips so pure,
Nor were the anemones about her hair
Soft, smooth, and wavering like the face beneath.

"What dost thou here?" Echion, half afraid,
Half angry, cried. She lifted up her eyes,
But nothing spake she. Rhaicos drew one step
Backward, for fear came likewise over him,
But not such fear; he panted, gasp'd, drew in
His breath, and would have turn'd it into words,
But could not into one.
              "O send away
That sad old man!" said she. The old man went
Without a warning from his master's son,
Glad to escape, for sorely he now fear'd,
And the axe shone behind him in their eyes.

Hamad. And would'st thou too shed the most innocent
    Of blood? No vow demands it; no god wills
    The oak to bleed.
Rhaicos. Who art thou? Whence? Why here?
    And whither would'st thou go? Among the robed
    In white or saffron, or the hue that most
    Resembles dawn or the clear sky, is none
    Array'd as thou art. What so beautiful
    As that grey robe which clings about thee close,
    Like moss to stones adhering, leaves to trees,
    Yet lets thy bosom rise and fall in turn,
    As, touch'd by zephyrs, fall and rise the boughs
    Of graceful platane by the river-side?
Hamad. Lovest thou well thy father's house?
Rhaicos.   Indeed
I love it, well I love it, yet would leave
For thine, where'er it be, my father's house,
With all the marks upon the door, that show
My growth at every birthday since the third,
And all the charms, o'erpowering evil eyes,
My mother nail'd for me against my bed,

And the Cydonian bow (which thou shalt see)
Won in my race last Spring from Eutychos.

Hamad. Bethink thee what it is to leave a home
Thou never yet hast left, one night, one day.

Rhaicos. No, 'tis not hard to leave it : 'tis not hard
To leave, O maiden, that paternal home
If there be one on earth whom we may love
First, last, for ever ; one who says that she
Will love for ever too.   To say which word,
Only to say it, surely is enough.
It shows such kindness—if 'twere possible
We at the moment think she would indeed.

Hamad. Who taught thee all this folly at thy age ?

Rhaicos. I have seen lovers and have learnt to love.

Hamad. But wilt thou spare the tree ?

Rhaicos.   My father wants
The bark ; the tree may hold its place awhile.

Hamad. Awhile ? thy father numbers then my days ?

Rhaicos. Are there no others where the moss beneath
Is quite as tufty ?   Who would send thee forth
Or ask thee why thou tarriest ?   Is thy flock
Anywhere near ?

Hamad.   I have no flock : I kill
Nothing that breathes, that stirs, that feels the air,
The sun, the dew.   Why should the beautiful
(And thou art beautiful) disturb the source
Whence springs all beauty.   Hast thou never heard
Of Hamadryads ?

Rhaicos.   Heard of them I have :
Tell me some tale about them.   May I sit
Beside thy feet ?   Art thou not tired ?   The herbs
Are very soft ; I will not come too nigh ;
Do but sit there, nor tremble so, nor doubt.
Stay, stay an instant : let me first explore
If any acorn of last year be left

Within it ; thy thin robe too ill protects
Thy dainty limbs against the harm one small
Acorn may do. Here's none. Another day
Trust me ; till then let me sit opposite.
Hamad. I seat me ; be thou seated, and content.
Rhaicos. O sight for gods ! ye men below ! adore
The Aphroditè. *Is* she there below ?
Or sits she here before me ? as she sate
Before the shepherd on those heights that shade
The Hellespont, and brought his kindred woe.
Hamad. Reverence the higher Powers ; nor deem amiss
Of her who pleads to thee, and would repay—
Ask not how much—but very much. Rise not.
No, Rhaicos, no ! Without the nuptial vow
Love is unholy. Swear to me that none
Of mortal maids shall ever taste thy kiss,
Then take thou mine ; then take it, not before.
Rhaicos. Hearken, all Gods above ! O Aphroditè,
O Herè, let my vow be ratified !
But wilt thou come into my father's house ?
Hamad. Nay : and of mine I cannot give thee part.
Rhaicos. Where is it ?
Hamad. In this oak.
Rhaicos.   Ay ; now begins
The tale of Hamadryad : tell it through.
Hamad. Pray of thy father never to cut down
My tree ; and promise him, as well thou may'st,
That every year he shall receive from me
More honey than will buy him nine fat sheep,
More wax than he will burn to all the Gods.
Why fallest thou upon thy face ? Some thorn
May scratch it, rash young man ! Rise up ; for
shame !
Rhaicos. For shame I cannot rise. O pity me !
I dare not sue for love—but do not hate !

Let me once more behold thee—not once more
But many days : let me love on—unloved !
I aimed too high : on my own head the bolt
Falls back, and pierces to the very brain.
Hamad. Go, rather go—than make me say I love.
Rhaicos. If happiness is immortality
 (And whence enjoy it else the Gods above ?)
 I am immortal too : my vow is heard—
 Hark ! on the left—Nay, turn not from me now,
 I claim my kiss.
Hamad.   Do men take first, then claim ?
 Do thus the seasons run their course with them ?
 Her lips were seal'd ; her head sank on his breast.
 'Tis said that laughs were heard within the wood :
 But who should hear them ? and whose laughs ? and
  why ?

ON HIS SEVENTY-FIFTH BIRTHDAY

I strove with none, for none was worth my strife,
 Nature I loved, and next to Nature, Art ;
I warmed both hands before the fire of life,
 It sinks, and I am ready to depart.

THOMAS CAMPBELL. 1777-1844

THE PARROT

The deep affections of the breast,
   That Heaven to living things imparts,
Are not exclusively possess'd
   By human hearts.

A parrot from the Spanish Main,
   Full young, and early caged, came o'er
With bright wings, to the bleak domain
   Of Mulla's shore.

To spicy groves where he had won
   His plumage of resplendent hue,
His native fruits, and skies and sun,
   He bade Adieu.

For these he changed the smoke of turf,
   A heathery land and misty sky,
And turn'd on rocks and raging surf
   His golden eye.

But petted in our climate cold
   He lived and chatter'd many a day;
Until with age, from green and gold
   His wings grew grey.

At last, when blind and seeming dumb,
   He scolded, laugh'd, and spoke no more,
A Spanish stranger chanced to come
   To Mulla's shore;

He hail'd the bird in Spanish speech,
   The bird in Spanish speech replied,
Flapp'd round his cage with joyous screech,
   Dropt down and died.

THE REV. GEORGE CROLY. 1780–1860

PERICLES

This was the ruler of the land,
  When Athens was the land of fame;
This was the light that led the band,
  When each was like a living flame;
The centre of earth's noblest ring—
  Of more than men the more than king!

Yet not by fetter, nor by spear,
  His sovereignty was held or won:
Feared—but alone as freemen fear,
  Loved—but as freemen love alone,
He waved the sceptre o'er his kind
  By Nature's first great title—Mind!

Resistless words were on his tongue—
  Then eloquence-first flashed below;
Full armed to life the portent sprung—
  Minerva from the Thunderer's brow!
And his the sole, the sacred hand
  That shook her ægis o'er the land.

And throned immortal by his side,
  A woman sits with eye sublime,—
Aspasia, all his spirit's bride;
  But, if their solemn love were crime,
Pity the Beauty and Sage,—
  Their crime was in their darkened age.

He perished, but his wreath was won,—
   He perished in his height of fame;
Then sunk the cloud on Athens' sun,
   Yet still she conquered in his name.
Filled with his soul, she could not die;
   Her conquest was posterity.

JAMES HENRY LEIGH HUNT. 1784–1859

CAPTAIN SWORD

Captain Sword got up one day,
Over the hills to march away,
Over the hills and through the towns,
They heard him coming across the downs,
Stepping in music and thunder sweet,
Which his drums sent before him into the street,
And lo ! 'twas a beautiful sight in the sun ;
For first came his foot, all marching like one,
With tranquil faces, and bristling steel,
And the flag full of honour as though it could feel,
And the officers gentle, the sword that hold
'Gainst the shoulder, heavy with trembling gold,
And the massy tread, that in passing is heard,
Though the drums and the music say never a word.

And then came his horse, a clustering sound,
Of shapely potency forward bound.
Glossy black steeds, and riders tall
Rank after rank, each looking like all ;
'Midst moving repose and a threatening calm,
With mortal sharpness at each right arm,
And hues that painters and ladies love,
And ever the small flag blushed above.

And ever and anon the kettledrums beat,
Hasty power 'midst order meet ;
And ever and anon the drums and fifes
Came like motion's voice, and life's ;
Or into the golden grandeurs fell
Of deeper instruments mingling well,

Burdens of beauty for winds to bear ;
And the cymbals kissed in the shining air,
And the trumpets their visible voices rear'd,
Each looking forth with its tapestried beard,
Bidding the heavens and earth make way
For Captain Sword and his battle array.

He, nevertheless, rode indifferent-eyed,
As if pomp were a toy to his manly pride,
Whilst the ladies loved him the more for his scorn,
And thought him the noblest man ever was born,
And tears came into the bravest eyes,
And hearts swell'd after him double their size,
And all that was weak, and all that was strong,
Seem'd to think wrong's self in him could not be wrong,
Such love, though with bosom about to be gored,
Did sympathy get for brave Captain Sword.

So half that night, as he stopped in the town,
'Twas all one dance going merrily down,
With lights in windows and love in eyes
And a constant feeling of sweet surprise ;
But all the next morning 'twas tears and sighs,
For the sound of his drums grew less and less,
Walking like carelessness off from distress ;
And Captain Sword went whistling gay,
" Over the hills and far away."

THOMAS LOVE PEACOCK. 1785–1866

LOVE AND AGE

I played with you 'mid cowslips blowing,
    When I was six and you were four;
When garlands weaving, flower-balls throwing,
    Were pleasures soon to please no more.
Through groves and meads, o'er grass and heather,
    With little playmates, to and fro
We wandered hand in hand together;
    But that was sixty years ago.

You grew a lovely roseate maiden,
    And still our early love was strong;
Still with no care our days were laden,
    They glided joyously along;
And I did love you, very dearly,
    How dearly words want power to show;
I thought your heart was touched as nearly;
    But that was fifty years ago.

Then other lovers came around you,
    Your beauty grew from year to year,
And many a splendid circle found you
    The centre of its glittering sphere.
I saw you then, first vows forsaking,
    On rank and wealth your hand bestow;
Oh, then I thought my heart was breaking;
    But that was forty years ago.

And I lived on, to wed another:
    No cause she gave me to repine;
And when I heard you were a mother,
    I did not wish the children mine.

My own young flock, in fair progression,
    Made up a pleasant Christmas row;
My joy in them was past expression;
    But that was thirty years ago.

You grew a matron plump and comely,
    You dwelt in fashion's brightest blaze;
My earthly lot was far more homely;
    But I too had my festal days.
No merrier eyes have ever glistened
    Around the hearthstone's wintry glow,
Than when my youngest child was christened:—
    But that was twenty years ago.

Time passed. My eldest girl was married,
    And I am now a grandsire grey;
One pet of four years old I've carried
    Among the wild-flowered meads to play.
In our old fields of childish pleasure,
    Where now, as then, the cowslips blow,
She fills her basket's ample measure,—
    And that is not ten years ago.

But though first love's impassioned blindness
    Has passed away in colder light,
I still have thought of you with kindness,
    And shall do, till our last good-night.
The ever-rolling silent hours
    Will bring a time we shall not know,
When our young days of gathering flowers
    Will be an hundred years ago.

THE REV. RICHARD HARRIS BARHAM.
1788–1845

AS I LAY A-THYNKYNGE

As I lay a-thynkynge, a-thynkynge, a-thynkynge,
Merrie sang the birde as she sat upon the spraye;
   There came a noble knyghte,
   With his hauberke shynynge bryghte,
   And his gallant heart was lyghte,
     Free and gaye:
As I lay a-thynkynge, he rode upon his waye.

As I lay a-thynkynge, a-thynkynge, a-thynkynge,
Sadly sang the birde as she sat upon the tree;
   There seem'd a crimson'd plain,
   Where a gallant knyghte lay slayne,
   And a steed with broken rein
     Ran free,
As I lay a-thynkynge, most pitiful to see.

As I lay a-thynkynge, a-thynkynge, a-thynkynge,
Merrie sang the birde as she sat upon the boughe;
   A lovely mayde came bye,
   And a gentil youth was nyghe,
   And he breathed many a syghe
     And a vowe,
As I lay a-thynkynge, her hearte was gladsome now.

As I lay a-thynkynge, a-thynkynge, a-thynkynge,
Sadly sang the birde as she sat upon the thorne;
   No more a youth was there,
   But a maiden rent her haire,
   And cried in sad despaire,
     "That I was borne!"
As I lay a-thynkynge, she perishèd forlorne.

As I lay a-thynkynge, a-thynkynge, a-thynkynge,
Sweetly sang the birde as she sat upon the briar;
    There came a lovely childe,
    And his face was meek and milde,
    Yet joyously he smiled
        On his sire;
As I lay a-thynkynge, a cherub mote admire.

As I lay a-thynkynge, a-thykynge, a-thynkyge,
Sadly sang the birde as it perched upon a bier;
    That joyous smile was gone,
    And the face was white and wan,
    As the downe upon the swan
        Doth appear;
As I lay a-thynkynge—oh! bitter flowed the tear.

As I lay a-thynkynge, the golden sun was sinking,
O, merrie sang that birde as it glitter'd on her breast;
    With a thousand gorgeous dyes
    While soaring to the skies,
    'Mid the stars she seemed to rise
        As to her nest;
As I lay a-thynkynge, her meaning was exprest:—

      " Follow, follow me away,
      It boots not to delay,"—
      'Twas so she seemed to saye,
        " Here is rest."

DEAN MILMAN. 1791–1868

THE NATIVITY

For Thou wert born of woman! Thou didst come,
O Holiest! to this world of sin and gloom,
Not in Thy dread omnipotent array;
    And not by thunders strew'd
    Was Thy tempestuous road,
Nor indignation burnt before Thee on Thy way;
    But Thee, a soft and naked child,
    Thy mother undefiled,
In the rude manger laid to rest
From off her virgin breast.

The heavens were not commanded to prepare
A gorgeous canopy of golden air,
Nor stoop'd their lamps th' enthroned fires on high:
    A single silent star
    Came wandering from afar,
Gliding unchecked and calm along the liquid sky;
    The Eastern sages leading on
    As at a kingly throne,
To lay their gold and odours sweet
Before Thy infant feet.

The Earth and Ocean were not hush'd to hear
Bright harmony from every starry sphere;
Nor at Thy presence brake the voice of song
    From all the cherub choirs
    And seraphs' burning lyres
Pour'd thro' the host of heaven the charmed clouds along,
    One angel troop the strain began,
    Of all the race of man
    By simple shepherds heard alone,
    That soft Hosanna's tone.

And when Thou didst depart, no car of flame
To bear Thee hence in lambent radiance came;
Nor visible Angels mourn'd with drooping plumes
  Nor didst Thou mount on high
  From fatal Calvary
With all thine own redeem'd out-bursting from their
    tombs.
  For Thou didst bear away from Earth
  But one of human birth,
  The dying felon by Thy side, to be
  In Paradise with Thee.

Nor o'er Thy cross the clouds of vengeance brake;
A little while the conscious earth did shake
At that foul deed by her fierce children done;
  A few dim hours of day
  The world in darkness lay,
Then bask'd in bright repose beneath the cloudless sun
  While Thou didst sleep within the tomb,
  Consenting to Thy doom;
  Ere yet the white-robed Angel shone
  Upon the sealèd stone.

THE REV. JOHN KEBLE.   1792-1866

THIRD SUNDAY IN ADVENT

What went ye out to seè
O'er the rude sandy lea,
Where stately Jordan flows by many a palm,
Or where Gennesaret's wave
Delights the flowers to lave,
That o'er her western slope breathe airs of balm?

All through the summer night
Those blossoms red and bright
Spread their soft breasts, unheeding to the breeze,
Like hermits watching still
Around the sacred hill,
Where erst our Saviour watched ı.pon His knees.

The Paschal moon above
Seems like a Saint to rove,
Left shining in the world with Christ alone;
Below, the lake's still face
Sleeps sweetly in th' embrace
Of mountains terraced high with mossy stone.

Here may we sit, and dream
Over the heavenly theme,
Till to our soul the former days return;
Till on the grassy bed,
Where thousands once He fed,
The world's incarnate Maker we discern.

O cross no more the main,
Wandering so wild and vain,
To count the reeds that tremble in the wind,
On listless dalliance bound
Like children gazing round,
Who on God's works no seal of Godhead find :—

Bask not in courtly bower,
Or sun-bright hall of power,
Pass Babel quick, and seek the holy land—
From robes of Tyrian dye
Turn with undazzled eye
To Bethlehem's glade, or Carmel's haunted strand.

Or choose thee out a cell
In Kedron's storied dell,
Beside the Springs of Love, that never die ;
Among the olives kneel
The chill night blast to feel,
And watch the moon that saw thy Master's agony.

Then rise at dawn of day,
And wind thy thoughtful way,
Where rested once the Temple's stately shade,—
With due feet tracing round
The city's northern bound,
To th' other holy garden, where the Lord was laid.

Who thus alternate see
His death and victory,
Rising and falling as on angel wings
They, while they seem to roam,
Draw daily nearer home—
Their heart untravell'd still adores the King of Kings.

TWENTIETH SUNDAY AFTER TRINITY

Where is thy favour'd haunt, eternal Voice,
    The region of thy choice,
Where, undisturb'd by sin and earth, the soul
    Owns thy entire control?
'Tis on the mountain's summit dark and high,
    When storms are hurrying by:
'Tis 'mid the strong foundations of the eartn,
    Where torrents have their birth.

No sounds of worldly toil ascending there
    Mar the full burst of prayer;
Lone Nature feels that she may freely breathe,
    And round us and beneath
Are heard her sacred tones: the fitful sweep
    Of winds across the steep,
Through wither'd bents—romantic note and clear,
    Meet for a hermit's ear.

The wheeling kite's wild solitary cry,
    And scarcely heard so high,
The dashing waters when the air is still
    From many a torrent rill
That winds unseen beneath the shaggy fell,
    Track'd by the blue mist well:
Such sounds as make deep silence in the heart
    For thought to do her part.

'Tis then we hear the voice of God within,
    Pleading with care and sin:
Child of my love! how have I wearied thee?
    Why wilt thou err from me?
Have I not brought thee from the house of slaves,
    Parted the drowning waves,
And set my saints before thee in the way,
    Lest thou should'st faint or stray?

What? was the promise made to thee alone?
　　Art thou th' excepted one?
An heir of glory without grief or pain?
　　O vision false and vain!
There lies thy cross; beneath it meekly bow;
　　It fits thy stature now;
Who scornful pass it with averted eye,
　　'Twill crush them by-and-by.

Raise thy repining eyes, and take true measure
　　Of thine eternal treasure;
The Father of thy Lord can grudge thee nought,
　　The world for thee was bought;
And as this landscape broad—earth, sea, and sky—
　　All centres in thine eye,
So all God does, if rightly understood,
　　Shall work thy final good.

CHRISTMAS DAY

What sudden blaze of song
　　Spreads o'er the expanse of Heaven?
In waves of light it thrills along
　　Th' angelic signal given—
" Glory to God!" from yonder central fire
Flows out the echoing lay beyond the starry quire;

　　Like circles widening round
　　　　Upon a clear blue river,
　　Orb after orb, the wondrous sound
　　　　Is echoed on for ever:
" Glory to God on high, on earth be peace,
" And love towards men of love—salvation and release."

Yet stay, before you dare
    To join that festal throng;
Listen and mark what gentle air
    First stirr'd the tide of song:
'Tis not, "the Saviour born in David's home
To whom for power and health obedient worlds should
      come."

'Tis not, "the Christ the Lord"—
    With fix'd adoring look
The choir of angels caught the word,
    Nor yet their silence broke:
But when they heard the sign, where Christ should be,
In sudden light they shone and heavenly harmony.

Wrapp'd in His swaddling bands,
    And in His manger laid,
The hope and glory of all lands
    Is come to the world's aid:
No peaceful home upon His cradle smil'd,
Guests rudely went and came, where slept the royal child.

But where Thou dwellest, Lord,
    No other thought should be,
Once duly welcom'd and ador'd,
    How should I part with Thee?
Bethlehem must lose Thee soon, but Thou wilt grace
The single-heart to be Thy sure abiding-place.

Thee, on the bosom laid
    Of a pure virgin mind,
In quiet ever, and in shade,
    Shepherd and sage may find;
They, who have bow'd untaught to Nature's sway,
And they, who follow Truth along her star-pav'd way.

The pastoral spirits first
   Approach Thee, Babe Divine,
For they in lowly thoughts are nurs'd,
   Meet for Thy lowly shrine :
Sooner than they should miss where Thou dost dwell,
Angels from Heaven will stoop to guide them to Thy cell.

Still, as the day comes round
   For Thee to be reveal'd,
By wakeful shepherds Thou art found,
   Abiding in the field.
All through the wintry heaven and chill night air,
In music and in light Thou dawnest on their prayer.

O faint not ye for fear—
   What though your wandering sheep,
Reckless of what they see and hear,
   Lie lost in wilful sleep ?
High Heaven in mercy to your sad annoy
Still greets you with glad tidings of immortal joy.

Think on th' eternal home,
   The Saviour left for you ;
Think on the Lord most holy, come
   To dwell with hearts untrue :
So shall ye tread untir'd His pastoral ways,
And in the darkness sing your carol of high praise.

FIRST SUNDAY AFTER EPIPHANY

Lessons sweet of Spring returning,
   Welcome to the thoughtful heart !
May I call ye sense or learning,
   Instinct pure, or heaven-taught art ?

Be your title what it may,
Sweet the lengthening April day,
While with you the soul is free,
Ranging wild o'er hill and lea.

Soft as Memnon's harp at morning
   To the inward ear devout,
Touch'd by light, with heavenly warning,
   Your transporting chords sing out.
Every leaf in every nook,
Every wave in every brook,
Chanting with a solemn voice,
Minds us of our better choice.

Needs no show of mountain hoary,
   Winding shore or deepening glen,
Where the landscape in its glory
   Teaches truth to wandering men.
Give true hearts but earth and sky,
And some flowers to bloom and die,—
Homely scenes and simple views
Lowly thoughts may best infuse.

SECOND SUNDAY AFTER EASTER

O for a sculptor's hand
That thou might'st take thy stand,
Thy wild hair floating on the eastern breeze,
Thy tranc'd yet open gaze
Fix'd on the desert haze,
As one who deep in heaven some airy pageant sees.

In outline, dim and vast,
Their fearful shadows cast
The giant forms of empires on their way
To ruin : one by one
They tower and they are gone,
Yet in the prophet's soul the dreams of avarice stay.

No sun or star so bright
In all the world of light
That they should draw to heaven his downward eye ;
He hears th' Almighty's word,
He sees the angel's sword,
Yet low upon the earth his heart and treasure lie.

Lo, from yon argent field,
To him and us reveal'd,
One gentle star glides down, on earth to dwell.
Chain'd as they are below
Our eyes may see it glow,
And as it mounts again, may track its brightness well.

To him it glar'd afar
A token of wild war,
The banner of his Lord's victorious wrath ;
But close to us it gleams,
Its soothing lustre streams
Around our home's green walls, and on our churchway path.

We in the tents abide
Which he at distance eyed,
Like goodly cedars by the waters spread,
While seven red altar-fires
Rose up in wavy spires,
Where on the mount he watch'd his sorceries dark and
dread.

He watch'd till morning's ray
On lake and meadow lay,
And willow-shaded streams, that silent sweep
Around the banner'd lines,
Where, by their several signs,
The desert-wearied tribes in sight of Canaan sleep.

He watch'd till knowledge came
Upon his soul like flame,
Not of those magic fires at random caught :
But, true prophetic light
Flash'd o'er him, high and bright,
Flash'd once, and died away, and left his darken'd
thought.

And can he choose but fear,
Who feels his God so near,
That when he fain would curse, his powerless tongue
In blessing only moves ?—
Alas ! the world he loves
Too close around his heart her tangling veil hath
flung.

Sceptre and Star divine,
Who in thine inmost shrine
Hast made us worshippers, O claim thine own ;
More than thy seers we know—
O teach our love to grow
Up to thy heavenly light, and ·reap what thou hast
sown.

FIRST SUNDAY AFTER TRINITY

Where is the land with milk and honey flowing,
   The promise of our God, our fancy's theme?
Here over shatter'd walls dank weeds are growing,
   And blood and fire have run in mingled stream;
      Like oaks and cedars all around
      The giant corses strew the ground,
And haughty Jericho's cloud piercing wall
Lies where it sank at Joshua's trumpet call.

These are not scenes for pastoral dance at even,
   For moonlight rovings in the fragrant glades,
Soft slumbers in the open eye of heaven,
   And all the listless joy of summer shades.
      We in the midst of ruins live,
      Which every hour dread warning give,
Nor may our household vine or fig-tree hide
The broken arches of old Canaan's pride.

Where is the sweet repose of hearts repenting,
   The deep calm sky, the sunshine of the soul,
Now heaven and earth are to our bliss consenting,
   And all the Godhead joins to make us whole?
      The triple crown of mercy now
      Is ready for the suppliant's brow,
By the Almighty Three for ever plann'd
And from behind the cloud held out by Jesus' hand.

" Now, Christians, hold your own—the land before ye
   Is open,—win your way, and take your rest."
So sounds our war-note; but our path of glory
   By many a cloud is darken'd and unblest;

And daily as we downward glide,
Life's ebbing stream on either side
Shows at each turn some mouldering hope or joy,
The Man seems following still the funeral of the Boy.

Open our eyes, thou Sun of life and gladness,
That we may see that glorious world of thine!
It shines for us in vain, while drooping sadness
Enfolds us here like mist: come Power benign,
Touch our chill'd hearts with vernal smile,
Our wintry course do Thou beguile,
Nor by the wayside ruins let us mourn,
Who have th' eternal towers for our appointed bourne.

SECOND SUNDAY AFTER TRINITY

The clouds that wrap the setting sun
When Autumn's softest gleams are ending,
Where all bright hues together run
In sweet confusion blending :—
Why, as we watch their floating wreath,
Seem they the breath of life to breathe?
To fancy's eye their motions prove
They mantle round the sun for love.

When up some woodland dale we catch
The many twinkling smile of ocean,
Or with pleas'd ear bewilder'd watch
His chime of restless motion;
Still as the surging waves retire
They seem to gasp with strong desire
Such signs of love old Ocean gives,
We cannot choose but think he lives.

Would'st thou the life of souls discern?
   Nor human wisdom nor divine
Helps thee by aught beside to learn;
   Love is life's only sign.
The Spring of the regenerate heart,
The pulse, the glow of every part,
Is the true love of Christ our Lord
As man embrac'd, as God ador'd.

But he, whose heart will bound to mark
   The full bright burst of summer morn,
Loves too each little dewy spark
   By leaf or flow'ret worn:
Cheap forms, and common hues, 'tis true,
Through the bright shower-drop meet his view;
The colouring may be of this earth;
The lustre comes of heavenly birth.

Even so, who loves the Lord aright,
   No soul of man can worthless find;
All will be precious in his sight,
   Since Christ on all hath shin'd:
But chiefly Christian souls; for they,
Though worn and soil'd with sinful clay,
Are yet, to eyes that see them true,
All glistening with baptismal dew.

Then marvel not, if such as bask
   In purest light of innocence,
Hope against hope, in love's dear task,
   Spite of all dark offence.
If they who hate the trespass most,
Yet, when all other love is lost,
Love the poor sinner, marvel not;
Christ's mark outwears the rankest blot.

No distance breaks the tie of blood;
   Brothers are brothers evermore;
Nor wrong, nor wrath of deadliest mood,
   That magic may o'erpower;
Oft, ere the common source be known,
The kindred drops will claim their own,
And throbbing pulses silently
Move heart towards heart by sympathy.

So is it with true Christian hearts;
   Their mutual share in Jesus' blood
An everlasting bond imparts
   Of holiest brotherhood:
Oh! might we all our lineage prove,
Give and forgive, do good and love,
By soft endearments in kind strife
Lightening the load of daily life!

There is much need; for not as yet
   Are we in shelter or repose,
The holy house is still beset
   With leaguer of stern foes;
Wild thoughts within, bad men without;
All evil spirits round about,
Are banded in unblest device,
To spoil Love's earthly paradise.

Then draw we nearer day by day,
   Each to his brethren, all to God,
Let the world take us as she may,
   We must not change our road;
Not wondering, though in grief to find
The martyr's foe still keep her mind;
But fix'd to hold Love's banner fast,
And by submission win at last.

SAINT MATTHEW

Ye brethren blest, ye holy maids,
   The nearest heaven on earth,
Who talk with God in shadowy glades,
   Free from rude care and mirth;
To whom some viewless teacher brings
The secret lore of rural things
The moral of each fleeting cloud and gale,
The whispers from above, that haunt the twilight vale.

Say, when in pity ye have gaz'd
   On the wreath'd smoke afar,
That o'er some town, like mist uprais'd,
   Hung hiding sun and star,
Then as ye turn'd your weary eye
To the green earth and open sky
Were ye not fain to doubt how Faith could dwell
Amid that dreary glare, in this world's citadel?

But Love's a flower that will not die
   For lack of leafy screen,
And Christian Hope can cheer the eye
   That ne'er saw vernal green,
Then be ye sure that Love can bless
Even in this crowded loneliness,
Where ever-moving myriads seem to say,
"Go—thou art nought to us, nor we to thee—away!"

There are in this loud stunning tide
   Of human care and crime,
With whom the melodies abide
   Of th' everlasting chime;

D

Who carry music in their heart
Through dusky lane and wrangling mart,
Plying their daily task with busier feet,
Because their secret souls a holy strain repeat.

How sweet to them, in such brief rest
    As thronging cares afford,
In thought to wander, fancy-blest
    To where their gracious Lord,
In vain, to win proud Pharisees,
Spake, and was heard by fell disease—
But not in vain, beside yon breezy lake,
Bade the meek Publican his gainful seat forsake.

At once he rose, and left his gold;
    His treasure and his heart
Transferr'd, where he shall safe behold
    Earth and her idols part:
While he beside his endless store
Shall sit, and floods unceasing pour
Of Christ's true riches o'er all time and space
First angel of his Church, first steward of his Grace.

Nor can ye not delight to think
    Where He vouchsaf'd to eat
How the Most Holy did not shrink
    From touch of sinner's meat;
What worldly hearts and hearts impure
Went with Him through the rich man's door,
That we might learn of Him lost souls to love,
And view His least and worst with hope to meet above.

These gracious lines shed Gospel light
    On Mammon's gloomiest cells
As on some city's cheerless night
    The tide of sunrise swells.

Till tower, and dome, and bridge-way proud
    Are mantled with a golden cloud,
And to wise hearts this certain hope is given ;
"No mist that man may raise, shall hide the eye of
    Heaven."

    And oh ! if even on Babel shine
        Such gleams of Paradise,
    Should not their peace be peace divine,
        Who day by day arise,
    To look on clearer Heavens, and scan
    The work of God untouch'd by man?
Shame on us, who about us Babel bear,
And live in Paradise, as if God was not there !

TWENTY-FIRST SUNDAY AFTER TRINITY

    The morning mist is clear'd away,
    Yet still the face of heaven is grey,
Nor yet th' autumnal breeze has stirr'd the grove,
    Faded, yet full, a paler green
    Skirts soberly the tranquil scene,
The redbreast warbles round this leafy cove.

    Sweet messenger of "calm decay," [1]
    Saluting sorrow as you may,
As one still bent to find or make the best,
    In thee, and in this quiet mead
    The lesson of sweet peace, I read,
Rather in all to be resign'd than blest.

    'Tis a low chant, according well
    With the soft solitary knell,

[1] See p. 54.

As homeward from some grave belov'd we turn,
    Or by some holy death-bed dear,
    Most welcome to the chasten'd ear
Of her whom Heaven is teaching how to mourn.

    O cheerful tender strain ! the heart
    That duly bears with you its part,
Singing so thankful to the dreary blast,
    Though gone and spent its joyous prime,
    And on the world's autumnal time,
'Mid wither'd hues and sere, its lot to cast :

    That is the heart for thoughtful seer,
    Watching, in trance nor dark nor clear,
Th' appalling Future as it nearer draws ;
    His spirit calm'd the storm to meet,
    Feeling the rock beneath his feet,
And tracing through the cloud th' eternal cause.

    That is the heart for watchman true
    Waiting to see what God will do,
As o'er the Church the gathering twilight falls :
    No more he strains his wistful eye,
    If chance the golden hours be nigh,
By youthful Hope seen beaming round her walls.

    Forc'd from his shadowy paradise,
    His thoughts to Heaven the steadier rise :
There seek his answer when the world reproves :
    Contented in his darkling round,
    If only he be faithful found
When from the east th' eternal morning moves.

THE GATHERING OF THE CHURCH

From the " Lyra Apostolica"

Wherefore shrink, and say, " 'Tis vain ;
In their hour hell-powers must reign ;
Vainly, vainly would we force
Fatal Error's torrent course ;
Earth is mighty, we are frail,
Faith is gone, and Hope must fail."

Yet along the Church's sky
Stars are scattered, pure and high ;
Yet her wasted gardens bear
Autumn violets, sweet and rare—
Relics of a spring-time clear,
Earnests of a bright new year.

Israel yet hath thousands sealed,
Who to Baal never kneeled ;
Seize the banner, spread its fold !
Seize it with no faltering hold !
Spread its foldings high and fair,
Let all see the Cross is there !

What, if to the trumpet's sound
Voices few come answering round ?
Scarce a votary swell the burst
When the anthem peals at first ?
God hath sown, and He will reap,
Growth is slow when roots are deep.

He will aid the work begun,
For the love of His dear Son ;
He will breathe in their true breath,
Who serene in prayer and faith,
Would our dying embers fan
Bright as when their glow began.

THE REV. GEORGE CORNISH.

TO THE REDBREAST

Unheard in Summer's flaring ray,
 Pour forth thy notes, sweet singer,
Wooing the stillness of the autumn day,
 Bid it a moment linger,
  Nor fly
Too soon from Winter's scowling eye.

The blackbird's song, at even-tide,
 And hers, who gay ascends,
Filling the heavens far and wide,
 Are sweet.   But none so blends
  As thine
With calm decay, and peace divine.

J. GIBSON LOCKHART. 1794–1854

LINES

When youthful faith hath fled,
  Of loving take thy leave ;
Be constant to the dead—
  The dead cannot deceive.

Sweet modest flowers of Spring,
  How fleet your balmy day !
And man's brief year can bring
  No secondary May.

No earthly burst again
  Of gladness out of gloom
Fond hope and vision vain,
  Ungrateful to the tomb.

But 'tis an old belief
  That on some solemn shore,
Beyond the sphere of grief,
  Dear friends shall meet once more.

Beyond the sphere of time,
  And Sin and Fate's control,
Serene in endless prime
  Of body and of soul.

That creed I fain would keep,
  That hope I'll not forego,
Eternal be the sleep,
  Unless to waken so.

GEORGE DARLEY. 1795–1846

"IT IS NOT BEAUTY I DEMAND

It is not beauty I demand,
  A crystal brow, the moon's despair,
Nor the snow's daughter, a white hand,
  Nor mermaid's yellow pride of hair.

Tell me not of your starry eyes,
  Your lips that seem on roses fed,
Your breasts, where Cupid tumbling lies,
  Nor sleeps for kissing of his bed :—

A blooming pair of vermeil cheeks,
  Like Hebe's in her ruddiest hours,
A breath that softer music speaks
  Than summer winds a-wooing flowers.

These are but gauds : nay, what are lips ?
  Coral beneath the ocean stream,
Whose brink, when your adventurer slips,
  Full oft he perisheth on them.

And what are cheeks but ensigns oft
  That wave hot youth to fields of blood ?
Did Helen's breast, though ne'er so soft,
  Do Greece or Ilium any good ?

Eyes can with baleful ardour burn ;
  Poison can breathe, that erst perfumed ;
There's many a white hand holds an urn,
  With lovers' hearts to dust consumed.

For crystal brows there's nought within ;
    They are but empty cells for pride ;
He who the Syren's hair would win
    Is mostly strangled in the tide.

Give me, instead of beauty's bust,
    A tender heart, a loyal mind,
Which with temptation I would trust,
    Yet never link'd with error find,—

One in whose gentle bosom I
    Could pour my secret heart of woes,
Like the care-burthen'd honey-fly
    That hides his murmurs in the rose,—

My earthly comforter ! whose love
    So indefeasible might be,
That, when my spirit wound above,
    Hers could not stay, for sympathy.

THOMAS CARLYLE. 1795–1881

SPEECH OF THE ERDGEIST IN "FAUST"

In Being's floods, in Action's storm,
 I walk, and work, above, beneath,
Work and weave in endless motion!
  Birth and Death
   An infinite Ocean;
  A seizing and giving
  The fire of the Living:
'Tis thus at the roaring Loom of Time I ply,
And weave for God the garment thou seest Him by.

TO-DAY

So here hath been dawning
 Another blue day:
Think wilt thou let it
 Slip useless away.

Out of Eternity
 This new is born;
Into Eternity
 At night will return.

Behold it aforetime
 No eye ever did;
So soon it for ever
 From all eyes is hid.

Here hath been dawning
 Another blue day:
Think wilt thou let it
 Slip useless away.

THOMAS HOOD. 1798–1845

FROM "THE HAUNTED HOUSE"

The wren had built within the porch, she found
  Its quiet loneliness so sure and thorough ;
And on the lawn,—within its turfy mound,
  The rabbit made his burrow.

The rabbit wild and grey, that flitted through
  The shrubby clumps, and frisk'd, and sat, and vanished,
But leisurely and bold, as if he knew
  His enemy was banished.

The wary crow,—the pheasant from the woods,—
  Lulled by the still and everlasting sameness,
Close to the mansion, like domestic broods,
  Fed with a "shocking tameness."

The coot was swimming in the reedy pond,
  Beside the water-hen, so soon affrighted ;
And in the weedy moat the heron, fond
  Of solitude, alighted.

The moping heron, motionless and stiff,
  That on a stone, as silently, as stilly,
Stood an apparent sentinel, as if
  To guard the water-lily.

No sound was heard, except, from far away,
  The ringing of the Whitwall's shrilly laughter,
Or now and then, the chatter of the jay,
  That Echo murmured after.

THE DEATHBED

We watched her breathing through the night,
  Her breathing soft and low,
As in her breast the wave of life
  Kept heaving to and fro.
So silently we seemed to speak,
  So slowly moved about,
As we had lent her half our powers
  To eke her living out.

Our very hopes belied our fears,
  Our fears our hopes belied—
We thought her dying when she slept,
  And sleeping when she died.
For when the morn came, dim and sad,
  And chill with early showers,
Her quiet eyelids closed—she had
  Another morn than ours.

LORD MACAULAY. 1800–1859

THE ARMADA

Attend, all ye who list to hear our noble England's praise ;
I tell of the thrice famous deeds she wrought in ancient
    days,
When that great fleet invincible against her bore in vain
The richest spoils of Mexico, the stoutest hearts of Spain.

   It was about the lovely close of a warm summer day,
There came a gallant merchant-ship full sail to Plymouth
    Bay ;
Her crew hath seen Castile's black fleet beyond Aurigny's
    isle
At earliest twilight on the waves lie heaving many a mile.
At sunrise she escaped their van, by God's especial grace ;
And the tall Pinta, till the noon, had held her close in
    chase.
Forthwith a guard at every gun was placed along the
    wall ;
The beacon blazed upon the roof of Edgecumbe's lofty
    hall ;
Many a light fishing-bark put out to pry along the coast,
And with loose rein and bloody spur rode inland many
    a post.
With his white hair unbonneted, the stout old sheriff
    comes ;
Behind him march the halberdiers ; before him sound
    the drums ;
His yeomen round the market-cross make clear an ample
    space ;
For there behoves him to set up the standard of Her
    Grace.

And haughtily the trumpets peal, and gaily dance the
   bells,
As slow upon the labouring wind the royal blazon swells.
Look how the Lion of the sea lifts up his ancient crown,
And underneath his deadly paw treads the gay lilies down.
So stalked he when he turned to flight, on that famed
   Picard field,
Bohemia's plume, and Genoa's bow, and Cæsar's eagle
   shield:
So glared he when at Agincourt in wrath he turned to
   bay,
And crushed and torn beneath his claws the princely
   hunters lay.
Ho! strike the flagstaff deep, Sir Knight: ho! scatter
   flowers, fair maids:
Ho! gunners, fire a loud salute: ho! gallants, draw
   your blades:
Thou sun, shine on her joyously; ye breezes, waft her
   wide:
Our glorious "Semper eadem," the banner of our pride.

The freshening breeze of eve unfurled that banner's
   massy fold,
The parting gleam of sunshine kissed that haughty scroll
   of gold;
Night sank upon the dusky beach, and on the purple sea,
Such night in England ne'er had been, nor e'er again
   shall be.
From Eddystone to Berwick bounds, from Lynn to
   Milford Bay,
That time of slumber was as bright and busy as the day;
For swift to east and swift to west the ghastly war-flame
   spread,
High on St. Michael's Mount it shone: it shone on
   Beachy Head.

Far on the deep the Spaniard saw, along each Southern
  shire,

Cape beyond cape, in endless range, those twinkling
  points of fire.

The fisher left his skiff to rock on 'Tamar's glittering
  waves :

The rugged miners poured to war from Mendip's sun-
  less caves :

O'er Longleat's towers, o'er Cranbourne's oaks, the fiery
  herald flew ;

He roused the shepherds of Stonehenge, the rangers of
  Beaulieu.

Right sharp and quick the bells rang out all night from
  Bristol town,

And ere the day three hundred horse had met on Clifton-
  down ;

The sentinel on Whitehall gate looked forth into the
  night,

And saw o'erhanging Richmond Hill the streak of blood-
  red light ;

Then bugle's note and cannon's roar the death-like
  silence broke,

And with one start, and with one cry, the royal city woke.

At once on all her stately gates arose the answering
  fires ;

At once the wild alarum clashed from all her reeling
  spires ;

From all the batteries of the Tower pealed loud the
  voice of fear ;

And all the thousand masts of Thames sent back a louder
  cheer ;

And from the farthest wards was heard the rush of
  hurrying feet,

And the broad streams of pikes and flags rushed down
  each roaring street ;

And broader still became the blaze, and louder still the
　　din,
As fast from every village round the horse came spurring
　　in :
And eastward straight from wild Blackheath the warlike
　　errand went,
And roused in many an ancient hall the gallant squires
　　of Kent.
Southward from Surrey's pleasant hills flew those bright
　　couriers forth ;
High on bleak Hampstead's swarthy moor they started
　　for the north ;
And on, and on, without a pause, untired, they bounded
　　still :
All night from tower to tower they sprang ; they sprang
　　from hill to hill :
Till the proud Peak unfurled the flag o'er Darwin's rocky
　　dales,
Till like volcanoes flared to heaven the stormy hills of
　　Wales,
Till twelve fair counties saw the blaze on Malvern's
　　lonely height,
Till streamed in crimson on the wind the Wrekin's crest
　　of light,
Till broad and fierce the star came forth on Ely's stately
　　fane,
And tower and hamlet rose in arms o'er all the boundless
　　plain ;
Till Belvoir's lordly terraces the sign to Lincoln sent,
And Lincoln sped the message on o'er the wide Vale of
　　Trent ;
Till Skiddaw saw the fire that burned on Gaunt's em-
　　battled pile,
And the red glare on Skiddaw roused the burghers of
　　Carlisle.

NASEBY

Oh! wherefore come ye forth in triumph from the
    north,
With your hands and your feet, and your raiment all
    red?
And wherefore doth your rout send forth a joyous shout?
And whence be the grapes of the wine-press that ye
    tread?

Oh! evil was the root, and bitter was the fruit,
And crimson was the juice of the vintage that we trod;
For we trampled on the throng of the haughty and the
    strong,
Who sate in the high places and slew the saints of God.

It was about the noon of a glorious day of June,
That we saw their banners dance and their cuirasses
    shine,
And the man of blood was there, with his long essenced
    hair,
And Astley, and Sir Marmaduke, and Rupert of the
    Rhine.

Like a servant of the Lord, with his Bible and his sword,
The general rode along us to form us for the fight;
When a murmuring sound broke out, and swelled into a
    shout
Among the godless horsemen upon the tyrant's right.

And hark! like the roar of the billows on the shore,
The cry of battle rises along the charging line!
For God! for the cause! for the Church! for the laws!
For Charles, King of England, and Rupert of the Rhine!

The furious German comes, with his clarions and his
    drums,
His bravos of Alsatia and pages of Whitehall;
They are bursting on our flanks! Grasp your pikes!
    Close your ranks!
For Rupert never comes, but to conquer, or to fall.

They are here—they rush on—we are broken—we are
    gone—
Our left is borne before them like stubble in the blast.
O Lord, put forth Thy might! O Lord, defend the right!
Stand back to back in God's name! and fight it to
    the last!

Stout Skippon hath a wound—the centre hath given
    ground,
Hark! hark! what means the trampling of horsemen on
    our rear?
Whose banner do I see, boys? 'Tis he! thank God!
    'tis he, boys!
Bear up another minute! Brave Oliver is here!

Their heads all stooping low, their points all in a row;
Like a whirlwind on the trees, like a deluge on the
    dykes,
Our cuirassiers have burst on the ranks of the accurst,
And at a shock have scattered the forest of his pikes.

Fast, fast, the gallants ride, in some safe nook to hide
Their coward heads, predestined to rot on Temple
    Bar;
And he—he turns! he flies! shame on those cruel
    eyes
That bore to look on torture, and dare not look on
    war!

Ho, comrades! scour the plain; and ere ye strip the
slain,
First give another stab to make your search secure;
Then shake from sleeves and pockets their broad-pieces
and lockets,
The tokens of the wanton, the plunder of the
poor.

Fools! your doublets shone with gold, and your hearts
were gay and bold,
When you kissed your lily hands to your lemans
to-day;
And to-morrow shall the fox from her chambers in the
rocks
Lead forth her tawny cubs to howl about the prey.

Where be your tongues, that late mocked at heaven,
and hell, and fate?
And the fingers that once were so busy with your
blades?
Your perfumed satin clothes, your catches and your
oaths?
Your stage plays and your sonnets, your diamonds
and your spades?

Down! down! for ever down, with the mitre and the
crown!
With the Belial of the Court, and the Mammon of the
Pope!
There is woe in Oxford halls, there is wail in Durham's
stalls;
The Jesuit smites his bosom, the bishop rends his
cope.

And she of the seven hills shall mourn her children's
    ills,
And tremble when she thinks on the edge of Eng-
    land's sword ;
And the kings of earth in fear shall shudder when they
    hear
What the hand of God hath wrought for the houses
    and the Word !

THE MUSTER

(From the " Lays of Ancient Rome ")

The horsemen and the footmen
    Are pouring in amain
From many a stately market-place ;
    From many a fruitful plain ;
From many a lonely hamlet,
    Which, hid by beech and pine,
Like an eagle's nest, hangs on the crest
    Of purple Apennine ;

From lordly Volaterræ,
    Where scowls the far-famed hold
Piled by the hands of giants
    For god-like kings of old ;
From sea-girt Populonia,
    Whose sentinels descry
Sardinia's snowy mountain-tops
    Fringing the Southern sky ;

From the proud mart of Pisæ,
    Queen of the western waves,
Where ride Massilia's triremes
    Heavy with fair-haired slaves ;

From where sweet Clanis wanders
   Through corn and vines and flowers
From where Cortona lifts to heaven
   Her diadem of towers.

Tall are the oaks whose acorns
   Drop in dark Auser's rill;
Fat are the stags that champ the boughs
   Of the Ciminian hill;
Beyond all streams Clitumnus
   Is to the herdsman dear;
Best of all pools the fowler loves
   The great Volsinian mere.

But now no stroke of woodman
   Is heard by Auser's rill;
No hunter tracks the stag's green path
   Up the Ciminian hill;
Unwatched along Clitumnus
   Grazes the milk-white steer;
Unharmed the water-fowl may dip
   In the Volsinian mere.

The harvests of Arretium,
   This year, old men shall reap;
This year, young boys in Umbro
   Shall plunge the struggling sheep;
And in the vats of Luna,
   This year, the must shall foam
Round the white feet of laughing girls,
   Whose sires have marched to Rome.

LINES WRITTEN IN AUGUST 1847

The day of tumult, strife, defeat, was o'er;
   Worn out with toil, and noise, and scorn, and spleen,
I slumbered, and in slumber saw once more
   A room in an old mansion, long unseen.

That room, methought, was curtained from the light;
   Yet through the curtains shone the moon's cold ray
Full on a cradle, where, in linen white,
   Sleeping life's first soft sleep, an infant lay.

Pale flickered on the hearth the dying flame,
   And all was silent in that ancient hall,
Save when by fits on the low night wind came
   The murmur of the distant waterfall.

And lo! the fairy queens who rule our birth
   Drew nigh to speak the new-born baby's doom:
With noiseless step which left no trace on earth,
   From gloom they came, and vanished into gloom.

Not deigning on the boy a glance to cast
   Swept careless by the gorgeous Queen of Gain;
More scornful still, the Queen of Fashion passed
   With mincing gait and sneer of cold disdain.

The Queen of Power tossed high her jewelled head;
   And o'er her shoulder threw a wrathful frown:
The Queen of Pleasure on the pillow shed
   Scarce one stray rose-leaf from her fragrant crown.

Still Fay in long procession followed Fay;
   And still the little couch remained unblest:
But, when those wayward sprites had passed away,
   Came One, the last, the mightiest, and the best.

Oh, glorious lady, with the eyes of light
  And laurels clustering round thy lofty brow,
Who by the cradle's side did'st watch that night,
  Warbling a sweet strange music, who wast thou?

"Yes, darling, let them go;" so ran the strain:
  "Yes; let them go, gain, fashion, pleasure, power,
And all the busy elves to whose domain
  Belongs the nether sphere, the fleeting hour.

"Without one envious sigh, one anxious scheme,
  The nether sphere, the fleeting hour resign.
Mine is the world of thought, the world of dream,
  Mine all the past, and all the future mine.

"Fortune, that lays in sport the mighty low,
  Age, that to penance turns the joys of youth,
Shall leave untouched the gifts which I bestow,
  The sense of beauty and the thirst of truth.

"Of the fair brotherhood who share my grace,
  I, from thy natal day, pronounce thee free;
And, if for some I keep a nobler place,
  I keep for none a happier than for thee.

"There are who, while to vulgar eyes they seem
  Of all my bounties largely to partake,
Of me as of some rival's handmaid deem,
  And court me but for gain's, power's, fashion's sake.

"To such, though deep their lore, though wide their fame,
  Shall my great mysteries be all unknown:
But thou, through good and evil, praise and blame,
  Wilt not thou love me for myself alone?

"Yes; thou wilt love me with exceeding love;
  And I will tenfold all that love repay,
Still smiling, though the tender may reprove,
  Still faithful, though the trusted may betray.

" For aye mine emblem was, and aye shall be,
　　The ever-during plant whose bough I wear,
Brightest and greenest then, when every tree
　　That blossoms in the light of time is bare.

" In the dark hour of shame, I deigned to stand
　　Before the frowning peers at Bacon's side :
On a far shore I smoothed with tender hand,
　　Through months of pain, the sleepless bed of Hyde :

" I brought the wise and brave of ancient days
　　To cheer the cell where Raleigh pined alone ;
I lighted Milton's darkness with the blaze
　　Of the bright ranks that guard the eternal throne.

" And even so, my child, it is my pleasure,
　　That thou not then alone should'st feel me nigh,
When in domestic bliss and studious leisure,
　　Thy weeks uncounted come, uncounted fly ;

" Not then alone, when myriads, closely pressed
　　Around thy car, the shout of triumph raise ;
Nor when in gilded drawing-rooms, thy breast
　　Swells at the sweeter sound of woman's praise.

" No : when on restless night dawns cheerless morrow,
　　When weary soul and wasting body pine,
Thine am I still, in danger, sickness, sorrow,
　　In conflict, obloquy, want, exile, thine ;

" Thine, where on mountain waves the snowbirds scream
　　Where more than Thule's winter barbs the breeze,
Where scarce, through lowering clouds, one sickly gleam
　　Lights the drear May-day of Antarctic seas ;

" Thine, when around thy litter's track all day
　　White sandhills shall reflect the blinding glare ;
Thine, when through forests breathing death, thy way
　　All night shall wind by many a tiger's lair.

"Thine most, when friends turn pale, when traitors fly,
  When, hard beset, thy spirit, justly proud,
For truth, peace, freedom, mercy, dares defy
  A sullen priesthood and a raving crowd.

"Amidst the din of all things fell and vile,
  Hate's yell, and Envy's hiss, and Folly's bray,
Remember me; and with an unforced smile
  See riches, baubles, flatterers pass away.

"Yes: they will pass away; nor deem it strange:
  They come and go, as comes and goes the sea:
And let them come and go: thou, through all change
  Fix thy firm gaze on virtue and on me."

EPITAPH ON A JACOBITE

To my true King I offered free from stain
Courage and faith; vain faith and courage vain;
For him I threw lands, honours, wealth away,
And one dear hope that was more prized than they.
For him I languished in a foreign clime,
Grey-haired with sorrow in my manhood's prime.
Heard in La Verna Scargill's whispering trees,
And pined by Arno for my lovelier Tees;
Beheld each night my home in fevered sleep,
Each morning started from that dream to weep,
Till God, who saw me tried too sorely, gave
The resting-place I asked, an early grave.
Oh, thou whom chance leads to this nameless stone
From that proud country which was once mine own,
By those white cliffs I never more must see,
By that dear language which I spake like thee,
Forget all feuds, and shed one English tear
O'er English dust: a broken heart lies here.

PART II

PART II

INTRODUCTORY NOTES

In the Second Part of this volume I have collected a number of specimens of poets who were born after the beginning of the nineteenth century, and became conspicuous in the reign of Queen Victoria. Amongst these the first place naturally belongs to John Henry, Cardinal Newman, born 21st February 1801, who, from 1837 onwards to 1896, exercised so potent an influence over a large portion of his countrymen. All his readers know how much of the poet he had in his composition; but of his verse very little save the well-known hymn, " Lead, Kindly Light," a production of his early life, and the " Dream of Gerontius," which was written in his old age, is generally familiar. I have taken an extract from the latter poem and several of the short pieces which appeared in the " Lyra Apostolica," along with those of others, of which none were more remarkable than that by Richard Hurrell Froude, called " Old Self and New Self." At a later period Newman published his own verses in a separate volume. Froude, I regret to say, died just before the reign of the Queen began, and falls accordingly outside my limit.

The extracts from NEWMAN *are followed by one*

from Mrs. Archer Clive (1801–1873), *whose name is closely connected with the commencement of the reign by her poem,* "The Queen's Ball," *from which I have quoted at some length. She was led to compose it by the accident of a friend having written to her that a hundred and fifty invitations to the first ball given at the palace after the accession of Queen Victoria had been issued to people who were dead. She imagines some of them to have accepted their invitations.*

The next place belongs to Mrs. Maclean, *née Letitia Landon* (1802–1838), *whose merits were very eagerly canvassed both in her lifetime and after her tragical death on the West Coast of Africa had caused a great sensation in the public mind.*

A man was born about the same time as the ill-fated L. E. L. who was destined to great and brilliant success in many lines of life. Lord Lytton (1803–1873), *considered, I believe, that as a poet he would be best remembered by his* "King Arthur," *but few will share that opinion.*

The extracts I have made are exclusively taken from the "New Timon" *and* "St. Stephen's," *in both of which he followed the lead of Pope. That of itself is disagreeable to many persons, but I hold that they take a prejudiced view. The* "New Timon" *contains many brilliant passages, though it is not, as a whole, to be compared with the other poem I have mentioned.* "St. Stephen's" *is a metrical criticism of the great English orators, from Sir John Eliot down to our own times, and a saner piece of criticism couched in more vigorous verse has not been seen in these latter days.*

WINTHROP MACKWORTH PRAED (1802–1839) *was hardly a Victorian poet, for his health began to fail in 1838, and he died the next year.   Had he lived he would probably, like his Cambridge rival, Macaulay, have exchanged the rhymes of his youth for more serious work.   I give two specimens of his verse, illustrating his gayer and his graver moods.*

Sir EDMUND HEAD (1805–1868) *was much better known to the world as an administrator than as a poet.   He became Governor of New Brunswick in 1847, and was promoted in 1854 to be Governor-General of Canada.   He returned to England in 1861, was appointed a Civil Service Commissioner in 1852, and died of heart disease in 1868.   He was a familiar figure in the most intelligent society of London, and all his friends would have subscribed to Ticknor's eulogy of him, " He was one of the most accurate and accomplished scholars I have ever known."*

FRANCIS MAHONY (1805–1866), *who wrote under the name of " Father Prout," was brought up by the Jesuits, and remained for a long time connected with the Great Order, for which, however, he eventually showed himself a good deal too hilarious.   Before he died he hardly retained anything of the priestly character save in his personal appearance.   He was a pillar of* Fraser's Magazine, *and wrote with equal facility in a humorous and in a pathetic vein.* One *of his mystifications, an imaginary French original of* Wolfe's *lines on the Death of Sir John Moore, found its way quite recently into the London press.* His *"* Bells of Shandon," *which I quote in the text, has many obvious faults, but as a strange and agreeable* tour de force *deserves, I think, the place I have given it.* When *its author died, Denis Florence M'Carthy published a very graceful poem about him in the same metre, from which I quote two verses :—*

" *The songs melodious, which—a new Harmodius—*
    Young Ireland wreathed round its rebel sword,
With deep vibrations and aspirations
    Fling a glorious madness o'er the festive board.
But to me seems sweeter the melodious metre
Of the simple lyric that we owe to thee—
        Of the ' Bells of Shandon,'
        That sound so grand on
The pleasant waters of the river Lee.

There's a grave that rises on thy sward, Devizes,
    Where Moore lies sleeping from his land afar ;
And a white stone flashes over Goldsmith's ashes
    In the quiet cloister of Temple Bar.
So where thou sleepest, with a love that's deepest
Shall thy land remember thy sweet song and thee,
        While the ' Bells of Shandon'
        Shall sound so grand on
The pleasant waters of the river Lee."

It would be idle to say anything about Mrs. BROWN-
ING (1806–1861), LORD TENNYSON (1809–1892),

or his friend, FitzGerald[1] (1809–1883), *whose*
"Omar Khayyám" *has had, in the last thirty years,*
so astonishing a success, after having begun its life
by what seemed to be an altogether hopeless failure.
All people, who care for poetry at all, have long since
made up their minds as to the position which they
would assign in the Temple of Fame to these three
authors.

Lady Dufferin (1807–1867), *whose beautiful*
lines addressed to her son on his twenty-first birthday
I have been allowed to republish, was the grand-
daughter of Richard Brinsley Sheridan, and Miss
Linley. Mrs. Norton (1808–1877) *was a year*
younger. *Both had the poetical faculty in a very*
high degree. *Perhaps the* "Lament of the Irish
Emigrant" *is the best known poem by the first, and*
the ballad beginning "A soldier of the Legion lay
dying in Algiers" *by the second; but I have pre-*
ferred to take the stanzas I have mentioned from the
writings of the one sister, and a passage from the
"Lady of La Garaye" *from those of the other.*

Richard Monckton Milnes, *the first Lord Hough-*
ton (1809–1885), *has suffered from having more*
genius than he quite knew what to do with, but he
must be acknowledged to have been a man of great
and many gifts, as well as to have done so many

---

[1] Some of my readers may not have seen the volume in which
Mr. Mallock has employed FitzGerald's method in dealing with
"Lucretius." I venture to call their attention to it.

*good deeds, as to make it very easy for him to
traverse the bridge of Es-Sirat.*

FRANCES ANN KEMBLE, *belonging to the great
theatrical family whose chief glory is Mrs. Siddons,
was born in 1809, and died in London a few years
ago at a very advanced age. She became the wife of
Mr. Pierce Butler, a Southern planter, but the mar-
riage was not a happy one, and was eventually dis-
solved. Towards the middle of the forties her poems
were a good deal read in England, and pleased very
fastidious judges, but of late they have been less
familiar, while her prose works have commanded a
wider audience.*

HENRY ALFORD (1810–1871), *whose name is
usually associated with his edition of the Greek Tes-
tament, which was a great advance upon any work of
the kind previously published in England, spent his
middle life as a parish priest in the country, but
removed to London in 1853, and became extremely
well known by his admirable lectures at Quebec
Chapel, in which, throwing over the absurd practice
of preaching a sermon whether he had anything
to say or not, he went regularly through one chapter
of the Bible after another, invariably bringing to
notice something which was new even to very well-
informed persons in his congregation. It is strange
that so excellent a precedent has not had more
followers. In 1857 he was made Dean of
Canterbury, and retained that position till he
died.*

HENRY OXENHAM (1829–1888) *began his educa-
tion at Harrow, gained the Balliol Scholarship when
he was only seventeen, and was a prominent figure
during all his residence in Oxford, where he was
intimately connected with the extreme section of the
High Church party. It was generally thought that
he would go over to Rome as soon as he had taken
his degree, but he deferred that step till* 1857, *and
after he had taken it, instead of throwing himself
into the central stream of Catholic life, he kept close
to the shore, thereby throwing away gifts which many
of his friends believed were likely to give him much
consideration amongst those whom he joined. Later
he became connected with Döllinger, and went some
little way with the adherents of the Old Catholic
party, from whom, however, he soon separated himself.
He was an assiduous writer on Catholic subjects
alike in books and newspapers, as well as the author
of the volume of poems from which I quote in the
text.*

WILLIAM BELL SCOTT (1811–1890) *was born at
Edinburgh, but passed most of his life in England,
partly in London, partly in Newcastle-on-Tyne, whither
he was sent by the Board of Trade to superintend the
Government School of Design. From that place as
a centre, his influence in matters of art extended all
over the northern counties. He wrote many volumes
of poetry, and edited not a few of the poetical works
of other people. While near the end of his life he
published his Reminiscences in two volumes, under the
title of* " Autobiographical Notes." *All this was in*

addition to a great deal of purely artistic work and of writing connected with Art.

ALFRED DOMETT (1811–1887) *wrote various poems when he was hardly over twenty.   In May 1842 he left London for New Zealand.   It was this departure which led to Browning's poem on "* Waring,*" for Domett was Waring.   His departure was, however, more satisfactory in its results than could have been expected, seeing that in his new country he filled nearly all the chief offices in the Administration, and wrote his name on the early annals of the Colony.   In 1871 he returned to London, and did not die till 1887.*

Of BROWNING *himself* (1812–1889), *or of* THACKERAY (1811–1863), *I need not speak.   Their names are household words, but few of my readers are likely to remember* THOMAS DAVIS (1814–1845), *whose poems in the* Nation *attracted in their day a good deal of attention.   He died when he was a little over thirty, and before he had freed himself from the crazy politics with which he became connected after leaving Trinity College, Dublin, where he took his degree at two-and-twenty.   His ballads on "* Fontenoy*" and on "* The Sack of Baltimore *" by Algerine pirates, are generally considered, I think, to be his best, but I prefer that on the "* Irish Brigade,*" which I have given below.*

FREDERICK WILLIAM FABER (1814–1863), *who died before he had quite reached the age of fifty, was,*

*next to Newman, the most interesting person whom
the Oxford Movement produced. Like Newman, he
was brought up amongst Evangelical surroundings,
and, like him, he died an Oratorian. His first
volume of poems,* "The Cherwell Water Lily,"
*was published when he was very young. Like all
his works, it contains a great deal that is valueless,
and not a little that is exceedingly beautiful. It was
of him that Wordsworth said,* "I have never met
any one who had so good an eye for Nature as I have
myself except a young man who was here last year,
Frederick Faber, and he had a better." *Any careful
student of his writings will see that this is not over-
praise, and that he could give the soul of a landscape
in a very few words. Unhappily, as he went on in
life and found great numbers of persons, in the
Church which he joined, delighted with everything he
wrote, he became a less and less severe critic alike of
his poetry and of his prose. Still, considering the com-
parative brevity of his life, he produced a great deal,
and deserves to be had in long remembrance not only
by those with whom he was connected by agreement of
opinion, but by many others who belong to entirely
different schools of thought. His life has been but
poorly written, with a view rather to edification than
information.*

Dr. CHARLES MACKAY (1814–1889) *was born
at Perth, and was chiefly known as a song writer.*
"There's a Good Time Coming," *which had so ex-
traordinary a popular success, was by him. He did
a prodigious amount of work as a journalist, wrote*

many prose works, and a good deal of poetry, of which I give one specimen.

JOHN CAMPBELL SHAIRP (1815–1885) *was educated at the Edinburgh Academy and at the University of Glasgow, whence he passed as a Snell Exhibitioner to Balliol. After leaving Oxford he became a Master at Rugby, but eventually succeeded James D. Forbes as Principal of the United College, St. Andrews, and held the Latin Chair in that University till* 1872. *He wrote much good prose, such as his* "Studies in Poetry." *The two poems which I have printed show him, I think, at his best, bringing into relief alike the English and Scottish elements in his character.*

The REV. THOMAS WHYTEHEAD (1815–1843) *was educated at Cambridge, where he obtained many distinctions, but he was admitted to an* ad eundem *degree at Oxford, 4th December* 1841, *and was closely allied with some persons there, more especially with Frederick Faber, to whom several of his poems were addressed. He went out as chaplain to Dr. Selwyn, Bishop of New Zealand; but his health broke down, and he died in* 1843. *Before leaving England he published a remarkable little book called* "College Life." *Dreamy as it is, it reflects as well as anything I know the* ethos *of the Tractarian Movement. The hymn which I have transferred to the text is as beautiful in its way as his friend Faber's* "Shadow of the Rock," *and the other slighter composition goes some way to repair a great injustice by rehabilitating the enemy of some of man's worst enemies.*

Of all the marvellously gifted and uncanny sister-hood who gave to the Rectory at Haworth so high a place in contemporary literature, EMILY BRONTË (1816–1855) *had far the most remarkable poetical gift. Dying at thirty, she had not time to produce any great amount of verse, but some of it is of the very highest interest. I give one example.*

GEORGE SYDNEY SMYTHE (1818–1857), *the last Lord Strangford but one, was a member of the small but brilliant group which gave a certain romantic interest to the Parliament of* 1841. *He was the intimate friend of Frederick Faber, and of the present Duke of Rutland, in whose poems, which have been quite unduly censured by political adversaries, there are verses addressed to him. He was at one time the friend, and later the bitter enemy, of Disraeli, who is said to have remarked, pointing to his picture, " If that man had lived I should never have been Prime Minister." That, however, was a totally erroneous criticism. George Smythe, though about as brilliant as he well could be, had few of the qualities which carried his critic so far——had, above all, none of that almost superhuman patience which even foes admired. He is understood to have been the Waldershare of " Endymion," and that picture of him is, I suspect, much nearer the reality than the remark which I have quoted above. A clever journalist of his day put his finger upon a weak point when he said, " But what could the House make of a young man who used to spring bolt upright in a foreign debate, shut his eyes, and pour forth a series of sentences which sounded like a translation from the French of Vergniaud?" Lord Aberdeen, whose Under-Secretary he was for a time, made a not less apposite observation when he said that his fault was "not reading enclosures." His book, "Historic Fancies," was emphatically the book of a man who did not "read enclosures," but all through it are snatches both of prose and verse which well deserve to live. Of the latter I have transferred a few specimens to these pages.*

I have given in my quotations from Newman and Faber some characteristic specimens of the poetry of the Oxford Movement. The brief connection with that movement of ARTHUR CLOUGH is well set forth in Shairp's poem on the "Balliol Scholars," which I have also given. It has always been said, and I believe it to be true, that the verses beginning

"As ships becalmed at eve that lay"

were written in relation to Clough's breach with W. G. Ward, along with whom he had gone a considerable way in the Newmanic direction. Anyhow, he may be considered as the pioneer of the Liberal movement in Oxford, which grew stronger and stronger from 1848 onwards until it became at last nearly all-powerful there. That change of opinion on the banks of the Isis marks a new departure in English thought, and I have accordingly given to Clough a very considerable place—a greater place than some may possibly think his due when considered solely as a poet.

JOHN WILLIAM BURGON (1813–1888) *went up late to Oxford, but the best piece of work which he did belonged to his earlier time there.   His Newdigate "Petra" has had few superiors.   He lived on to be in elderly life a compendium of all the prejudices which grew and flourished in his University before the hand of Reform was laid upon its venerable abuses, and died as Dean of Chichester without ever producing again anything so good as the prize poem of his youthful days.*

It is not by his verse that CHARLES KINGSLEY (1819–1875) *is best remembered in the present generation, but some of it may outlive his novels as long as these have outlived his rather confused theology.   The impression of his fresh bright personality will remain as long as those who knew him survive, but their number is rapidly dwindling.*

From RUSKIN (1819–1900) *I have taken nothing save a few lines, of surpassing beauty, which describe one of those little shrines of the Blessed Virgin on which one comes amid the lagunes of Venice.*

MISS SMEDLEY (1820–1877), *who wrote the sonnet about Bishop Patteson which I have reprinted, lived most of her life at Tenby, where she wrote, and wrote exceedingly well, both in prose and poetry.   Patteson has become a sort of Anglican saint, and quite deservedly.   My recollections of him belong to his time as an undergraduate at Balliol, and none of us who knew him even at that early period would, I appre-*

hend, think that to speak of him as "clarum et venerabile nomen" *was at all excessive.*

Professor AYTOUN (1813–1865) *was the son of a Writer to the Signet in Edinburgh. At first it seemed probable that he would follow his father's profession, but he went later to the Scotch Bar, where he succeeded fairly, and obtained from his political party (he was a High Tory) the well-deserved Sheriffship of Orkney. He was a successful teacher of rhetoric and literature in Edinburgh, co-operated with Sir Theodore Martin in writing the extremely amusing* " Bon Gaultier Ballads," *published the* " Lays of the Scottish Cavaliers," *a book which has had very many editions, but died at the comparatively early age of fifty-two.*

FREDERICK LOCKER (1821–1895), *as we all called him forty years ago, but whom a very happy marriage later turned into Locker-Lampson, was one of the most successful pupils in the school of Praed. He wrote much and well in the style of his master, became famous on both sides of the Atlantic not only as the writer of excellent verse, but as one of the first of bibliophiles, a taste in which he has been emulated by his son, whose Appendix to his father's Catalogue of the Rowfant Library is a truly remarkable performance for so young a man.*

If I am blamed for giving so much space to MATTHEW ARNOLD (1822–1888), *I can only say, without attempting in the slightest degree to impugn the general verdict which puts Tennyson first, and Browning second, amongst the poets of the Victorian Age, that Arnold's poems say more to me individually than those of either of his two great rivals.*

Full of wisdom as are his prose works, they often contain things which one would wish away ; but with his poetry it is not so. If we put on one side a few things which, like " Merope," *may be considered mere* tours de force, *it is all but perfect. I should have preferred* " Thyrsis " *to the* " Scholar-Gipsy," *and have added* " Calais Sands," " Stanzas from Carnac," " Westminster Abbey," *and* " A Southern Night," *if they had been* publici juris.

JOHN O'HAGAN (1822–1890) *was an Irish lawyer, and the son-in-law of Lord O'Hagan, who was so much better known on this side of St. George's Channel. The highest office filled by him was that of Judicial Commissioner under the not very successful Irish Land Act of* 1881, *but he had a very considerable literary faculty, and was connected in early youth with the rather foolish but very vigorous polemics of the* Nation. *The poem I have selected has, however, nothing to do with polemics, but treats of a subject much more generally interesting.*

SYDNEY THOMPSON DOBELL (1824–1874) *was the son of a wine merchant residing in Kent, who, however, removed to Cheltenham while his son was still a boy. All through his life he carried on more or less his father's business, but the strength of his mind went chiefly to literature. In* 1850 *he made a considerable success by a poem called* " The Roman," *and in* 1856 *he published a collection called* " England in Time of War," *containing the poem which will be found on a subsequent page.   He wrote a great deal which was much more admired forty years ago than it is now, but was sometimes even then. very sharply criticised, as, for instance, in Aytoun's* " Firmilian." *He appears, too, to have been a very useful man in Gloucestershire, where he usually lived when on this side of the Channel.   Starting with wildly Radical ideas, he gradually sobered into a sensible, steady-going Liberal.*

WILLIAM CORY (1823–1892), *better known by his former name of Johnson, was long an Eton Master, and published in the year* 1858 *a small volume called* " Ionica," *from which I take what is perhaps the most beautiful of many beautiful pieces, a translation from* " Callimachus."

ADELAIDE ANN PROCTER (1825–1864) *was the eldest daughter of Mr. Procter, best known as Barry Cornwall.   She joined the Latin Church in* 1851, *and published a good deal in* Household Words *and other publications without either her own family or their intimate friend, Mr. Dickens, knowing who* " Mary Berwick" *really was.   In* 1858 *her poems were collected and published.   The one which I have selected has become extremely familiar as a song. She never had strong health, and died before she was forty.*

Her father, who was born in 1787, *outlived his gifted child, dying only in* 1874.   *He did not absolutely abandon the writing of verse after the Queen's accession, but he was too essentially a poet of the earlier decades of the century to make it desirable to include him in this collection.*

The remarkable poem, "Crowned and Discrowned," *by* Canon BRIGHT (1825–1901), *who died a few months ago, was published originally, if my memory serves me correctly, in the* Rugby Miscellany. *If it was reprinted I never chanced to see it, and the copy in this volume is taken from a manuscript written out for me many years ago by Professor Conington.*

DINAH MARIA CRAIK (1826–1887) *was known in her early days as Miss Mulock, and the authoress of* "Olive," *a novel which had a deserved success. In* 1857 *she published a work which was even more admired,* "John Halifax, Gentleman." *Her poems, some of which first appeared in* 1852, *were collected in* 1881. *The one which I have quoted belongs to her earlier life, and seems to me very lovely.*

MORTIMER COLLINS (1827–1876) *was born at Plymouth, where his father was a solicitor. He became a Mathematical Master in Guernsey when he was still very young, but left the island and devoted himself to literature in* 1856. *He was a most prolific writer both in verse and prose, a violent Tory and devotee of Aristophanes, extremely fond of Bohemian society, a good ornithologist, a great walker, a lover of dogs, and altogether the sort of open-air person who would have been a prominent figure among the adherents of the King in the Great Civil War.*

The poem which I have quoted from him shows extremely well this side of his character.

DANTE GABRIEL ROSSETTI (1828–1882), *best known as a painter, had succeeded as a poet before he took to art, for* "The Blessed Damozel," *on the whole his most memorable poem, was written about* 1847, *though not published till a year or two later. It was only in* 1848 *that he became the pupil of Ford Madox Brown, and laid the foundation of his artistic fame. The years from* 1850 *to* 1860 *seem to be thought those in which he achieved most in painting. His collected poems had been buried with his wife in* 1862, *but were exhumed by permission of Henry Bruce, later Lord Aberdare, when he was Home Secretary, and published in* 1870.

Strange to say, his poetical powers which had slumbered for a great many years, thanks to bad health and other causes, blazed up again, and he published in 1880 *some very remarkable work, including the* "Ballad of the White Ship." *No other Englishman has achieved so much success in the combined characters of painter and poet.*

ELLEN MARY PATRICK DOWNING (1828–1869), *known in her day as* "Mary of the Nation," *has been rescued from oblivion, at least on this side of the Irish Channel, by Mr. Stopford Brooke's valuable collection of Irish poetry in the English tongue. The poem which I have reprinted is said to have been the last written by its authoress before she went into a convent in* 1849. *It stands out delightfully from the political ravings with which it was originally associated.*

CHRISTINA GEORGINA ROSSETTI (1830–1894) *succeeded brilliantly in more than one totally different kind of poetry, and above all in her intensely mystic poems, which are very numerous, and which make some critics regard her as far superior to any English poetess, with the exception, perhaps, of Mrs. Browning. I should not myself agree with that verdict; but she certainly deserves a high place. She was the sister of Dante Gabriel Rossetti, and hardly less gifted.*

JEAN INGELOW (1830–1897) *was a most prolific writer alike of poems and novels. Several of the former are so admirable that I have found much difficulty in choosing the one I like best, the second place, if not the first, belonging certainly to the very exquisite lines entitled "Requiescat in Pace." I have, however, settled finally on "The High Tide on the Coast of Lincolnshire,* 1571."

EDWARD ROBERT BULWER LYTTON (1831–1892), *first Earl of Lytton, began his education at Harrow, studied at Bonn, entered the Diplomatic Service, and had a very distinguished career in it. When he was Minister at Lisbon in* 1876 *he was, much to his surprise, offered the Viceroyalty of India. He retained that great office for four years, but resigned in* 1880. *He returned in* 1887 *to his old profession, becoming Ambassador in Paris, a post in which he was emi-*

nently successful. He published " Clytemnestra and other Poems" *as early as* 1855, " The Wanderer" *in* 1859, " Lucile" *in* 1860, *and continued publishing poetry from time to time through the whole of his active and brilliant life.*

CHARLES STUART CALVERLEY (1831–1884), *the best of parodists, early showed an extraordinary power of writing Latin verse, and won the Balliol Scholarship in* 1850. *He soon, however, quarrelled with the authorities, disappeared from Oxford and went to Cambridge, where he managed his affairs better, but died prematurely in* 1884, *leaving less behind him than might have been expected from so very clever a man.*

ADAM LINDSAY GORDON (1833–1870) *was educated at Cheltenham College, and kept some terms at Merton, but went out in* 1853 *to South Australia, where he became a trooper in the Mounted Police, and led a wild life, which ended unhappily. He wrote some exceedingly vigorous ballads, from one of which I have taken a very striking verse.*

RODEN BERKELEY WRIOTHESLEY NOEL (1834–1894) *was the fourth son of the first Lord Gainsborough. He was educated at Trinity, Cambridge, and took his degree in* 1858. *He wrote a great many volumes of poetry, was much interested in philosophy, and became a member of the Metaphysical Society, but died suddenly while travelling in Germany.*

JAMES THOMSON (1834–1882) *was born at Port-Glasgow, was appointed, while still very young, an assistant-schoolmaster in the army. When stationed near Cork he became acquainted with a young girl who seems to have exercised a most extraordinary and most salutary influence over him; but died, unhappily, before they were married. In* 1868 *he left the army, and was offered a home by Mr. Bradlaugh at Tottenham. While he lived near London (or, as was the case later in it) he wrote a great deal. His* "City of Dreadful Night" *first won him fame, but ere fame came he had, unfortunately, taken to drinking. He went to live in Leicester, but removed, just before his death, once more to London, where he died very sadly.*

WILLIAM MORRIS (1834–1899) *would have been a useful person in his generation if he had done nothing more than give a powerful and enduring impulse to the beautifying of our houses; but as far back as* 1858 *he was recognised as a true poet. In* 1867 *appeared the* "Life and Death of Jason," *while in* 1873 *came the book by which he is best known,* "The Earthly Paradise." *Many may wish that he had kept to work of this class, and had not wasted his time over Socialistic follies.*

The most remarkable thing about Lord DE TABLEY (1835–1895) *was the extraordinary range of subjects which he not only knew, but knew well. He was a most assiduous student of poetry as well as a poet himself. He was minutely acquainted with English botany, and an authority upon Greek coins. In* 1865 *he fought Mid-Cheshire in the Liberal interest as well as he skated, and he skated as well as he wrote about book-plates! It was one of his characteristics that he was never satisfied with doing anything great or small by halves. If he took up a subject he mastered it thoroughly. Whether his taking up so many subjects was to the advantage of his fame with the general public may be a question, but those who knew him would not have wished him in any respect, save that of health, other than what he was.*

AUGUSTA WEBSTER (1837 – 1894) *was the daughter of Vice-Admiral Davies, married a Fellow and Law Lecturer at Trinity, Cambridge, and lived long there. Endowed with a very powerful intelligence, great industry, and poetical power, she wrote* "Dramatic Studies," *and much else, but comparatively little which is suited to a collection like this. I have chosen a sonnet, very good of its kind, and on a dignified subject.*

JOHN ADDINGTON SYMONDS (1840–1893) *was one of the most interesting men of letters who has lived in our days, thanks to his heroic and really magnificent struggle with health which would have reduced most men to absolute idleness. He was educated at Balliol, coming early under the influence of Conington and then of Jowett. Later, he was elected a Fellow of Magdalen, but married, while still young, the second daughter of Mr. Frederick North, long a familiar figure in the House of Commons. His first book appeared in* 1871, *and from that date to the end he poured forth work in verse and prose, all of a very high order of merit, though some of his prose compositions will probably live the longest. There is an admirable notice of him by Mr. Herbert Warren, the President of Magdalen, in Mr. Miles's* "Poets and Poetry of this Century." *I have hesitated between the sonnet I have cited and the very beautiful verses on* "The Crocus and the Soldanella," *deciding in favour of the former merely on considerations of space.*

FREDERIC MYERS (1843–1900) *was a son of the author of* "Catholic Thoughts," *one of the first pioneers of Broad Church ideas in the Anglican Communion, who, however, kept his light under a bushel for many years, circulating his Essays only in private. Frederic Myers was long an inspector of schools, but is best known to the public from his connection with the Society for Psychical Research and for a supremely good essay upon Virgil.* "St. Paul" *was the first of his poems which attracted general attention. I have quoted from the last few stanzas of it.*

EDWARD BOWEN, *younger brother of Lord Bowen, whose sudden death saddened a very wide circle in the spring of* 1901, *will long be remembered for his* "Harrow Songs," *two of which I have printed.*

COSMO MONKHOUSE (1840–1901) *was born in London, was educated at St. Paul's School, and entered the Board of Trade at the age of seventeen. He wrote much and well in verse, published a novel, and became one of the best known of English art critics.   A poem which I quote below is quite up to the best level of contemporary poetry, and another of his pieces called "The Dead March" is hardly inferior to it.*

ROBERT LOUIS STEVENSON's (1850–1894) *poetry is not put, even by his most enthusiastic admirers, at all on the same level with his prose.   Still, some of it is very good, and I have selected two verses which seem as strong as anything he has left behind him.*

JAMES KENNETH STEPHEN (1859–1892), *second son of Sir J. Fitzjames Stephen, won a great reputation at Cambridge, wrote much brilliant and playful verse, developing other powers of a high order. A career of unusual promise was cut short by an accident which ruined his health.*

PART II

JOHN HENRY CARDINAL NEWMAN. 1801–1890

KNOWLEDGE

"Weep not for me :—
Be blithe as wont, nor tinge with gloom
The stream of love that circles home,
        Light hearts and free !
Joy in the gifts Heaven's bounty lends,
Nor miss my face, dear friends !

"I still am near ;—
Watching the smiles I prized on earth,
Your converse mild, your blameless mirth ;
        Now, too, I hear
Of whisper'd sounds the tale complete—
Low prayers and musings sweet.

"A sea before
The throne is spread ; its pure still glass
Pictures all earth scenes as they pass ;
        We on its shore
Share in the bosom of our rest
God's knowledge, and are blest !"

REST

"They are at rest.
We may not stir the heaven of their repose
By rude invoking voice, or prayer addrest
 In waywardness to those
Who in the mountain grots of Eden lie,
And hear the fourfold river as it murmurs by.

 "They hear it sweep
In distance down the dark and savage vale ;
But they at rocky bed, or current deep,
 Shall never more grow pale.
They hear, and meekly muse, as fain to know
How long untired, unspent, that giant stream shall
 flow.

 "And soothing sounds
Blend with the neighbouring waters as they glide ;
Posted along the haunted garden's bounds,
 Angelic forms abide
Echoing, as words of watch, o'er lawn and grove,
The verses of that hymn which seraphs chant above."

FROM "THE DREAM OF GERONTIUS"

I went to sleep ; and now I am refreshed,
A strange refreshment ; for I feel in me
An inexpressible lightness and a sense
Of freedom, as I were at length myself,
And ne'er had been before. How still it is !
I hear no more the busy beat of time,
No, nor my fluttering breath, nor struggling pulse ;

Nor does one moment differ from the next.
I had a dream; yes, some one softly said,
"He's gone"; and then a sigh went round the room.
And then I surely heard a priestly voice
Cry "Subvenite": and they knelt in prayer.
I seem to hear him still; but thin and low
And fainter and more faint the accents come
As at an ever-widening interval.
Ah, whence is this?   What is this severance?
This silence pours a solitariness
Into the very essence of my soul;
And the deep rest, so soothing and so sweet,
Hath something too of sternness and of pain.

MRS. ARCHER CLIVE. 1801–1873

FROM "THE QUEEN'S BALL"

One phantom was a girl, who here
Had glitter'd in her eighteenth year,
So heavenly fair in those bright hours,
With quaint device of dress and flowers,
That the eye dwelt on her surprised,
As on a fable realised;
One, spellbound, most of all, had burn'd
With love, which frankly she return'd:
But while their silken courtship sped,
   Did sudden clouds a storm unroll;
And 'twixt them left a gulf so dread
   As frightened from its place her soul.
The world, whose fragile ornament
   She for a time so brief had been,
Heard, faintly, of some dark event
   That hid her from its festive scene;
Heard all that was, and what was not;
Inquired, conjectured and forgot.
Meantime the maiden's life took wing;
   Beneath Existence's strife it died;
And, like a fountain of the Spring,
It met the Summer's sun and died;
Her lover watch'd with broken heart
   (Or what to him and her seem'd broken),
   And the last words that she heard spoken,
Were, "Not for long, my Life, we part."
She heard, and smiled, in death to be
Love's victim, and its victory.
She came this night and, unseen, moved
Where she had glitter'd, triumph'd, loved;

And 'mid new beauties, sought for one
Who should lament for her that's gone.
She found him straight; but, ah! no dream
Of her, the dead, there seem'd for him;
He moved among the fair and gay,
His smile and ready word had they,
He touch'd soft hands, and breathed a sigh,
And sought and found an answering eye;
And in the dance he mix'd with many,
As happy and as light as any.
Then on his breast the phantom rush'd,
Her phantom hair his bosom brush'd,
Her fond fantastic arms she wound
Beseechingly his form around.

   Her airy lips his visage kiss'd;
In vain, in vain, no thought he cast
Back on the memory of the past,
And she must let it go at last,
   The cherish'd hope that she was miss'd.

A ghost went gliding round, who'd been
The guest of guests, in such a scene;
Without *his* wit, the feast was cross'd;
Without *his* pen, the scene was lost;
He came to earth, to weep their lot,
Who wanted him and found him not.
But where were they?   Did none recall
His presence needful once to all.

New wits were risen—new words were said,
And his, like him, were of the dead.
Yet Genius is a deathless light,
That still burns on through thickest night;
It fires a steady lamp whose rays
Descend through time, like stars through space,

Though twice a thousand years be fled,
We still repeat what Æsop said.
Thus he, sad ghost! slow circling there,
By many an all-unconscious ear,
Caught at the last the dearest name,
His own,—the hold he had on Fame.
"Poor ——," the speaker said, "his mot,
The witty soul! was—so and so."
He heard,—he drank the praise they gave,
And went the easier to his grave.

A ghost was there, who died in age,
Not wearied yet with pilgrimage;
A soul so kindly and so slight,—
So guileless in the world's despite,
    So void of thought, yet rightly feeling,
It could have no descending weight,—
'Twould flutter up to heaven's gate,
Like down, on rising breezes, stealing.
And yet she sighed to see the ray
    Of gem and gold, her own of late,
Which on a younger bosom lay,
    The owner of her name and state.
Not all forgotten, she; for one
Whom the new lady smiled upon,
Said, "Is it true, then, that at last
The Ancient Dame away has pass'd?"
She heard, and turned her to the tomb,
And said—"Alas! your turn will come."

WINTHROP MACKWORTH PRAED. 1802–1839

(Verses on seeing the Speaker asleep in his chair.)

Sleep, Mr. Speaker, 'tis surely fair,
If you mayn't in your bed, that you should in
    your chair;
Louder and longer still they grow,
Tory and Radical, Aye and No;
Talking by night and talking by day:
Sleep, Mr. Speaker,—sleep while you may.

Sleep, Mr. Speaker; slumber lies
Light and brief on a Speaker's eyes.
Fielden or Finn in a minute or two
Some disorderly thing will do;
Riot will chase repose away—
Sleep, Mr. Speaker,—sleep while you may!

Sleep, Mr. Speaker.   Sweet to men
Is the sleep that cometh but now and then,
Sweet to the weary, sweet to the ill,
Sweet to the children that work in the mill.
You have more need of repose than they,—
Sleep, Mr. Speaker,—sleep while you may!

Sleep, Mr. Speaker, Harvey will soon
Move to abolish the sun and the moon;
Hume will no doubt be taking the sense
Of the House on a question of sixteenpence.
Statesmen will howl, and patriots bray,—
Sleep, Mr. Speaker,—sleep while you may!

Sleep, Mr. Speaker, and dream of the time,
When loyalty was not quite a crime,

When Grant was a pupil in Canning's school,
And Palmerston fancied Wood a fool.
Lord, how principles pass away,—
Sleep, Mr. Speaker,—sleep while you may!

THE DYING GIRL TO HER LOVER

Fare thee well, love, fare thee well,
  From the world I pass away,
Where the brightest things that dwell
  All deceive and all decay;
Cheerfully I fall asleep
  As by some mysterious spell,
Yet I weep to see thee weep—
  Fare thee well, love, fare thee well.

Tell of me, love, tell of me,
  Not amid the heartless throng,
Not when passion bends the knee,
  Not where pleasure trills the song.
But when some most cherish'd one
  By your side at eve shall be,
Ere your twilight tales are done,
  Tell of me, love, tell of me!

Leave me now, love, leave me now,
  Not with sorrow, not with sighs,
Not with clouds, love, on thy brow,
  Not with tears, love, in thine eyes.
We shall meet, we know not where,
  And be blest, we dream not how,
With a kiss and with a prayer
  Leave me now, love, leave me now!

L. E. MACLEAN (L. E. L.).   1802–1838

FELICIA HEMANS

Thou art gone from us, and with thee departed,
　　How many lovely things have vanished too;
Deep thoughts that at thy will to being started,
　　And feelings, teaching us our own were true.
Thou hast been round us, like a viewless spirit,
　　Known only by the music on the air;
The leaf or flowers which thou hast named inherit
　　A beauty known but from thy breathing there:
For thou didst on them fling thy strong emotion,
　　The likeness from itself the fond heart gave;
As planets from afar look down on ocean,
　　And give their own sweet image to the wave.

And thou didst bring from foreign lands their treasures
　　As floats thy various melody along;
We know the softness of Italian measures,
　　And the grave cadence of Castilian song.
A general bond of union is the poet,
　　By its immortal verse is language known,
And for the sake of song do others know it—
　　One glorious poet makes the world his own.
And thou—how far thy gentle sway extended!
　　The heart's sweet empire over land and sea;
Many a stranger and far flower was blended
　　In the soft wreath that glory bound for thee.
The echoes of the Susquehanna's waters
　　Paused in the pine-woods words of thine to hear;
And to the wide Atlantic's younger daughters
　　Thy name was lovely, and thy song was dear.

Was not this purchased all too dearly? never
　　Can fame atone for all that fame hath cost.
We see the goal, but know not the endeavour,
　　Nor what fond hopes have on the way. been lost.
What do we know of the unquiet pillow,
　　By the worn cheek and tearful eyelid prest,
When thoughts chased thoughts, like the tumultuous
　　　　billow,
　　Whose very light and foam reveals unrest?
We say, the song is sorrowful, but know not
　　What may have left that sorrow on the song;
However mournful words may be, they show not
　　The whole extent of wretchedness and wrong.
They cannot paint the long sad hours, passed only
　　In vain regrets o'er what we feel we are.
Alas! the kingdom of the lute is lonely—
　　Cold is the worship coming from afar.

　　　.　　　.　　　.　　　.　　　.　　　.　　　.

What on this earth could answer thy requiring,
　　For earnest faith—for love, the deep and true,
The beautiful, which was thy soul's desiring,
　　But only from thyself its being drew.
How is the warm and loving heart requited
　　In this harsh world, where it awhile must dwell,
Its best affections wronged, betrayed, and slighted—
　　Such is the doom of those who love too well.
Better the weary dove should close its pinion,
　　Fold up its golden wings and be at peace:
Enter, O Ladye, that serene dominion,
　　Where earthly cares and earthly sorrows cease.
Fame's troubled hour has cleared, and now replying,
　　A thousand hearts their music ask of thine.
Sleep with a light, the lovely and undying,
　　Around thy grave—a grave which is a shrine.

LORD LYTTON. 1803–1873

ST. JAMES'S STREET ON A SUMMER MORNING

(*From the " New Timon"*)

O'er royal London in luxuriant May,
While lamps yet twinkled dawning crept the day,
Home from the hell the pale-eyed gamester steals,
Home from the ball flash jaded beauty's wheels.
The lean grimalkin, who since night began
Has hymned to love amid the wrath of man,
Scared from his raptures by the morning star,
Flits finely by and threads the area bar.
From fields suburban rolls the early cart,
As rests the revel so awakes the mart.
Transfusing Mocha from the beans within,
Bright by the crossing gleams the alchemic tin.
There halts the craftsman ; there with envious sigh
The houseless vagrant looks and limps foot-weary by.
Behold that street, the Omphalos of Town,
Where the grim palace wears the prison's frown,
As mindful still, amid a gaudier race,
Of the veil'd genius of that mournful place,
Of floors no majesty but grief's has trod,
And weary limbs that only knelt to God.
What tales, what morals of the elder day,
If stones had language could that street convey !
Along that space the bloodhound crowd arrayed,
Howled round the shrine where last the Stuart prayed ;
See to that spot the self-same bloodhounds run,
To lick the feet of Stuart's viler son.
There through the dusk-red towers amidst his ring
Of Vans and Mynheers rode the Dutchman king,

And there did England's Goneril thrill to hear
The shouts that triumph'd o'er her crownless Lear.
There where the gaslight streams o'er Crockford's
    door
Bluff Henry chuckled at the jests of More.
There, where you gaze upon the last H. B.,
Swift paused and muttered — "Shall I have that
    See?"
There where yon pile for party's common weal
Knits votes that serve with hearts abhorring Peel,
Blunt Walpole seized and roughly bought his man,
Or, tired of Polly, St. John lounged to Anne.

LORD JOHN RUSSELL

But see our Statesman when the steam is on,
And languid Johnny glows to glorious John.
When Hampden's thought by Falkland's muses
    drest,
Lights the pale cheek and swells the generous breast;
When the pent heat expands the quickening soul,
And foremost in the race the wheels of genius roll.
What gives the past the haunting charms that please
Sage, Scholar, Bard—the shades of men like these.
Seen in our walks, with vulgar blame or praise,
Reviled or worshipped as our faction sways.
Some centuries hence and from that praise or blame,
As light from vapour breaks the steady flame,
And the trite present, which while acted seems
Life's dullest prose, fades in the land of dreams.

CONSEQUENCES OF THE REFORMATION

(From " St. Stephen's ")

Faith thus dislodged from ancient schools and creeds,
Question to question, doubt to doubt succeeds—
Clouds gathering flame for thunders soon to be,
And glass'd on Shakespeare as upon a sea.
Each guess of others into worlds unknown
Shakespeare revolves, but guards conceal'd his own—
As in the Infinite hangs poised his thought,
Surveying all things, and asserting nought.

And now, transferr'd from singer and from sage,
Stands in full day the Spirit of the Age—
Inquiry !—She, so coy when first pursued
In her own ancient, arduous solitude,
Seized by the crowd, and dragged before their bar,
Changes her shape, and towers transform'd to war ;
Inscribes a banner, flings it to the gales—
Cries, " I am Truth, and Truth when arm'd prevails !"
Up leaps the zealot—Zeal must clear her way,
And fell the forests that obscure the day.
To guard the Bible flashes forth the sword,
And Cromwell rides, the servant of the Lord.
Twin-born with Freedom, then with her took breath,
That Art whose dying will be Freedom's death.
From thought's fierce clash, in lightning broke the word ;
Ungagg'd at last the Isle's strong man was heard :
Still in their sheaths the direful swords repose ;
Voice may yet warn : The Orator arose !
Founders of England's slow-built eloquence—
Truth's last adornment as her first defence—
Pass—but as shadows ! Nevermore again
May the land need, yet reel beneath, such men.

H

Lo, where from haunted floors the phantoms rise
Pale through the mists which cleared for us the skies,
There, but one moment lingering in the hall,
The earliest, hardiest Orator of all,
Young Eliot wanes upon the verge of War,
As day, in redd'ning, slays its own bright star.
There flits by Waller of the silvery tongue,
And faith as ductile as the lyre he strung.
There, wise to warn, yet impotent to guide,
And sad with foresight, moves the solemn Hyde.
Mark in the front, fit leader of the van,
Yon large, imperfect, necessary man;
With all the zeal a cause conflicting needs,
And all the craft by which the cause succeeds,
Iron as Ludlow, yet as Villiers trim,
'Twixt saint and sinner—Atlas-shouldered Pym.
Behind, pure, chill, and lonely as a star,
Ruthless as angels, when destroying, are,
Sits Vane, and dreams Utopian isles to be,
While swells the storm, and sea but spreads on sea;
Still in a mirage he discerns a shore,
And acts with Hampden from belief in More.
Nor less alone, nor less a dreamer, there
Wan Falkland looks through space with gloomy
        stare
Pondering that question which no wise man's voice
Ever solved yet, to guide the brave man's choice,
When the dread present, as on an abyss,
Splits, in two paths, the frowning precipice—
That, to lost towers which tides already whelm;
This, through dark gorges to an unknown realm;
Hard to decide! each future has its crime;
Each past its wreck: here, how control the time?
There, how rekindle dust?   Between the two
At least choose quick.   Life is the verb "To do!"

SIR ROBERT WALPOLE

Burly and bluff, in St. John's vacant place,
The land's new leader lifts his jovial face.
Alas! poor Nine—a dreary time for you!
King George the First, Sir Robert Walpole too!
Sir Robert waits;—those shrewd coarse features scan,
How strong the sense, how English is the man!—
English, if left to all plain sense bestows,
And stripp'd of all that Man to genius owes.
He sets no flowers, but each dry stubble gleans—
Statesman in ends, but huckster in the means—
Boldly he nears his hacks, extends the chaff,
And flings the halter with an ostler's laugh.
Corruptly frank, he buys or bullies all,
And is what placemen style "the practical."
Is this man eloquent?   The man creates
New ground, now ours—the level of debates.
Eloquent?—Yes, in parliamentary sense,
The skilful scorn of what seems eloquence;
Adroit, familiar, fluent, easy, free,
And each quick point as quick to seize as see;
Shielding the friend, but covering from the foe,
And ne'er above his audience nor below:
Arm'd in finance, blow up with facts the speech,
And rows of figures bristle in the breach.
Soft in his tones, seductive in his sighs,
When doom'd to take "a vote upon supplies;"
At times a proser, at no time a prater,
And six feet high—in short, a great debater.
And is that all?—Nay, truth must grant much more;
The bluff old Whig was Briton to the core.
With this strong purpose, whatsoe'er he plann'd,
To save from Pope and Papist kings the land.

His heart was mild, it slew not nor proscribed;
His tenets loose, in clemency he bribed.
A town conspires in secret :—he sends down
Cannon—tut! candidates to buy the town.
Sly Jesuits have a senator misled,
He hints a pension, and he saves a head.
While since adventure outlets must obtain,
In closing war he frees the roads to gain ;
Shows teeming marts, and says to Hope, " Behold,
'Tis Peace that guards the avenues to gold."
So blent with good and evil all the springs
Which move in states the wheels of human things,
That, though the truth must be with pain confest,
Men not too good may suit mankind the best ;
So leave Sir Robert " buttoned to the chin,
Broadcloth without, and a warm heart within ! "

FOX

Men live who tell us what no books can teach,
How spoke the speaker—what his style of speech.
Our Fox's voice roll'd no melodious stream—
It rose in splutter and went off in scream,
Yet could it vary in appropriate place,
From the sharp alto to the rumbling bass.
Such sudden changes when you'd least expect,
Secured to dissonance a stage effect,
Striking you most when into talk-like ease
Slid the wild gamut down the cracking keys.
The Action? what Quintilian would have shock'd ;
The huge fist thunder'd, and the huge frame rock'd,

As clattering down, *immenso ore*, went
Splinters and crags of crashing argument.
Not for neat reasonings, subtle and refined,
Paused the strong logic of that rushing mind;
It tore from out the popular side of Truth
Fragments, the larger because left uncouth—
Hands, if less strong, more patient than his own,
Perfect the statue, his heaved forth the stone,
And in the rock his daring chisel broke,
Hew'd the bold outlines with a hasty stroke.
But on this force, with its disdain of rule,
No safe good sense would like to found a school;
And (drop the image) he who leads mankind
Must seek to soothe and not to shock the mind.
The chief whose anger all the angry cheer,
Thins his own ranks—the temperate disappear;
They shake their heads, and in a sober fright
Groan, "What a passion he was in to-night!"
"Men in a passion must be in the wrong;"
"And, heavens! how dangerous when they're made so
      strong!"
Thus is it strange, with all his genius, zeal,
Such head to argue, and such heart to feel,
That the great Whig, amidst immense applause,
Scared off his clients and bawled down his cause;
Undid reform by lauding revolution,
Till cobblers cried, "God save the Constitution!"
Met by deserters in his own approaches,
He fled: his followers filled three hackney coaches!
Leave we the orator but track the man,
May clothes with bloom the orchard of St. Anne;
Under the blossoms, stirr'd by the meek wind,
See that large form so quietly reclined;
Those black brows bent o'er learning's calmest tome,
That smile whose peace floods, as with sunlight, home.

There see him taste, far from life's reek and din,
Toil without strife, and pleasure without sin;
Glow o'er some golden song, or pause perplext
By some dry scholiast or some doubtful text;
Charm kindred ears with Attic lore and wit,
And rapt to Pindus, leave mankind to Pitt.

PITT

The lone proud man! for him no graces smiled,
No love the pause from jaded toil beguiled;
No twilight tryst exchanged the youthful vow;
No tender lips kissed trouble from that brow!
His sole Egeria (O supreme caprice!)
A crack'd, uncanny war-witch of a niece,
Who, at his death, found Syrian sands alone
Replace the lost grand desert she had known,
For rule in wastes by previous empire fit,
Had she not ruled a lonelier world in Pitt?
Yet all strong natures have affections strong
Barr'd the free vents which to man's life belong;
Still springs well up, concentre sudden force,
And glad the waves of which they swell the course.
These are the minds that serve some abstract
        creed—
The Church Ignatius, Fame the Royal Swede;
More hot the ideal, human love unknown,
As chaste Pygmalion hugg'd to life a stone.
Pitt's human passion, his ideal dream,
His soul's twin Arcady and Academe,
Was England!—Not more rooted to the deep
The stubborn isle round which the tempests sweep,

Than he to England; call him, if you will,
Too fond of power—'twas power for England still.
Through this he ruled; he spoke, and this was
    shown;
The Laws, the Land, the Altar and the Throne,
Mere words with others, were to him the all
Left man to prize and strive for since the Fall.

LORD MELBOURNE

In stalwart contrast, large of heart and frame,
Destined for power, in youth more bent on fame,
Sincere, yet deeming half the world a sham,
Mark the rude handsome manliness of Lamb!
None then foresaw his rise; ev'n now but few
Guess right the man so many thought they knew;
Gossip accords him attributes like these—
A sage good-humour based on love of ease,
A mind that most things undisturb'dly weigh'd,
Nor deem'd their metal worth the clink it made.
Such was the man, in part, to outward show;
Another man lay coil'd from sight below—
As mystics tell us that this fleshly form
Enfolds a subtler which escapes the worm,
And is the true one which the Maker's breath
Quicken'd from dust, and privileged from death.
His was a restless, anxious intellect;
Eager for truth and pining to detect,
Each ray of light that mind can cast on soul,
Chequering its course, or shining from its goal,
Each metaphysic doubt—each doctrine dim—
Plato or Pusey—had delight for him.

His mirth, though genial, came by fits and starts—
The man was mournful in his heart of hearts.
Oft would he sit, or wander forth alone ;
Sad—why ? I know not ; was it ever known ?
Tears came with ease to those ingenuous eyes—
A verse, if noble, bade them nobly rise.
Hear him discourse, you'd think he scarcely felt ;
No heart more facile to arouse or melt ;
High as a knight's in some Castilian lay,
And tender as a sailor's in a play.

O'CONNELL

Hear him in senates, second-rate at best,
Clear in a statement, happy in a jest ;
Sought he to shine, then certain to displease ;
Tawdry yet coarse-grain'd, tinsel upon frieze :
His Titan strength must touch what gave it birth ;
Hear him to mobs, and on his mother earth !

Once to my sight the giant thus was given,
Wall'd by wide air, and roof'd by boundless heaven ;
Beneath his feet the human ocean lay,
And wave on wave flow'd into space away.
Methought no clarion could have sent its sound
Even to the centre of the hosts around ;
And as I thought rose the sonorous swell,
As from some church tower swings the silvery bell.
Aloft and clear, from airy tide to tide,
It glided, easy as a bird may glide ;
To the last verge of that vast audience sent,
It play'd with each wild passion as it went.

Now stirr'd the uproar, now the murmur still'd,
And sobs or laughter answered as it will'd.

Then did I know what spells of infinite choice,
To rouse or lull, has the sweet human voice;
Then did I seem to seize the sudden clue
To the grand troublous Life Antique—to view
Under the rock-stand of Demosthenes
Mutable Athens heave her noisy seas.

THE ORATOR

Loud as a scandal on the ears of town,
And just as brief, the orator's renown!
Year after year debaters blaze and fade—
Scarce mark'd the dial ere departs the shade;
Words die so soon when fit but to be said,
Words only live when worthy to be read.

Already Fox is silent to our age,
Burke quits the rostrum to illume the page.
He did not waste his treasure as he went,
But hoarded wealth to pile his monument.
Now voice and manner can offend no more,
And pure from dross shines out the golden ore—
Down to oblivion sinks each rude defect,
And soars anneal'd, the eternal intellect.

Thus is a torrent, if we stand too near,
Rough to the sight, and jarring to the ear;
But heard afar, when dubious of the way,
In paths perplex'd where forests dim the day,

Mellow'd from every discord, o'er the ground,
As from an unseen spirit, comes the sound—
That sound the step unconsciously obeys,
And, lured to light by music, threads the maze.

THE SUCCESSFUL POLITICIAN

Few, who at ease their Members' speeches read,
Guess the hard life of Members who succeed;
Pass by the waste of youthful golden days,
And the dread failure of the first essays—
Grant that the earlier steeps and sloughs are past,
And Fame's broad highway stretches smooth at last;
Grant the success, and now behold the pains:
Eleven to three—Committee upon Drains!
From three to five—self-commune and a chop;
From five to dawn—a bill to pass or stop;
Which, stopt or pass'd, leaves England much the same.
Alas for genius staked in such a game!
When as "the guerdon" in the grasp appears,
"Comes the blind Fury with the abhorred shears."

SIR EDMUND HEAD. 1805–1868

TRANSLATION FROM PROPERTIUS

Vex not the grave with tears : its shadows deep
    Repulse the mourner and exclude the day ;
The bourne is passed : cease, Paulus, cease to weep ;
    A gate of adamant hath barred the way.

Prayer dies in echoes 'mid these gloomy bowers,
    And floats in vain round sullen Pluto's ear :
Prayer moves the Gods above : th' infernal powers
    Nor list the suppliant voice, nor heed the tear.

Such were the truths taught by the trumpet's blare,
    When o'er my bier curl'd up the funeral flame ;
What booted then our troth, or lineage fair,
    Or those bright pledges which have graced our name?

Could I thus 'scape from Fate's unbending laws?
    No ! five small fingers now may lift my dust.
All young and spotless let me plead my cause
    To Æacus and Minos—stern, yet just.

If any maid could vaunt her sires in Rome,
    Ancestral fame was mine on either side ;
For Spain and Carthage deck'd with spoils the home
    Where Scipio's blood was match'd with Libo's pride.

A girl, dear Paulus, on our wedding-day,
    I wreath'd the bridal fillet in my hair :
And soon, too soon, in death thus snatch'd away,
    No second name upon my tomb I bear.

Shades of our fathers ! ye whose titles tell
    Of Afric shorn of empire at your feet ;
And how the braggart race of Perseus fell—
    Achilles' sons hurl'd from Achilles' seat—

Stand forth, and witness that no sland'rer's breath
    E'er tainted on the Censor's roll my name ;
Between the bridal torch and torch of death
    We liv'd and lov'd in wedded faith the same.

It needed not a judge or law to guide
    One, in whose veins the blood of all her race
Swell'd with the instinct of a conscious pride,
    And bade maintain a Roman matron's place.

I shrink from none.   If ancient tales be true,
    When Vesta's fire was quench'd, Emilia's hand
Her linen garment o'er the ashes threw,
    And show'd beneath its folds the kindled brand

We know that Claudia's slender girdle mov'd
    The mighty Mother's ship : their vestal pride
Will hail the faith in steadfast wedlock prov'd,
    And great Cornelia seated at their side.

Thou, too, Scribonia, gentle mother, say,
    Now thou art weeping o'er thy daughter's tomb,
What is there in my course to wish away,
    Save that I met in death an early doom ?

'Tis something for a mother, when she dies,
    To leave no barren hearth, no desert home ;
I joy to think that sons have clos'd my eyes
    Who live to bear their ancient name in Rome.

My daughter ! let the world retrace in thee
    The even tenour of thy mother's life :
Like me, prolong thy line, and die like me,
    Firm in thy plighted troth, but once a wife.

A woman's brighter triumph is attain'd
    When blame no more can wound nor flatt'ry move,
When praise from all, unbrib'd and unrestrain'd,
    Meets o'er her bier the tears of those who love.

Still, Paulus, in my ashes lives one care ;
    Our children of their mother are bereft :
The household charge we both were wont to share
    In undivided weight on thee is left.

Affection's duty now devolves on thee !
    Oh ! let them not a mother's fondness miss,
But when they clasp thy neck or climb thy knee,
    Add to their sire's caress a mother's kiss.

Be careful, if thou e'er for me shall weep,
    That they may never mark the tears thus shed ;
Let it suffice thyself to mourn in sleep
    The wife whose spirit hovers o'er thy bed ;

Or in thy chamber, if thou wilt, aloud
    Address that wife as if she could reply ;
Dim not our children's joys with sorrow's cloud,
    But dry the tear, and check the rising sigh.

You, too, my children, at your father's side,
    In after years a step-dame if you see,
Let no rash word offend her jealous pride,
    Nor indiscreetly wound by praising me.

Obey his will in all : and should he bear
    In widow'd solitude the woes of age,
Let it be yours to prop his steps with care,
    And with your gentle love those woes assuage.

I lost no child : 'twas mine in death to see
    Their faces cluster'd round : nor should I grieve
If but the span of life cut off from me
    Could swell the years in store for those I leave.

My cause is pleaded and my tale is told :
    Pronounce me worthy of the meed I claim,
And give me, where my fathers sleep of old,
    Such honour as befits Cornelia's house and name.

FRANCIS MAHONY ("FATHER PROUT"). 1805–66

THE SHANDON BELLS

With deep affection,
And recollection,
I often think of
  Those Shandon bells,
Whose sounds so wild would,
In the days of childhood,
Fling round my cradle
  Their magic spells.
On this I ponder
Where'er I wander,
And thus grow fonder,
  Sweet Cork, of thee;
With thy bells of Shandon,
That sound so grand on
The pleasant waters
  Of the river Lee.

I've heard bells chiming
Full many a clime in,
Tolling sublime in,
  Cathedral shrine,
While at a glib rate
Brass tongues would vibrate—
But all their music
  Spoke nought like thine;
For memory dwelling
On each proud swelling
Of the belfry knelling
  Its bold notes free,
Made the bells of Shandon
Sound far more grand on
The pleasant waters
  Of the river Lee.

I've heard bells tolling
Old "Adrian's Mole" in,
Their thunder rolling
    From the Vatican,
And cymbals glorious
Swinging uproarious
In the gorgeous turrets
    Of Nôtre Dame;
But thy sounds were sweeter
Than the dome of Peter
Flings o'er the Tiber,
    Pealing solemnly;—
O! the bells of Shandon
Sound far more grand on
The pleasant waters
    Of the river Lee.

There's a bell in Moscow
While on tower and kiosk O!
In Saint Sophia
    The Turkman gets;
And loud in air
Calls men to prayer
From the tapering summit
    Of tall minarets.
Such empty phantom
I freely grant them;
But there is an anthem
    More dear to me,—
'Tis the bells of Shandon
That sound so grand on
The pleasant waters
    Of the river Lee,

MRS. BROWNING. 1806-1861

SLEEP

Of all the thoughts of God that are
Borne inward into souls afar,
   Along the Psalmist's music deep,
Now tell me if that any is,
For gift or grace, surpassing this—
   " He giveth His belovèd sleep ? "

What would we give to our beloved ?
The hero's heart to be unmoved,
   The poet's star-tuned harp to sweep,
The patriot's voice to teach and rouse,
The monarch's crown to light the brows ?—
   " He giveth His belovèd sleep."

What do we give to our beloved ?
A little faith all undisproved,
   A little dust to oversweep,
And bitter memories to make
The whole earth blasted for our sake :
   He giveth His belovèd sleep.

"Sleep soft, beloved ! " we sometimes say,
Who have no tune to charm away
   Sad dreams that through the eyelids creep :
But never doleful dream again
Shall break the happy slumber when
   He giveth His belovèd sleep.

I

O earth, so full of dreary noises!
O men, with wailing in your voices!
  O delvèd gold, the wailers heap!
O strife, O curse, that o'er it fall!
God strikes a silence through you all,
  And giveth His belovèd sleep.

His dews drop mutely on the hill;
His cloud above it saileth still,
  Though on its slope men sow and reap;
More softly than the dew is shed,
Or cloud is floated overhead,
  He giveth His belovèd sleep!

Ay, men may wonder while they scan
A living, thinking, feeling man,
  Confirmed in such a rest to keep;
But angels say—and through the word
I think their happy smile is heard—
  He giveth His belovèd sleep!

For me, my heart that erst did go
Most like a tired child at a show
  That sees through tears the mummers leap,
Would now its wearied vision close,
Would childlike on His love repose,
  Who giveth His belovèd sleep!

And friends!—dear friends—when it shall be
That this low breath is gone from me,
  And round my bier ye come to weep,—
Let one most loving of you all,
Say, "Not a tear must o'er her fall—
  He giveth His belovèd sleep!"

FROM A VISION OF POETS

Lucretius—nobler than his mood:
Who dropped his plummet down the broad
Deep universe, and said, "No God."

Finding no bottom: he denied
Divinely the divine, and died
Chief poet on the Tiber-side.

A MUSICAL INSTRUMENT

What was he doing, the great god Pan,
    Down in the reeds by the river?
Spreading ruin and scattering ban,
Splashing and paddling with hoofs of a goat,
And breaking the golden lilies afloat
    With the dragon-fly on the river.

He tore out a reed, the great god Pan,
    From the deep cool bed of the river;
The limpid water turbidly ran,
And the broken lilies a-dying lay,
And the dragon-fly had fled away,
    Ere he brought it out of the river.

High on the shore sate the great god Pan,
    While turbidly flowed the river;
And hacked and hewed as a great god can,
With his hard bleak steel at the patient reed,
Till there was not a sign of the leaf indeed
    To prove it fresh from the river.

He cut it short, did the great god Pan,
  (How tall it stood in the river !)
Then drew the pith, like the heart of a man,
Steadily from the outside ring,
And notched the poor dry empty thing
  In holes, as he sate by the river.

"This is the way," laughed the great god Pan,
  (Laughed while he sate by the river),
"The only way, since gods began
To make sweet music, they could succeed !"
Then dropping his mouth to a hole in the reed,
  He blew in power by the river.

Sweet, sweet, sweet, O Pan !
  Piercing sweet by the river !
Blinding sweet, O great god Pan !
The sun on the hill forgot to die,
And the lilies revived, and the dragon-fly
  Came back to dream on the river.

Yet half a beast is the great god Pan,
  To laugh as he sits by the river,
Making a poet out of a man :
The true gods sigh for the cost and pain,—
For the reed which grows nevermore again
  As a reed with the reeds in the river.

TO L. E. L. ON THE DEATH OF
FELICIA HEMANS

Thou bay-crowned living One that o'er the bay-crowned
    Dead art bowing,
And o'er the shadeless, moveless brow the vital shadow
    throwing,

And o'er the sighless, songless lips the wail and music
    wedding,
Dropping above the tranquil eyes the tears not of their
    shedding!—

Take music from the silent Dead, whose meaning is
    completer;
Reserve thy tears for living brows where all such tears
    are meeter;
And leave the violets in the grass to brighten where thou
    treadest!
No flowers for her! no need of flowers—albeit "bring
    flowers" thou saidest.

Yes, flowers, to crown the "cup and lute!" since both
    may come to breaking:
Or flowers, to greet the "bride"! the heart's own beating
    works its aching:
Or flowers, to sooth the "captive's" sight, from earth's
    free bosom gathered,
Reminding of his earthly hope, then withering as it
    withered!

But bring not near the solemn corse, the type of human
    seeming!
Lay only dust's stern verity upon the dust undreaming!
And while the calm perpetual stars shall look upon it
    solely,
Her spherèd soul shall look on *them* with eyes more
    bright and holy.

Nor mourn, O living One, because her part in life was
    mourning
Would she have lost the poet's fire for anguish of the
    burning?—

The minstrel harp, for the strained string? the tripod
    for the afflated
Woe? or the vision, for those tears in which it shone
    dilated?

Perhaps she shuddered while the world's cold hand her
    brow was wreathing,
But never wronged that mystic breath which breathed in
    all her breathing
Which drew from rocky earth and man, abstractions high
    and moving—
Beauty, if not the beautiful, and love, if not the loving.

Such visionings have paled in sight: the Saviour she
    descrieth,
And little recks *who* wreathed the brow which on His
    bosom lieth,
The whiteness of His innocence o'er all her garments
    flowing,
There learneth she the sweet "new song" she will not
    mourn in knowing.

Be happy, crowned and living One! and, as thy dust
    decayeth,
May thine own England say for thee, what now for Her it
    sayeth—
"Albeit softly in our ears her silver song was ringing,
The footfall of her parting soul is softer than her
    singing!"

E. FITZGERALD. 1809–1883

RUBÁIYÁT OF OMAR KHAYYÁM

They say the Lion and the Lizard keep
The Courts where Jamshýd gloried and drank deep;
    And Bahrám, that great Hunter—the Wild Ass
Stamps o'er his Head, but cannot break his sleep.

I sometimes think that never blows so red
The Rose as where some buried Cæsar bled;
    That every Hyacinth the Garden wears
Dropt in her lap from some once lovely Head.

And this reviving Herb whose tender Green
Fledges the River-Lip on which we lean—
    Ah, lean upon it lightly! for who knows
From what once lovely Lip it springs unseen!

Ah, my Belovèd, fill the Cup that clears,
To-day of past Regrets and Future Fears:
    To-morrow!—Why, to-morrow I may be
Myself with Yesterday's sev'n thousand years.

For some we loved, the loveliest and the best
That from his Vintage rolling Time hath prest,
    Have drunk their Cup a Round or two before,
And one by one crept silently to rest.

And we, that now make merry in the Room
They left, and Summer dresses in new bloom,
    Ourselves must we beneath the Couch of Earth
Descend—ourselves to make a Couch—for whom?

Ah, make the most of what we yet may spend,
Before we too into the Dust descend;
   Dust into Dust, and under Dust to lie
Sans Wine, sans Song, sans Singer, and—sans End.

Alike for those who for To-day prepare,
And those that after some To-morrow stare,
   A Muezzin from the Tower of Darkness cries,
"Fools! your Reward is neither Here nor There."

Why, all the Saints and Sages who discuss'd
Of the two worlds so wisely—they are thrust
   Like foolish Prophets forth; their Words to scorn
Are scatter'd, and their Mouths are stopt with Dust.

Myself when young did eagerly frequent
Doctor and Saint, and heard great argument
   About it and about; but evermore
Came out by the same door where in I went.

With them the seed of Wisdom did I sow,
And with mine own hand wrought to make it grow;
   And this was all the Harvest that I reap'd—
"I came like Water, and like Wind I go."

LORD TENNYSON. 1809–1892

CIRCUMSTANCE

Two children in two neighbour villages
Playing mad pranks along the heathy leas ;
Two strangers meeting at a festival ;
Two lovers whispering by an orchard wall ;
Two lives bound fast in one with golden ease ;
Two graves grass-green beside a gray church-tower,
Wash'd with still rains and daisy blossomèd ;
Two children in one hamlet born and bred ;
So runs the round of life from hour to hour.

MORTE D'ARTHUR

So all day long the noise of battle roll'd
Among the mountains by the winter sea ;
Until King Arthur's table, man by man,
Had fallen in Lyonnesse about their Lord,
King Arthur : then, because his wound was deep,
The bold Sir Bedivere uplifted him,
Sir Bedivere, the last of all his knights,
And bore him to a chapel nigh the field,
A broken chancel with a broken cross,
That stood on a dark strait of barren land.
On one side lay the Ocean, and on one
Lay a great water, and the moon was full.
    Then spake King Arthur to Sir Bedivere :
"The sequel of to-day unsolders all
The goodliest fellowship of famous knights
Whereof this world holds record.   Such a sleep

They sleep—the men I loved.   I think that we
Shall never more, at any future time,
Delight our souls with talk of knightly deeds,
Walking about the gardens and the halls
Of Camelot, as in the days that were.
I perish by this people which I made,—
Tho' Merlin sware that I should come again
To rule once more—but let what will be, be,
I am so deeply smitten thro' the helm
That without help I cannot last till morn.
Thou therefore take my brand Excalibur,
Which was my pride : for thou rememberest how
In those old days, one summer noon, an arm
Rose up from out the bosom of the lake,
Clothed in white samite, mystic, wonderful,
Holding the sword—and how I row'd across
And took it, and have worn it, like a king :
And, wheresoever I am sung or told
In aftertime, this also shall be known :
But now delay not : take Excalibur,
And fling him far into the middle mere :
Watch what thou seest, and lightly bring me word.''

    To him replied the bold Sir Bedivere :
" It is not meet, Sir King, to leave thee thus,
Aidless, alone, and smitten thro' the helm.
A little thing may harm a wounded man.
Yet I thy hest will all perform at full,
Watch what I see, and lightly bring thee word."

    So saying, from the ruin'd shrine he stept
And in the moon athwart the place of tombs,
Where lay the mighty bones of ancient men,
Old knights, and over them the sea-wind sang
Shrill, chill, with flakes of foam. He, stepping down
By zig-zag paths, and juts of pointed rock,
Came on the shining levels of the lake.

There drew he forth the brand Excalibur,
And o'er him, drawing it, the winter moon,
Brightening the skirts of a long cloud, ran forth
And sparkled keen with frost against the hilt:
For all the haft twinkled with diamond sparks,
Myriads of topaz-lights, and jacinth-work
Of subtlest jewellery. He gazed so long
That both his eyes were dazzled, as he stood,
This way and that dividing the swift mind,
In act to throw: but at the last it seem'd
Better to leave Excalibur conceal'd
There in the many-knotted waterflags,
That whistled stiff and dry about the marge.
So strode he back slow to the wounded King.

Then spake King Arthur to Sir Bedivere:
"Hast thou perform'd my mission which I
     gave?
What is it thou hast seen? or what hast heard?"

And answer made the bold Sir Bedivere:
"I heard the ripple washing in the reeds,
And the wild water lapping on the crag!"

To whom replied King Arthur, faint and pale:
"Thou hast betray'd thy nature and thy name,
Not rendering true answer, as beseem'd
Thy fealty, nor like a noble knight;
For surer sign had follow'd, either hand,
Or voice, or else a motion of the mere.
This is a shameful thing for men to lie.
Yet now, I charge thee, quickly go again
As thou art lief and dear, and do the thing
I bad thee, watch, and lightly bring me word!"

Then went Sir Bedivere the second time
Across the ridge, and paced beside the mere,
Counting the dewy pebbles, fix'd in thought;
But when he saw the wonder of the hilt,

How curiously and strangely chased, he smote
His palms together, and he cried aloud,
   "And if indeed I cast the brand away,
Surely a precious thing, one worthy note,
Should thus be lost for ever from the earth,
Which might have pleased the eyes of many men.
What good should follow this, if this were done?
What harm, undone? deep harm to disobey,
Seeing obedience is the bond of rule.
Were it well to obey then, if a king demand
An act unprofitable, against himself?
The king is sick, and knows not what he does.
What record, or what relic of my lord
Should be to aftertime, but empty breath
And rumours of a doubt? but were this kept,
Stored in some treasure-house of mighty kings,
Some one might show it at a joust of arms,
Saying, 'King Arthur's sword, Excalibur,
Wrought by the lonely maiden of the Lake.
Nine years she wrought it, sitting in the deeps
Upon the hidden bases of the hills.'
So might some old man speak in the aftertime
To all the people, winning reverence.
But now much honour and much fame were lost!"
   So spake he, clouded with his own conceit,
And hid Excalibur the second time,
And so strode back slow to the wounded King.
   Then spoke King Arthur, breathing heavily:
"What is it thou hast seen? or what hast heard?"
   And answer made the bold Sir Bedivere:
"I heard the water lapping on the crag,
And the long ripple washing in the reeds."
   To whom replied King Arthur much in wrath:
"Ah, miserable and unkind, untrue,
Unknightly, traitor-hearted! Woe is me!

Authority forgets a dying king,
Laid widow'd of the power in his eye
That bow'd the will. I see thee what thou art,
For thou, the latest-left of all my knights,
In whom should meet the offices of all,
Thou wouldst betray me for the precious hilt;
Either from lust of gold, or like a girl
Valuing the giddy pleasure of the eyes.
Yet, for a man may fail in duty twice,
And the third time may prosper, get thee hence:
But, if thou spare to fling Excalibur,
I will arise and slay thee with my hands."
  Then quickly rose Sir Bedivere, and ran,
And, leaping down the ridges lightly, plunged
Among the bulrush-beds, and clutch'd the sword,
And strongly wheel'd and threw it. The great brand
Made lightnings in the splendour of the moon,
And flashing round and round, and whirl'd in an arch,
Shot like a streamer of the Northern morn,
Seen where the moving isles of winter shock
By night, with noises of the Northern Sea.
So flash'd and fell the brand Excalibur:
But ere he dipt the surface, rose an arm
Clothed in white samite, mystic, wonderful,
And caught him by the hilt, and brandish'd him
Three times, and drew him under in the mere.
And lightly went the other to the King.
  Then spoke King Arthur, drawing thicker breath:
"Now see I by thine eyes that this is done.
Speak out: what is it thou hast heard, or seen?"
  And answer made the bold Sir Bedivere:
"Sir King, I closed mine eyelids, lest the gems
Should blind my purpose, for I never saw,
Nor shall see, here or elsewhere, till I die,
Not tho' I live three lives of mortal men,

So great a miracle as yonder hilt.
Then with both hands I flung him, wheeling him ;
But when I look'd again, behold an arm,
Clothed in white samite, mystic, wonderful,
That caught him by the hilt, and brandish'd him
Three times, and drew him under in the mere."

    And answer made King Arthur, breathing hard :
"My end draws nigh ; 'tis time that I were gone.
Make broad thy shoulders to receive my weight,
And bear me to the margin ; yet I fear
My wound hath taken cold, and I shall die."

    So saying, from the pavement he half rose,
Slowly, with pain, reclining on his arm,
And looking wistfully with wide blue eyes
As in a picture.   Him Sir Bedivere
Remorsefully regarded thro' his tears,
And would have spoken, but he found not words,
Then took with care, and kneeling on one knee,
O'er both his shoulders drew the languid hands,
And rising bore him thro' the place of tombs.

    But, as he walk'd, King Arthur panted hard,
Like one that feels a nightmare on his bed
When all the house is mute.   So sigh'd the King,
Muttering and murmuring at his ear, " Quick, quick !
I fear it is too late, and I shall die."
But the other swiftly strode from ridge to ridge,
Clothed with his breath, and looking, as he walk'd,
Larger than human on the frozen hills.
He heard the deep behind him, and a cry
Before.   His own thought drove him, like a goad.
Dry clash'd his harness in the icy caves
And barren chasms, and all to left and right
The bare black cliff clang'd round him, as he based
His feet on juts of slippery crag that rang
Sharp-smitten with the dint of armed heels—

And on a sudden, lo ! the level lake,
And the long glories of the winter moon.

   Then saw they how there hove a dusky barge,
Dark as a funeral scarf from stem to stern,
Beneath them ; and descending they were ware
That all the decks were dense with stately forms
Black-stoled, black-hooded, like a dream—by these
Three Queens with crowns of gold—and from them rose
A cry that shiver'd to the tingling stars,
And, as it were one voice an agony
Of lamentation, like a wind, that shrills
All night in a waste land, where no one comes,
Or hath come, since the making of the world.

   Then murmur'd Arthur, " Place me in the barge."
And to the barge they came. There those three Queens
Put forth their hands, and took the King, and wept.
But she, that rose the tallest of them all
And fairest, laid his head upon her lap,
And loosed the shatter'd casque, and chafed his hands,
And call'd him by his name, complaining loud,
And dropping bitter tears against his brow
Striped with dark blood : for all his face was white
And colourless, and like the wither'd moon
Smote by the fresh beam of the springing east ;
And all his greaves and cuisses dash'd with drops
Of onset ; and the light and lustrous curls—
That made his forehead like a rising sun
High from the daïs-throne—were parch'd with dust ;
Or, clotted into points and hanging loose,
Mix'd with the knightly growth that fringed his lips.
So like a shatter'd column lay the King ;
Not like that Arthur who, with lance in rest,
From spur to plume a star of tournament,
Shot thro' the lists at Camelot, and charged
Before the eyes of ladies and of kings.

Then loudly cried the bold Sir Bedivere,
" Ah ! my Lord Arthur, whither shall I go ?
Where shall I hide my forehead and my eyes ?
For now I see the true old times are dead,
When every morning brought a noble chance,
And every chance brought out a noble knight.
Such times have been not since the light that led
The holy Elders with the gift of myrrh.
But now the whole Round Table is dissolved
Which was an image of the mighty world ;
And I, the last, go forth companionless,
And the days darken round me, and the years,
Among new men, strange faces, other minds."

    And slowly answered Arthur from the barge :
" The old order changeth, yielding place to new,
And God fulfils Himself in many ways,
Lest one good custom should corrupt the world.
Comfort thyself : what comfort is in me ?
I have lived my life, and that which I have done
May He within Himself make pure ! but thou,
If thou shouldst never see my face again,
Pray for my soul.   More things are wrought by
    prayer
Than this world dreams of.   Wherefore, let thy voice
Rise like a fountain for me night and day.
For what are men better than sheep or goats
That nourish a blind life within the brain,
If, knowing God, they lift not hands of prayer
Both for themselves and those who call them friend ?
For so the whole round earth is every way
Bound by gold chains about the feet of God.
But now, farewell.   I am going a long way
With these thou seest—if indeed I go—
(For all my mind is clouded with a doubt)
To the island-valley of Avilion,

Where falls not hail, or rain, or any snow,
Nor ever wind blows loudly ; but it lies
Deep-meadow'd, happy, fair, with orchard-lawns
And bowery hollows crown'd with summer sea,
Where I will heal me of my grievous wound."
   So said he, and the barge with oar and sail
Moved from the brink, like some full-breasted swan
That, fluting a wild carol ere her death,
Ruffles her pure cold plume, and takes the flood
With swarthy webs.   Long stood Sir Bedivere
Revolving many memories, till the hull
Look'd one black dot against the verge of dawn,
And on the mere the wailing died away.

LOVE AND DUTY

Of love that never found his earthly close,
What sequel ?   Streaming eyes and breaking hearts ?
Or all the same as if he had not been ?
   Not so.   Shall Error in the round of time
Still father Truth ?   Oh, shall the braggart shout
For some blind glimpse of freedom work itself
Thro' madness, hated by the wise, to law,
System, and empire ?   Sin itself be found
The cloudy porch oft opening on the Sun ?
And only be, this wonder, dead, become
Mere highway dust ? or year by year alone
Sit brooding in the ruins of a life,
Nightmare of youth, the spectre of himself ?
   If this were thus, if this, indeed, were all,
Better the narrow brain, the stony heart,
The staring eye glazed o'er with sapless days,

K

The long mechanic pacings to and fro,
The set grey lite and apathetic end.
But am I not the nobler thro' thy love?
O three times less unworthy! likewise thou
Art more thro' love, and greater than thy years,
The Sun will run his orbit, and the Moon
Her circle. Wait, and Love himself will bring
The drooping flower of knowledge changed to fruit
Of wisdom. Wait: my faith is large in Time,
And that which shapes it to some perfect end.

Will some one say, Then why not ill for good?
Why took ye not your pastime? To that man
My work shall answer, since I knew the right
And did it; for a man is not as God,
But then most Godlike being most a man.
—So let me think 'tis well for me and thee—
Ill-fated that I am, what lot is mine,
Whose foresight preaches peace, my heart so slow
To feel it! For how hard it seem'd to me,
When eyes, love-languid thro' half-tears would dwell
One earnest, earnest moment upon mine,
Then not to dare to see! when thy low voice,
Faltering, would break its syllables, to keep
My own full-tuned,—hold passion in a leash,
And not leap forth and fall about thy neck,
And on thy bosom (deep desired relief!)
Rain out the heavy mist of tears, that weigh'd
Upon my brain, my senses and my soul!

For Love himself took part against himself
To warn us off, and Duty loved of Love—
Oh, this world's curse—beloved but hated—came
Like Death betwixt thy dear embrace and mine,
And crying, "Who is this? behold thy bride,"
She pushed me from thee.

                              If the sense is hard
To alien ears, I did not speak to these—
No, not to thee, but to thyself in me:
Hard is my doom and thine: thou knowest it all.

    Could Love part thus? was it not well to speak,
To have spoken once?   It could not but be well.
The slow sweet hours that bring us all things good,
The slow sad hours that bring us all things ill,
And all good things from evil, brought the night,
In which we sat together and alone,
And to the want, that hollow'd all the heart,
Gave utterance by the yearning of an eye,
That burn'd upon its object thro' such tears
As flow but once a life.

                              The trance gave way
To those caresses, when a hundred times
In that last kiss, which never was the last,
Farewell, like endless welcome, lived and died.
Then follow'd counsel, comfort, and the words
That make a man feel strong in speaking truth;
Till now the dark was worn, and overhead
The lights of sunset and of sunrise mix'd
In that brief night; the summer night, that paused
Among her stars to hear us; stars that hung
Love-charm'd to listen: all the wheels of Time
Spun round in station, but the end had come.

    O then, like those, who clench their nerves to rush
Upon their dissolution, we too rose,
There—closing like an individual life—
In one blind cry of passion and of pain,
Like bitter accusation ev'n to death,
Caught up the whole of love and utter'd it,
And bade adieu for ever.

                              Live—yet live—
Shall sharpest pathos blight us, knowing all

Life needs, for life is possible to will—
Live happy; tend thy flowers; be tended by
My blessing! Should my shadow cross thy thoughts
Too sadly for their peace, remand it thou
In calmer hours to Memory's darkest hold,
If not to be forgotten—not at once—
Not all forgotten. Should it cross thy dreams,
O might it come like one that looks content,
With quiet eyes unfaithful to the truth,
And point thee forward to a distant light,
Or seem to lift a burthen from thy heart
And leave thee freer, till thou wake refresh'd.
Then when the first low matin-chirp hath grown
Full quire, and morning driv'n her plough of pearl
Far furrowing into light the mounded rack,
Beyond the fair green field and eastern sea.

ULYSSES

It little profits that an idle king,
By this still hearth, among these barren crags,
Matched with an aged wife, I mete and dole
Unequal laws unto a savage race,
That hoard, and sleep, and feed, and know not me,
I cannot rest from travel: I will drink
Life to the lees: all times I have enjoyed
Greatly, have suffered greatly, both with those
That loved me and alone; on shore, and when
Thro' scudding drifts the rainy Hyades
Vext the dim sea: I am become a name;
For always roaming with a hungry heart,
Much have I seen and known; cities of men

And manners, climates, councils, governments,
Myself not least, but honour'd of them all ;
And drunk delight of battle with my peers,
Far on the ringing plains of windy Troy.
I am a part of all that I have met ;
Yet all experience is an arch wherethro'
Gleams that untravell'd world, whose margin fades
For ever and for ever when I move ;
How dull it is to pause, to make an end,
To rust unburnished, not to shine in use !
As tho' to breathe were life.   Life piled on life
Were all too little, and of one to me
Little remains : but every hour is saved
From that eternal silence, something more,
A bringer of new things ; and vile it were
For some three suns to store and hoard myself,
And this gray spirit yearning in desire
To follow knowledge, like a sinking star,
Beyond the utmost bound of human thought.

   This is my son, mine own Telemachus,
To whom I leave the sceptre and the isle—
Well-loved of me, discerning to fulfil
This labour, by slow prudence to make mild
A rugged people, and thro' soft degrees
Subdue them to the useful and the good.
Most blameless is he, centred in the sphere
Of common duties, decent not to fail
In offices of tenderness, and pay
Meet adoration to my household gods
When I am gone.   He works his work, I mine.

   There lies the port : the vessel puffs her sail :
There gloom the dark broad seas.   My mariners,
Souls that have toil'd and wrought and thought with
        me—
That ever with a frolic welcome took

The thunder and the sunshine, and opposed
Free hearts, free foreheads—you and I are old;
Old age hath yet his honour and his toil;
Death closes all; but something ere the end,
Some work of noble note, may yet be done
Not unbecoming men that strove with gods.
The lights begin to twinkle from the rocks:
The long day wanes: the slow moon climbs: the deep
Moans round with many voices.   Come, my friends,
'Tis not too late to seek a newer world.
Push off, and sitting well in order, smite
The sounding furrows; for my purpose holds
To sail beyond the sunset and the baths
Of all the western stars, until I die.
It may be that the gulfs will wash us down;
It may be we shall touch the Happy Isles,
And see the great Achilles, whom we knew.
Tho' much is taken, much abides; and tho'
We are not now that strength which in old days
Moved earth and heaven, that which we are, we are;
One equal temper of heroic hearts,
Made weak by time and fate, but strong in will
To strive, to seek, to find, and not to yield.

EVE OF ST. AGNES

Deep on the convent-roof the snows
    Are sparkling to the moon:
My breath to heaven like vapour goes:
    May my soul follow soon!
The shadows of the convent towers
    Slant down the snowy sward,
Still creeping with the creeping hours
    That lead me to my Lord:

Make Thou my spirit pure and clear
  As are the frosty skies,
Or this first snowdrop of the year
  That in my bosom lies.

As these white robes are soil'd and dark,
  To yonder shining ground ;
As this pale taper's earthly spark,
  To yonder argent round ;
So shows my soul before the Lamb,
  My spirit before Thee ;
So in mine earthly house I am,
  To that I hope to be.
Break up the heavens, O Lord ! and far,
  Thro' all yon starlight keen,
Draw me, Thy bride, a glittering star,
  In raiment white and clean.

He lifts me to the golden doors ;
  The flashes come and go ;
All heaven bursts her starry floors,
  And strows her lights below,
And deepens on and up ! the gates
  Roll back, and far within
For me the Heavenly Bridegroom waits,
  To make me pure of sin.
The sabbaths of Eternity,
  One sabbath deep and wide—
A light upon the shining sea—
  The Bridegroom with his bride !

IN MEMORIAM

XIX

The Danube to the Severn gave
 The darken'd heart that beat no more ;
 They laid him by the pleasant shore,
And in the hearing of the wave.

There twice a day the Severn fills ;
 The salt sea-water passes by,
 And hushes half the babbling Wye
And makes a silence in the hills.

The Wye is hush'd nor moved along,
 And hush'd my deepest grief of all,
 When fill'd with tears that cannot fall,
I brim with sorrow drowning song.

The tide flows down, the wave again
 Is vocal in its wooded walls ;
 My deeper anguish also falls,
And I can speak a little then.

XXIV

And was the day of my delight
 As pure and perfect as I say ?
 The very source and fount of Day
Is dash'd with wandering isles of night.

If all was good and fair we met,
 This earth had been the Paradise
 It never look'd to human eyes
Since Adam left his garden yet.

And is it that the haze of grief
    Makes former gladness loom so great?
    The lowness of the present state
That sets the past in this relief?

Or that the past will always win
    A glory from its being far;
    And orb into the perfect star
We saw not, when we moved therein?

XXXIII

O Thou that after toil and storm
    Mayst seem to have reach'd a purer air,
    Whose faith has centre everywhere,
Nor cares to fix itself to form.

Leave thou thy sister when she prays,
    Her early Heaven, her happy views;
    Nor thou with shadow'd hint confuse
A life that leads melodious days.

Her faith thro' form is pure as thine,
    Her hands are quicker unto good;
    Oh, sacred be the flesh and blood
To which she links a truth divine!

See thou, that countest reason ripe
    In holding by the law within,
    Thou fail not in a world of sin,
And ev'n for want of such a type.

LXVII

When on my bed the moonlight falls,
    I know that in thy place of rest
    By that broad water of the west,
There comes a glory on the walls:

Thy marble bright in dark appears,
    As slowly steals a silver flame
    Along the letters of thy name,
And o'er the number of thy years.

The mystic glory swims away;
    From off my bed the moonlight dies;
    And closing eaves of wearied eyes
I sleep till dusk is dipt in gray:

And then I know the mist is drawn
    A lucid veil from coast to coast,
    And in the chancel like a ghost
Thy tablet glimmers to the dawn.

LXXXIII

Dip down upon the northern shore,
    O sweet new-year delaying long;
    Thou doest expectant nature wrong;
Delaying long, delay no more.

What stays thee from the clouded noons,
    Thy sweetness from its proper place?
    Can trouble live with April days,
Or sadness in the summer moons?

Bring orchis, bring the foxglove spire,
    The little speedwell's darling blue,
    Deep tulips dash'd with fiery dew,
Laburnums, dropping-wells of fire.

O thou, new-year, delaying long,
    Delayest the sorrow in my blood,
    That longs to burst a frozen bud,
And flood a fresher throat with song.

CI

Unwatch'd, the garden bough shall sway,
 The tender blossom flutter down,
 Unloved, that beech will gather brown,
This maple burn itself away ;

Unloved, the sun-flower, shining fair,
 Ray round with flames her disc of seed,
 And many a rose-carnation feed
With summer spice the humming air ;

Unloved, by many a sandy bar,
 The brook shall babble down the plain,
 At noon, or when the lesser wain
Is twisting round the polar star ;

Uncared for, gird the windy grove,
 And flood the haunts of hern and crake,
 Or into silver arrows break
The sailing moon in creek and cove.

Till from the garden and the wild
 A fresh association blow,
 And year by year the landscape grow
Familiar to the stranger's child ;

As year by year the labourer tills
 His wonted glebe, or lops the glades ;
 And year by year our memory fades
From all the circle of the hills.

OH, THAT 'TWERE POSSIBLE

Oh, that 'twere possible,
After long grief and pain,
To find the arms of my true love
Round me once again !

When I was wont to meet her
In the silent woody places
By the home that gave me birth,
We stood 'tranced in long embraces
Mixt with kisses, sweeter, sweeter
Than anything on earth.

A shadow flits before me,
Not thou, but like to thee ;
Ah Christ, that it were possible
For one short hour to see
The souls we loved, that they might tell us
What and where they be !

It leads me forth at evening,
It lightly winds and steals
In a cold white robe before me,
When all my spirit reels
At the shouts, the leagues of lights,
And the roaring of the wheels.

Half the night I waste in sighs,
Half in dreams I sorrow after
The delight of early skies ;
In a wakeful doze I sorrow
For the hand, the lips, the eyes—
For the meeting of the morrow,
The delight of happy laughter,
The delight of low replies.

'Tis a morning pure and sweet,
And a dewy splendour falls
On the little flower that clings
To the turrets and the walls;
'Tis a morning pure and sweet,
And the light and shadow fleet;
She is walking in the meadow
And the woodland echo rings
In a moment we shall meet;
She is singing in the meadow,
And the rivulet at her feet
Ripples on in light and shadow
To the ballad that she sings.

Do I hear her sing as of old,
My bird with the shining head,
My own dove with the tender eye?
But there rings on a sudden a passionate cry—
There is some one dying or dead;
And a sullen thunder is rolled;
For a tumult shakes the city,
And I wake—my dream is fled;
In the shuddering dawn, behold,
Without knowledge, without pity,
By the curtains of my bed
That abiding phantom cold!

Get thee hence, nor come again:
Mix not memory with doubt,
Pass, thou deathlike type of pain,
Pass and cease to move about!
'Tis the blot upon the brain
That will show itself without.

Then I rise; the eave-drops fall,
And the yellow vapours choke
The great city sounding wide;
The day comes—a dull red ball
Wrapt in drifts of lurid smoke
On the misty river-tide.

Through the hubbub of the market
I steal, a wasted frame;
It crosses here, it crosses there,
Through all that crowd confused and loud
The shadow still the same;
And on my heavy eyelids
My anguish hangs like shame.

Alas! for her that met me,
That heard me softly call,
Came glimmering through the laurels
At the quiet evenfall,
In the garden by the turrets
Of the old manorial hall!

Would the happy spirit descend
From the realms of light and song,
In the chamber or the street,
As she looks among the blest,
Should I fear to greet my friend,
Or to say, "Forgive the wrong,"
Or to ask her, "Take me, sweet,
To the regions of thy rest?"

But the broad light glares and beats,
And the shadow flits and fleets,
And will not let me be;
And I loathe the squares and streets,
And the faces that one meets,
Hearts with no love for me;

Always I long to creep
Into some still cavern deep,
There to weep, and weep, and weep
My whole soul out to thee.

FROM "ELAINE"

So when the ghostly man had come and gone,
She, with a face bright as for sin forgiven,
Besought Lavaine to write as she devised
A letter, word for word; and when he asked,
"Is it for Lancelot, is it for my dear lord?
Then will I bear it gladly," she replied,
"For Lancelot and the Queen and all the world,
But I myself must bear it." Then he wrote
The letter she devised; which being writ
And folded, "O sweet father, tender and true,
Deny me not," she said—"You never yet
Denied my fancies—this, however strange,
My latest: lay the letter in my hand
A little ere I die, and close the hand
Upon it; I shall guard it even in death.
And when the beat is gone from out my heart,
Then take the little bed on which I died
For Lancelot's love, and deck it like the Queen's
For richness, and me also like the Queen
In all I have of rich, and lay me on it.
And let there be prepared a chariot-bier
To take me to the river, and a barge
Be ready on the river, clothed in black.
I go in state to court, to meet the Queen.
There surely I shall speak for mine own self,
And none of you can speak for me so well.

And therefore let our dumb old man alone
Go with me; he can steer and row, and he
Will guide me to that palace, to the doors."

She ceased; her father promised; whereupon
She grew so cheerful that they deem'd her death
Was rather in the fantasy than the blood.
But ten slow mornings past, and on the eleventh
Her father laid the letter in her hand,
And closed the hand upon it, and she died.
So that day there was dole in Astolat.

But when the next sun brake from underground,
Then, those two brethren slowly with bent brows
Accompanying, the sad chariot-bier
Passed like a shadow thro' the field, that shone
Full summer, to that stream whereon the barge,
Pall'd all its length in blackest samite, lay.
There sat the lifelong creature of the house,
Loyal, the dumb old servitor, on deck,
Winking his eyes, and twisted all his face.
So those two brethren from the chariot took
And on the black decks laid her in her bed,
Set in her hand a lily, o'er her hung
The silken case with braided blazonings,
And kiss'd her quiet brows, and saying to her,
"Sister, farewell for ever," and again,
"Farewell, sweet sister," parted all in tears.
Then rose the dumb old servitor, and the dead
Steer'd by the dumb went upward with the flood—
In her right hand the lily, in her left
The letter—all her bright hair streaming down—
And all the coverlid was cloth of gold
Drawn to her waist, and she herself in white,
All but her face, and that clear-featured face
Was lovely, for she did not seem as dead
But fast asleep, and lay as though she smiled.

LADY DUFFERIN.   1807–1867

TO MY DEAR SON

On his 21st Birthday, with a Silver Lamp, " Fiat Lux."

How shall I bless thee?   Human love
  Is all too poor in passionate words ;
The heart aches with a sense above
  All language that the lip affords :
Therefore a symbol shall express
  My love,—a thing not rare or strange,
But yet—eternal—measureless—
  Knowing no shadow and no change.
Light ! which of all the lovely shows
  To our poor world of shadows given,
The fervent Prophet-voices chose
  Alone, as attribute of heaven !

At a most solemn pause we stand,
  From this day forth, for evermore,
The weak but loving human hand
  Must cease to guide thee as of yore.
Then, as thro' life thy footsteps stray,
  And earthly beacons dimly shine,
" Let there be light " upon thy way,
  And holier guidance far than mine !
" Let there be light " in thy clear soul,
  When passion tempts and doubts assail ;
When grief's dark tempests o'er thee roll,
    " Let there be light " that shall not fail !

L

So, Angel-guarded, may'st thou tread
　　The narrow path which few may find,
And at the end look back, nor dread
　　To count the vanished years behind!
And pray that she, whose hand doth trace
　　This heart-warm prayer,—when life is past—
May see and know thy blessed face,
　　In God's own glorious light at last!

MRS. NORTON. 1808–1877

THE LADY OF LA GARAYE

Oh! woodland paths she ne'er again may see,
Oh! tossing branches of the forest tree,
Oh! loveliest banks in all the land of France,
Glassing your shadows in the silvery Rance;
Oh! river with your swift yet quiet tide,
Specked with white sails that seem in dreams to glide;
Oh! ruddy orchards, basking on the hills,
Whose plenteous fruit the thirsty flagon fills;
And oh! ye winds, which free and unconfined,
No sickness poisons, and no art can bind,—
Restore her to enjoyment of the earth!
Echo again her songs of careless mirth,
Those little Breton songs so wildly sweet,
Fragments of music strange and incomplete,
Her small red mouth went warbling by the way
Through the glad roamings of her active day.

It may not be!   Blighted are summer hours!
The bee goes booming through the plats of flowers;
The butterfly its tiny mate pursues
With rapid fluttering of its painted hues;
The thin-winged gnats their transient time employ
Reeling through sunbeams in a dance of joy;
The small field-mouse with wide transparent ears
Comes softly forth, and softly disappears;
The dragon-fly hangs glittering on the reed;
The spider swings across his filmy thread;
And gleaming fishes, darting to and fro,
Make restless silver in the pools below.

All these poor lives—these lives of small account,
Feel the ethereal thrill within them mount ;
But the great human life,—the life Divine,—
Rests in dull torture, heavy and supine,—
And the bird's song by Garaye's walls of stone,
Crosses within, the irrepressible moan !
The slow salt tears, half weakness and half grief,
That sting the eyes before they bring relief,
And which with weary lids she strives in vain
To prison back upon her aching brain,
Fall down the lady's cheek,—her heart is breaking ;
A mournful sleep is hers : a hopeless waking ;
And oft, in spite of Claud's beloved rebuke,
When first the awful wish her spirit shook,—
She dreams of Death,—and of that quiet shore
In the far world where eyes shall weep no more,
And where the soundless feet of angels pass,
With floating lightness o'er the sea of glass.

R. M. MILNES (LORD HOUGHTON). 1809–1885

THE GREEK AT CONSTANTINOPLE

The cypresses of Scutari,
  In stern magnificence look down
On the bright lake and stream of sea,
  And glittering theatre of town :
Above the throng of rich kiosks,
  Above the towers in triple tire,
Above the domes of loftiest mosques
  These pinnacles of death aspire.

It is a wilderness of tombs,—
  Where white and gold and brilliant hue
Contrast with Nature's gravest glooms ;
  As these again with heaven's clear blue :
The city's multitudinous hum,
  So far, yet strikes the listening ear,—
But what are thousands to the sum
  Of millions calmly sleeping here?

For here, whate'er his life's degree,
  The Moslem loves to rest at last,
Loves to recross the band of sea
  That parts him from his people's past.
'Tis well to live and lord o'er those
  By whom his sires were most renowned ;
But his fierce heart finds best repose
  In the traditionary ground.

From this funereal forest's edge
  I gave my sight full range below,
Reclining on a grassy ledge,
  Itself a grave, or seeming so :

And that huge city flaunting bright,
    That crowded port and busy shore,
With roofs and minarets steeped in light,
    Seemed but a gaudy tomb the more.

I thought of what one might have hoped
    From Greek and Roman power combined,
From strength, that with a world had coped,
    Matched to the Queen of human mind ;—
From all the wisdom, might and grace,
    That Fancy's gods to man had given,
Blent in one empire and one race,
    By the true faith in Christ and Heaven.

The finest webs of earthly fate
    Are soonest and most harshly torn ;
The wise could scarce discriminate
    That evening splendour from the morn ;
Though we, sad students of the past,
    Can trace the lurid twilight line
That lies between the first and last,
    Who bore the name of Constantine.

Such were my thoughts and such the scene,
    When I perceived that by me stood
A Grecian youth of earnest mien,
    Well-suiting my reflective mood :
And when he spake, his words were tuned
    Harmonious to my present mind,
As if his spirit had communed
    With mine, while I had there reclined.

Stranger ! whose soul has strength to soar
    Beyond the compass of the eye,
And on a spot like this can more
    Than charms of form and hue descry—

Take off this mask of beauty,—scan
   The face of things with truth severe,
Think, as becomes a Christian man,
   Of us thy Christian brethren here.

Think of that age's awful birth,
   When Europe echoed, terror-riven,
That a new foot was on the earth,
   And a new name come down from Heaven:
When over Calpe's straits and steeps
   The Moor had bridged his royal road,
And Othman's sons from Asia's deeps
   The conquests of the Cross o'erflowed.

Think if the arm of Charles Martel
   Had failed upon the plain of Tours,
The fate, whose course you know so well,
   This foul subjection had been yours:
Where then had been the long renown
   France can from sire to son deliver?
Where English freedom rolling down,
   One widening, one continuous river?

Think with what passionate delight
   The tale was told in Christian halls,
How Sobieski turned to flight
   The Moslem from Vienna's walls:
How, when his horse triumphant trod
   The burgher's richest robes upon,
The ancient words rose loud—" From God
   A man was sent whose name was John."

Think not that time can ever give
   Prescription to such doom as ours,
That Grecian hearts can ever live
   Contented serfs of barbarous powers:

More than six hundred years had passed
  Since Moorish hosts could Spain o'erwhelm,
Yet Boabdil was thrust at last
  Lamenting from Granada's realm.

And if to his old Asian seat,
  From this usurped, unnatural throne,
The Turk is driven, 'tis surely meet
  That we again should hold our own.
Be but Byzantium's native sign
  Of Cross on Crescent once unfurled,
And Greece shall guard by right divine
  The portals of the Eastern world.

Before the small Athenian band
  The Persian myriads stood at bay,
The spacious East lay down unmanned
  Beneath the Macedonians' sway:
Alas! that Greek could turn on Greek—
  Fountain of all our woes and shame—
Till men knew scarcely where to seek
  The fragments of the Grecian name.

Know ye the Romans of the North?
  The fearful race, whose infant strength
Stretches its arms of conquest forth,
  To grasp the world in breadth and length?
They cry, "That ye and we are old,
  And worn with luxuries and cares,
And they alone are fresh and bold,
  Time's latest and most honoured heirs!"

Alas for you! alas for us!
  Alas for men that think and feel,
If once beside this Bosphorus
  Shall stamp Sclavonia's frozen heel!

Oh ! place us boldly in the van,
   And ere we yield this narrow sea,
The past shall hold within its span
   At least one more Thermopylæ.

ON THE DEATH OF ——

I'm not where I was yesterday,
   Though my home be still the same,
For I have lost the veriest friend
   Whom ever a friend could name;
I'm not where I was yesterday,
   Though change there be little to see,
For a part of myself has lapsed away
   From Time to Eternity.

I have lost a thought that many a year
   Was most familiar food
To my inmost mind, by night or day,
   In merry or plaintive mood ;
I have lost a hope, that many a year
   Looked far on a gleaming way,
When the walls of Life were closing round,
   And the sky was sombre grey.

For long, too long, in distant climes
   My lot was cast, and then,
A frail and casual intercourse
   Was all I had with men ;
But lonelily in distant climes
   I was well content to roam,
And felt no void, for my heart was full,
   Of the friend it had left at home.

And now I was close to my native shores,
　　And I felt him at my side,
His spirit was in that homeward wind,
　　His voice in that homeward tide :
For what were to me my native shores,
　　But that they held the scene,
Where my youth's most genial flowers had blown,
　　And affection's root had been ?

I thought, how should I see him first,
　　How should our hands first meet,
Within his room,—upon the stair,—
　　At the corner of the street ?
I thought, where should I hear him first,
　　How catch his greeting tone,—
And thus I went up to his door,
　　And they told me he was gone !

Oh ! what is Life but a sum of love,
　　And Death but to lose it all ?
Weeds be for those that are left behind,
　　And not for those that fall !
And now how mighty a sum of love
　　Is lost for ever to me . . .
. . . No, I'm not what I was yesterday,
　　Though change there be little to see.

MOMENTS

I lie in a heavy trance,
　　With a world of dreams without me
Shapes of shadow dance,
　　In wavering bands about me ;

But, at times, some mystic things
    Appear in this phantom lair,
That almost seem to me visitings
    Of Truth known elsewhere :
The world is wide,—these things are small,
They may be nothing, but they are All.

A prayer in an hour of pain,
    Begun in an undertone,
Then lowered, as it would fain
    Be heard by the heart alone ;
A throb, when the soul is entered
    By a light that is lit above,
Where the God of Nature has centered
    The Beauty of Love—
The world is wide,—these things are small,
They may be nothing, but they are All.

A look that is telling a tale,
    Which looks alone dare tell,—
When "a cheek is no longer pale,"
    That has caught the glance, as it fell ;
A touch, which seems to unlock
    Treasures unknown as yet,
And the bitter-sweet first shock,
    One can never forget ;—
The world is wide,—these things are small,
They may be nothing, but they are All.

A sense of an earnest Will
    To help the lowly-living,—
And a terrible heart-thrill,
    If you " have no power of giving ; "

An arm of aid to the weak,
    A friendly hand to the friendless,
Kind words, so short to speak,
    But whose echo is endless :
The world is wide,—these things are small,
They may be nothing, but they are All.

The moment we think we have learnt
    The love of the All-wise One,
By which we could stand unburnt,
    On the ridge of the seething sun :
The moment we grasp at the clue,
    Long lost and strangely riven,
Which guides our Soul to the True,
    And the Poet to Heaven.
The world is wide, —these things are small,—
If they be nothing, what is there at all ?

FRANCES ANNE KEMBLE. 1809–1893

EVENING

Now in the west is spread
A golden bed ;
Great purple curtains hang around,
With fiery fringes bound,
And cushions, crimson red,
For Phœbus' lovely head ;
And as he sinks through waves of amber light,
Down to the crystal halls of Amphitrite,
Hesper leads forth his starry legions bright
Into the violet fields of air—Good-night !

ART THOU ALREADY WEARY?

Art thou already weary of the way
  Thou who hast yet but half the way gone o'er?
  Get up and lift thy burthen ; lo, before
Thy feet the road goes stretching far away.
  If thou already faint who art but come
Through half thy pilgrimage, with fellows gay,
  Love, youth, and hope under the rosy bloom,
And temperate airs of early breaking day—
  Look yonder, how the heavens stoop and gloom !
There cease the trees to shade, the flowers to spring,
  And the angels leave thee.   What wilt thou become
Through yon drear stretch of dismal wandering,
  Lonely and dark !—*I shall take courage, friend,*
    For comes not every step more near the end ?

HENRY ALFORD. 1810–1871

LADY MARY

Thou wert fair, Lady Mary,
  As the lily in the sun:
And fairer yet thou mightest be,
  Thy youth was but begun:
Thine eye was soft and glancing,
  Of the deep bright blue;
And on the heart thy gentle words
  Fell lighter than the dew.

They found thee, Lady Mary,
  With thy palms upon thy breast,
Even as thou hadst been praying,
  At thine hour of rest:
The cold pale moon was shining
  On thy cold pale cheek;
And the morn of the Nativity
  Had just begun to break.

They carved thee, Lady Mary,
  All of pure white stone,
With thy palms upon thy breast
  In the chancel all alone;
And I saw thee when the winter moon
  Shone on thy marble cheek,
And the morn of the Nativity
  Had just begun to break.

But thou kneelest, Lady Mary,
  With thy palms upon thy breast,
Among the perfect spirits,
  In the land of rest:

Thou art even as they took thee
    At thine hour of prayer,
Save the glory that is on thee
    From the sun that shineth there.

We shall see thee, Lady Mary,
    On that shore unknown,
A pure and happy angel
    In the presence of the throne;
We shall see thee when the light divine
    Plays freshly on thy cheek,
And the resurrection morning
    Hath just begun to break.

FILIOLÆ DULCISSIMÆ

Say, wilt thou think of me when I'm away,
Borne from the threshold and laid in the clay,
Past and forgotten for many a day?

Wilt thou remember me when I am gone,
Further each year from thy vision withdrawn,
Thou in the sunset and I in the dawn?

Wilt thou remember me when thou shalt see
Daily and nightly encompassing thee,
Hundreds of others but nothing of me?

All that I ask is a tear in thine eye,
Sitting and thinking when no one is by.
"Thus she looked on me—thus rang her reply."

'Tis not to die though the path be obscure,
Grand is the conflict, the victory sure,
Past though the peril, there's one can secure.

'Tis not to land in the region unknown
Thronged by bright spirits, all strange and alone,
Waiting the doom from the Judge on the Throne.

But 'tis to feel the cold touch of decay,
'Tis to look back on the wake of one's way,
Fading and vanishing, day after day.

This is the bitterness, none can be spared ;
This the oblivion the greatest have shared ;
This the true death for ambition prepared.

Thousands are round us, toiling as we,
Living and loving, whose lot is to be
Passed and forgotten like waves on the sea.

Once in a lifetime is uttered a word
That doth not vanish as soon as 'tis heard :
Once in an age is humanity stirred.

Once in a century springs forth a deed
From the dark bonds of forgetfulness freed,
Destined to shine, and to help, and to lead.

Yet not e'en thus escape we our lot :
The deed lasts in memory, the doer is not :
The word liveth on but the voice is forgot.

Who knows the forms of the mighty of old ?
Can bust or can portrait the spirit unfold,
Or the light of the eye by description be told ?

Nay even He who our Ransom became,
Bearing the Cross, despising the shame,
Earning a name above every name,—

They who had handled Him while He was here,
Kept they in memory His lineaments clear,
Could they command them at will to appear?

They who had heard Him and lived on His voice,
Say, could they always recall at their choice
The tone and the cadence which made them rejoice?

Be we content then to pass into shade,
Visage and voice in oblivion laid,
And live in the light that our actions have made.

Yet do thou think of me, child of my soul:
That, when the waves of forgetfulness roll,
Part may survive in the wreck of the whole.

Still let me count on the tear in thine eye,
"Thus she bent o'er me, thus went her reply,
Sitting and thinking when no one was nigh."

M

HENRY NUTCOMBE OXENHAM.   1829–1888

"THE EARTH, WITH ITS BRIGHT AND GLORIOUS THINGS"

" Wir müssen nach der Heimath gehn
Um diese heilige Zeit zu sehn."
—NOVALIS.

The earth, with its bright and glorious things,
  With its blue and green and gold;
The unseen depth of the Ocean springs,
  With its treasure of gems untold.

The sunset sky, with its ruby glow;
  The snow-clad mountains hoary;
The moons, that on Summer midnights throw
  O'er the wave their golden glory.

The wonders of Art, that man has piled,
  In the cities, where myriads dwell;
The secrets of Science, which gleam unveiled
  In the student's hidden cell.

The burning dream of the poet's soul;
  The trance of the painter's eye;
The musical sounds, whose vibrations roll
  In their cycles of mystery.

The sweetness the smiles of home can impart,
  And Affection's dearest kiss—
They have power to subdue the believing heart,
  But they are not our own true bliss.

The Souls of the Holy their vigils keep,
  Through the dawn of Eternity,
In a stiller abode than the Ocean deep,
  Where the beds of coral lie.

The ruddy gold of the sunset heaven,
  The green of the twilight grove,
Are a light to the eye of the wayfarer given,
  To point to his home above.

The inspired voice in the poet's dreams,
  Breathes a message half unspoken ;
The heaven-sent ray on the artist gleams,
  With its earthly reflection broken.

The secrets of Science, genius may buy,
  Thro' a life-toil of many years ;—
They have power to light up the speaking eye,
  But they cannot draw our tears.

The dearest gift that is given on earth
  Is the smile of those we love ;
But the spirit of man feels a conscious dearth
  Which that smile cannot remove.

The Soul cannot rest, till it gains that shore,
  Where, blent in one heavenly vision,
The dreams of Affection and Knowledge and Power
  Are lost in their endless fruition.

W. BELL SCOTT.   1811–1890

BELOW THE OLD HOUSE

Beneath those buttressed walls with lichen grey,
  Beneath the slopes of trees whose flickering shade
  Darkens the pools by dun green velveted,
The stream leaps like a living thing at play,—
In haste it seems: it cannot, cannot stay!
  The great boughs changing there from year to year,
  And the high jackdaw-haunted eaves, still hear
The burden of the rivulet—*Passing away!*

And some time certainly that oak no more
  Will keep the winds in check; his breadth of beam
Will go to rib some ship for some far shore;
  Those coigns and eaves will crumble, while that
     stream
Will still run whispering, whispering night and day,
That oversong of Father Time—*Passing away!*

ALFRED DOMETT. 1811–1887

THE NATIVITY

It was the calm and silent night!
  Seven hundred years and fifty-three,
Had Rome been growing up to light,
  And now was queen of land and sea.
No sound was heard of clashing oars—
  Peace brooded o'er the hushed domain:
Apollo, Pallas, Jove, and Mars
  Held undisturbed their ancient reign,
    In the solemn midnight
      Centuries ago.

'Twas in the calm and silent night!
  The Senator of haughty Rome,
Impatient, urged his chariot's flight,
  From lordly revel rolling home;
Triumphal arches, gleaming, swell
  His breast with thoughts of boundless sway;
What recked the Roman what befell
  A paltry province far away,
    In the solemn midnight
      Centuries ago?

Within that province far away,
  Went plodding home a weary boor;
A streak of light before him lay,
  Fallen through a half-shut stable door
Across his path. He passed—for naught
  Told what was going on within;
How keen the stars, his only thought—
  The air how calm, and cold, and thin,
    In the solemn midnight
      Centuries ago!

Oh, strange indifference ! low and high
   Drowsed over common joys and cares ;
The earth was still—but knew not why
   The world was listening, unawares.
How calm a moment may precede
   One that shall thrill the world for ever !
To that still moment, none would heed,
    Man's doom was linked no more to sever—
      In the solemn midnight
        Centuries ago !

It is the calm and solemn night !
   A thousand bells ring out, and throw
Their joyous peals abroad, and smite
   The darkness—charmed and holy now !
The night that erst no name had worn,
   To it a happy name is given ;
For in that stable lay, new-born,
    The peaceful Prince of earth and heaven,
      In the solemn midnight
        Centuries ago !

ROBERT BROWNING. 1812–1889

MY LAST DUCHESS

That's my last Duchess painted on the wall,
Looking as if she were alive.   I call
That piece a wonder, now : Frà Pandolf's hands
Worked busily a day, and there she stands.
Will 't please you sit and look at her?   I said
" Frà Pandolf " by design : for never read
Strangers like you that pictured countenance,
The depth and passion of its earnest glance,
But to myself they turned (since none puts by
The curtain I have drawn for you, but I)
And seemed as they would ask me, if they durst,
How such a glance came there ; so, not the first
Are you to turn and ask thus.   Sir, 'twas not
Her husband's presence only, called that spot
Of joy into the Duchess' cheek : perhaps
Frà Pandolf chanced to say " Her mantle laps
Over my lady's wrist too much," or " Paint
Must never hope to reproduce the faint
Half-flush that dies along her throat : " such stuff
Was courtesy, she thought, and cause enough
For calling up that spot of joy.   She had
A heart—how shall I say?—too soon made glad,
Too easily impressed ; she liked whate'er
She looked on, and her looks went everywhere.
Sir, 'twas all one !   My favour at her breast,
The dropping of the daylight in the West,
The bough of cherries some officious fool
Broke in the orchard for her, the white mule
She rode with round the terrace—all and each
Would draw from her alike the approving speech,

Or blush, at least. She thanked men,—good ! but
    thanked
Somehow—I know not how—as if she ranked
My gift of a nine-hundred-years-old name
With anybody's gift.   Who'd stoop to blame
This sort of trifling ?   Even had you skill
In speech—(which I have not)—to make your will
Quite clear to such an one, and say, " Just this
Or that in you disgusts me ; here you miss,
Or there exceed the mark "—and if she let
Herself be lessoned so, nor plainly set
Her wits to yours, forsooth, and made excuse,
—E'en then would be some stooping ; and I choose
Never to stoop.   Oh, sir, she smiled, no doubt,
Whene'er I passed her ; but who passed without
Much the same smile ?   This grew ; I gave commands ;
Then all smiles stopped together.   There she stands
As if alive.   Will 't please you rise ?   We'll meet
The Company below, then.   I repeat,
The Count, your master's, known munificence
Is ample warrant that no just pretence
Of mine for dowry will be disallowed ;
Though his fair daughter's self, as I avowed
At starting, is my object.   Nay, we'll go
Together down, sir.   Notice Neptune, though,
Taming a sea-horse, thought a rarity,
Which Claus of Innsbruck cast in bronze for me !

INCIDENT OF THE FRENCH CAMP

You know, we French stormed Ratisbon :
    A mile or so away,
On a little mound, Napoleon
    Stood on our storming-day ;

With neck out-thrust, you fancy how,
    Legs wide, arms locked behind,
As if to balance the prone brow
    Oppressive with its mind.

Just as perhaps he mused " My plans
    That soar, to earth may fall,
Let once my army-leader Lannes
    Waver at yonder wall "—
Out 'twixt the battery-smoke there flew
    A rider, bound on bound
Full galloping ; nor bridle drew
    Until he reached the mound.

Then off there flung in smiling joy,
    And held himself erect
By just his horse's mane, a boy :
    You hardly could suspect—
(So tight he kept his lips compressed,
    Scarce any blood came through)
You looked twice ere you saw his breast
    Was all but shot in two.

"Well," cried he, " Emperor, by God's grace
    We've got you Ratisbon !
The Marshal's in the market-place,
    And you'll be there anon
To see your flag-bird flap his vans
    Where I, to heart's desire,
Perched him ! "   The chief's eye flashed ; his plans
    Soared up again like fire.

The chief's eye flashed ; but presently
    Softened itself, as sheathes
A film the mother-eagle's eye
    When her bruised eaglet breathes.

" You're wounded ! "   " Nay," the soldier's pride
   Touched to the quick, he said :
" I'm killed, Sire !   And his chief beside,
   Smiling the boy fell dead.

HOME THOUGHTS FROM ABROAD

Oh, to be in England now that April's there,
And whoever wakes in England sees, some morning,
   unaware,
That the lowest boughs and the brushwood sheaf
Round the elm-tree bole are in tiny leaf,
While the chaffinch sings on the orchard bough
In England—now !
And after April, when May follows,
And the white-throat builds, and all the swallows !
Hark, where my blossomed pear-tree in the hedge
Leans to the field and scatters on the clover
Blossoms and dewdrops—at the bent spray's edge—
That's the wise thrush : he sings each song twice over,
Lest you should think he never could recapture
The first fine careless rapture !
And, though the fields look rough with hoary dew,
All will be gay when noontide wakes anew
The buttercups, the little children's dower
—Far brighter than this gaudy melon-flower.

"DE GUSTIBUS"

Your ghost will walk, your lover of trees,
    (If our loves remain)
    In an English lane,
By a cornfield-side a-flutter with poppies.
Hark, those two in the hazel coppice—
A boy and a girl, if the good fates please,
    Making love, say—
    The happier they!
Draw yourself up from the light of the moon,
And let them pass as they will too soon,
    With the bean-flower's boon,
    And the blackbird's tune,
    And May and June!

What I love best in all the world
Is a castle, precipice-encurled,
In a gash of the wind-grieved Apennine.
Or look for me, old fellow of mine,
(If I get my head from out the mouth
O' the grave, and loose my spirit's bands,
And come again to the land of lands)—
In a sea-side house to the farther South,
Where the baked cicala dies of drouth,
And one sharp tree—'tis a cypress—stands,
By the many hundred years red-rusted,
Rough iron-spiked, ripe fruit, o'er-crusted,
My sentinel to guard the sands
To the water's edge.   For, what expands
Before the house, but the great opaque
Blue breadth of sea without a break?
While, in the house, for ever crumbles

Some fragment of the frescoed walls,
From blisters where a scorpion sprawls.
A girl barefooted brings, and tumbles
Down on the pavement, green-flesh melons,
And says there's news to-day—the king
Was shot at, touched in the liver-wing,
Goes with his Bourbon arm in a sling:
She hopes they have not caught the felons.
Italy, my Italy!
Queen Mary's saying serves for me—
        (When fortune's malice
        Lost her, Calais)—
Open my heart and you will see
Graved inside of it, " Italy."
Such lovers old are I and she:
So it always was, so shall ever be!

EVELYN HOPE

Beautiful Evelyn Hope is dead!
    Sit and watch by her side an hour.
That is her bookshelf, this her bed;
    She plucked that piece of geranium-flower,
Beginning to die too, in the glass;
    Little has yet been changed, I think;
The shutters are shut, no light may pass
    Save two long rays thro' the hinge's chink.

Sixteen years old when she died!
    Perhaps she had scarcely heard my name;
It was not her time to love; beside,
    Her life had many a hope and aim,

Duties enough and little cares,
   And now was quiet, now astir,
Till God's hand beckoned unawares—
   And the sweet white brow is all of her.

Is it too late then, Evelyn Hope?
   What, your soul was pure and true,
The good stars met in your horoscope,
   Made you of spirit, fire and dew—
And, just because I was thrice as old,
   And our paths in the world diverged so wide,
Each was nought to each, must I be told?
   We were fellow mortals, nought beside?

' No indeed! for God above
   Is great to grant, as mighty to make,
And creates the love to reward the love :
   I claim you still, for my own love's sake!
Delayed it may be for more lives yet,
   Through worlds I shall traverse, not a few :
Much is to learn, much to forget
   Ere the time be come for taking you.

But the time will come, at last it will,
   When, Evelyn Hope, what meant (I shall say)
In the lower earth, in the years long still
   That body and soul so pure and gay?
Why your hair was amber, I shall divine,
   And your mouth of your own geranium's red—
And what you would do with me, in fine,
   In the new life come in the old one's stead.

I have lived (I shall say) so much since then,
   Given up myself so many times,
Gained me the gains of various men,
   Ransacked the ages, spoiled the climes;
Yet one thing, one, in my soul's full scope,
   Either I missed or itself missed me;
And I want and find you, Evelyn Hope!
   What is the issue? let us see!

I loved you, Evelyn, all the while!
   My heart seemed full as it could hold;
There was place and to spare for the frank young smile,
   And the red young mouth, and the hair's young gold.
So, hush,—I will give you this leaf to keep:
   See, I shut it inside the sweet cold hand!
There, that is our secret; go to sleep!
   You will wake, and remember, and understand.

A GRAMMARIAN'S FUNERAL

Let us begin and carry up this corpse,
     Singing together.
Leave we the common crofts, the vulgar thorpes,
     Each in its tether,
Sleeping safe on the bosom of the plain,
     Cared-for till cock-crow;
Look out if yonder be not day again
     Rimming the rock-row!
That's the appropriate country; there, man's thought,
     Rarer, intenser,
Self-gathered for an outbreak, as it ought,
     Chafes in the censer.

Leave we the unlettered plain, its herd and crop ;
    Seek we sepulture
On a tall mountain, citied to the top,
    Crowded with culture !
All the peaks soar, but one the rest excels ;
    Clouds overcome it ;
No, yonder sparkle is the citadel's
    Circling its summit.
Thither our path lies ; wind we up the heights :
    Wait ye the warning ?
Our low life was the level's and the night's ;
    He's for the morning.
Step to a tune, square chests, erect each head,
    'Ware the beholders !
This is our master, famous, calm, and dead,
    Borne on our shoulders.

Sleep, crop and herd ! sleep, darkling thorpe and croft,
    Safe from the weather !
He, whom we convoy to his grave aloft,
    Singing together,
He was a man born with thy face and throat,
    Lyric Apollo !
Long he lived nameless ; how should spring take note
    Winter would follow ?
Till lo, the little touch, and youth was gone !
    Cramped and diminished.
Moaned he, " New measures, other feet anon !
    My dance is finished ? "
No, that's the world's way (keep the mountain-side,
    Make for the city !)
He knew the signal, and stepped on with pride
    Over men's pity ;

Left play for work, and grappled with the world,
      Bent on escaping:
"What's in the scroll," quoth he, "thou keepest
    furled?
      Show me their shaping.
Theirs who most studied man, the bard and sage.—
      Give!"—So, he gowned him.
Straight got by heart that book to its last page:
      Learned we found him,—
Yea, but we found him bald too, eyes like lead,
      Accents uncertain;
"Time to taste life," another would have said,
      "Up with the curtain!"
This man said rather, "Actual life comes next?
      Patience a moment!
Grant I have mastered learning's crabbed text,
      Still there's the comment.
Let me know all! Prate not of most or least,
      Painful or easy!
Even to the crumbs I'd fain eat up the feast,
      Ay, nor feel queasy."
Oh, such a life as he resolved to live,
      When he had learned it,
When he had gathered all books had to give!
      Sooner, he spurned it.
Image the whole, then execute the parts—
      Fancy the fabric
Quite, ere you build, ere steel strike fire from quartz,
      Ere mortar dab brick!

(Here's the town-gate reached; there's the market-
    place
      Gaping before us.)
Yea, this in him was the peculiar grace
      (Hearten our chorus!)

That before living he'd learn how to live—
    No end to learning;
Earn the means first—God surely will contrive
    Use for our earning.
Others mistrust and say, "But time escapes!
    Live now or never!"
He said, "What's time? Leave Now for dogs and apes!
    Man has Forever."
Back to his book then: deeper drooped his head:
    Calculus racked him:
Leaden before, his eyes grew dross of lead:
    Tussis attacked him.
"Now, master, take a little rest!"—not he!
    (Caution redoubled!
Step two abreast, the way winds narrowly!)
    Not a whit troubled,
Back to his studies, fresher than at first,
    Fierce as a dragon
He (soul-hydroptic with a sacred thirst)
    Sucked at the flagon.
Oh, if we draw a circle premature,
    Heedless of far gain,
Greedy for quick returns of profit, sure
    Bad is our bargain!
Was it not great? did he not throw on God
    (He loves the burthen)—
God's task to make the heavenly period
    Perfect the earthen?
Did he not magnify the mind, show clear
    Just what it all meant?
He would not discount life, as fools do here,
    Paid by instalment.
He ventured neck or nothing—heaven's success
    Found, or earth's failure:
"Wilt thou trust death or not?" He answered "Yes:
    Hence with life's pale lure!"

That low man seeks a little thing to do,
    Sees it and does it:
This high man, with a great thing to pursue,
    Dies ere he knows it.
That low man goes on adding one to one,
    His hundred's soon hit:
This high man aiming at a million,
    Misses an unit.
That, has the world here—should he need the next,
    Let the world mind him!
This throws himself on God, and unperplexed
    Seeking shall find him.
So, with the throttling hands of death at strife,
    Ground he at grammar;
Still, thro' the rattle, parts of speech were rife:
    While he could stammer
He settled Hoti's business—let it be!—
    Properly based Oun—
Gave us the doctrine of the inclitic De,
    Dead from the waist down.
Well, here's the platform, here's the proper place:
    Hail to your purlieus,
All ye highfliers of the feathered race,
    Swallows and curlews!
Here's the top-peak; the multitude below
    Live, for they can, there:
This man decided not to Live but Know—
    Bury this man here?
Here—here's his place, where meteors shoot, clouds form,
    Lightnings are loosened,
Stars come and go! Let joy break with the storm,
    Peace let the dew send!
Lofty designs must close in like effects:
    Loftily lying,
Leave him—still loftier than the world suspects,
    Living and dying.

"HOW THEY BROUGHT THE GOOD NEWS FROM GHENT TO AIX"

I sprang to the stirrup, and Joris, and he ;
I galloped, Dirck galloped, we galloped all three ;
"Good speed!" cried the watch, as the gate-bolts
    undrew ;
"Speed!" echoed the wall to us galloping through ;
Behind shut the postern, the lights sank to rest,
And into the midnight we galloped abreast.

Not a word to each other; we kept the great pace
Neck by neck, stride by stride, never changing our place ;
I turned in my saddle and made its girths tight,
Then shortened each stirrup, and set the pique right,
Rebuckled the cheek-strap, chained slacker the bit,
Nor galloped less steadily Roland a whit.

'Twas moonset at starting ; but while we drew near
Lokeren, the cocks crew and twilight dawned clear ;
At Boom, a great yellow star came out to see ;
At Düffeld, 'twas morning as plain as could be ;
And from Mechlin church-steeple we heard the half chime,
So Joris broke silence with, "Yet there is time!"

At Aerschot, up leaped of a sudden the sun,
And against him the cattle stood black every one,
To stare thro' the mist at us galloping past,
And I saw my stout galloper Roland at last,
With resolute shoulders, each butting away
The haze, as some bluff river headland its spray :

And his low head and crest, just one sharp ear bent back
For my voice, and the other pricked out on his track ;
And one eye's black intelligence,—ever that glance
O'er its white edge at me, his own master, askance !
And the thick heavy spume-flakes which aye and anon
His fierce lips shook upwards in galloping on.

By Hasselt, Dirck groaned; and cried Joris, "Stay spur!
Your Roos galloped bravely, the fault's not in her,
We'll remember at Aix"—for one heard the quick wheeze
Of her chest, saw the stretched neck and staggering knees,
And sunk tail, and horrible heave of the flank,
As down on her haunches she shuddered and sank.

So, we were left galloping, Joris and I,
Past Looz and past Tongres, no cloud in the sky;
The broad sun above laughed a pitiless laugh,
'Neath our feet broke the brittle bright stubble like chaff;
Till over by Dalhem a dome-spire sprang white,
And "Gallop," gasped Joris, "for Aix is in sight!"

"How they'll greet us!" and all in a moment his roan
Rolled neck and croup over, lay dead as a stone;
And there was my Roland to bear the whole weight
Of the news which alone could save Aix from her fate,
With his nostrils like pits full of blood to the brim,
And with circles of red for his eye-sockets' rim.

Then I cast loose my buffcoat, each holster let fall,
Shook off both my jack-boots, let go belt and all,
Stood up in the stirrup, leaned, patted his ear,
Called my Roland his pet-name, my horse without peer;
Clapped my hands, laughed and sang, any noise, bad or
　　good,
Till at length into Aix Roland galloped and stood.

And all I remember is, friends flocking round
As I sat with his head 'twixt my knees on the ground;
And no voice but was praising this Roland of mine,
As I poured down his throat our last measure of wine,
Which (the burgesses voted by common consent)
Was no more than his due who brought good news from
　　Ghent.

THE LOST LEADER

Just for a handful of silver he left us,
  Just for a riband to stick in his coat—
Found the one gift of which fortune bereft us,
  Lost all the others, she lets us devote;
They, with the gold to give, doled him out silver,
  So much was theirs who so little allowed:
How all our copper had gone for his service!
  Rags,—were they purple, his heart had been proud!
We that had loved him so, followed him, honoured him,
  Lived in his mild and magnificent eye,
Learned his great language, caught his clear accents,
  Made him our pattern to live and to die!
Shakespeare was of us, Milton was for us,
  Burns, Shelley, were with us,—they watch from their
      graves!
He alone breaks from the van and the freemen,
  He alone sinks to the rear and the slaves!

We shall march prospering,—not thro' his presence;
  Songs may inspirit us,—not from his lyre;
Deeds will be done,—while he boasts his quiescence,
  Still bidding crouch whom the rest bid aspire.
Blot out his name then, record one lost soul more,
  One task more declined, one more footpath untrod,
One more devils'-triumph and sorrow for angels,
  One wrong more to man, one more insult to God!
Life's night begins: let him never come back to us!
  There would be doubt, hesitation, and pain,
Forced praise on our part—the glimmer of twilight,
  Never glad confident morning again!
Best fight on well, for we taught him—strike gallantly,
  Menace our heart ere we master his own;
Then let him receive the new knowledge and wait us,
  Pardoned in heaven, the first by the throne!

MEETING AT NIGHT

The grey sea and the long black land ;
And the yellow half-moon large and low ;
And the startled little waves that leap
In fiery ringlets from their sleep,
As I gain the cove with pushing prow,
And quench its speed i' the slushy sand.

Then a mile of warm sea-scented beach ;
Three fields to cross till a farm appears ;
A tap at the pane, the quick sharp scratch
And blue spurt of a lighted match,
And a voice less loud, through joys and fears,
Than the two hearts beating each to each !

PARTING AT MORNING

Round the cape of a sudden came the sea,
And the sun looked over the mountain's rim :
And straight was a path of gold for him,
And the need of a world of men for me.

THE BISHOP ORDERS HIS TOMB AT SAINT PRAXED'S CHURCH

Vanity saith the preacher, vanity !
Draw round my bed : is Anselm keeping back ?
Nephews—sons mine . . . ah God, I know not ! Well—
She, men would have to be your mother once,

Old Gandolf envied me, so fair she was !
What's done is done, and she is dead beside,
Dead long ago, and I am Bishop since,
And as she died, so must we die ourselves,
And thence ye may perceive the world's a dream.
Life, how and what is it ?   As here I lie
In this state-chamber, dying by degrees,
Hours and long hours in the dead night, I ask
" Do I live, am I dead ? "   Peace, peace, seems all.
Saint Praxed's ever was the church for peace ;
And so about this tomb of mine.   I fought
With tooth and nail to save my niche, ye know :
—Old Gandolf cozened me, despite my care ;
Shrewd was that snatch from out the corner South
He graced his carrion with, God curse the same !
Yet still my niche is not so cramped, but thence
One sees the pulpit on the epistle-side,
And somewhat of the choir, those silent seats,
And up into the aëry dome where live
The angels, and a sunbeam's sure to lurk :
And I shall fill my slab of basalt there,
And 'neath my tabernacle take my rest,
With those nine columns round me, two and two,
The odd one at my feet where Anselm stands :
Peach-blossom marble all, the rare, the ripe
As fresh-poured red wine of a mighty pulse.
—Old Gandolf with his paltry onion-stone,
Put me where I may look at him !   True peach,
Rosy and flawless : how I earned the prize !
Draw close : that conflagration of my church
—What, then ?   So much was saved if aught were
    missed !
My sons, ye would not be my death ?   Go, dig
The white-grape vineyard where the oil-press stood,
Drop water gently till the surface sink,

And if ye find. . . . Ah! God, I know not, I! . . .
Bedded in store of rotten fig-leaves soft;
And corded up in a tight olive-frail,
Some lump, ah God! of *lapis lazuli.*
Big as a Jew's head cut off at the nape,
Blue as a vein o'er the Madonna's breast. . . .
Sons, all have I bequeathed you, villas, all,
That brave Frascati villa with its bath,
So let the blue lump poise between my knees,
Like God the Father's globe on both his hands
Ye worship in the Jesu Church so gay.
For Gandolf shall not choose but see and burst!
Swift as a weaver's shuttle fleet our years:
Man goeth to the grave, and where is he?
Did I say, basalt for my slab, sons?   Black—
'Twas ever antique-black I meant!   How else
Shall ye contrast my frieze to come beneath?
The bas-relief in bronze ye promised me,
Those Pans and Nymphs ye wot of, and perchance
Some tripod, thyrsus, with a vase or so,
The Saviour at His sermon on the mount,
Saint Praxed, in a glory, and one Pan
Ready to twitch the Nymph's last garment off,
And Moses with the tables . . . but I know
Ye mark me not!   What do they whisper thee
Child of my bowels, Anselm?   Ah! ye hope
To revel down my villas while I gasp
Bricked o'er with beggar's mouldy travertine,
Which Gandolf from his tomb-top chuckles at!
Nay, boys, ye love me—all of jasper, then!
'Tis jasper ye stand pledged to, lest I grieve.
My bath must needs be left behind, alas!
One block, pure green as a pistachio-nut,
There's plenty jasper somewhere in the world—
And have I not Saint Praxed's ear to pray

Horses for ye, and brown Greek manuscripts,
And mistresses with great smooth marbly limbs?
—That's if ye carve my epitaph aright,
Choice Latin, picked phrase, Tully's every word,
No gaudy ware like Gandolf's gaudy second line—
Tully, my masters? Ulpian serves his need!
And then how I shall lie through centuries,
And hear the blessed mutter of the mass,
And see God made and eaten all day long,
And feel the steady candle-flame, and taste
Good strong thick stupefying incense-smoke!
For as I lie here, hours of the dead night,
Dying in state and by such slow degrees,
I fold my arms as if they clasped a crook,
And stretch my feet forth as straight stone can point,
And let the bedclothes, for a mort-cloth, drop
Into great laps and folds of sculptor's work:
And as yon tapers dwindle, and strange thoughts
Grow, with a certain humming in my ears,
About the life before I lived this life,
And this life, too, popes, cardinals, and priests,
Saint Praxed at his sermon on the mount,
Your tall, pale mother with her talking eyes,
And new-found agate urns as fresh as day,
And marble's language, Latin pure, discreet
—Aha, Elucescebat quoth our friend?
No Tully, said I, Ulpian at the best!
Evil and brief hath been my pilgrimage.
All *lapis*, all, sons! Else I give the Pope
My villas! Will ye ever eat my heart?
Ever your eyes were as a lizard's quick,
They glitter like your mother's for my soul,
Or ye would heighten my impoverished frieze,
Piece out its starved design, and fill my vase
With grapes, and add a vizor and a Term,

And to the tripod ye would tie a lynx
That in his struggle throws the thyrsus down,
To comfort me on my entablature
Whereon I am to lie till I must ask,
"Do I live, am I dead?"   There, leave me, there!
For ye have stabbed me with ingratitude
To death: ye wish it—God, ye wish it!   Stone—
Gritstone, a-crumble!   Clammy squares which sweat
As if the corpse they keep were oozing through—
And no more *lapis* to delight the world!
Well, go!   I bless ye.   Fewer tapers there,
But in a row: and, going, turn your backs
—Ay, like departing altar-ministrants,
And leave me in my church, the church for peace,
That I may watch at leisure if he leers—
Old Gandolf at me, from his onion-stone,
As still he envied me, so fair she was!

FROM "HOLY CROSS DAY"

But now while the scapegoats leave our flock,
And the rest sit silent and count the clock,
Since forced to muse the appointed time
On these precious facts and truths sublime,—
Let us fitly employ it, under our breath,
In saying Ben Ezra's Song of Death.

For Rabbi Ben Ezra, the night he died,
Called sons and sons' sons to his side,
And spoke, "This world has been harsh and strange;
Something is wrong: there needeth a change,
But what, or where? at the last or first?
In one point only we sinned, at worst.

" The Lord will have mercy on Jacob yet,
And again in His border see Israel set.
When Judah beholds Jerusalem,
The stranger-seed will be joined to them :
To Jacob's House shall the Gentiles cleave.
So the Prophet saith and his sons believe.

" Ay, the children of the chosen race
Shall carry and bring them to their place :
In the land of the Lord shall lead the same
Bondsmen and handmaids.   Who shall blame,
When the slaves enslave, the oppressed ones o'er
The oppressor triumph for evermore ?

" God spake and gave us the word to keep :
Bade never fold the hands nor sleep
'Mid a faithless world,—at watch and ward,
Till Christ at the end relieve our guard.
By His servant Moses the watch was set :
Though near upon cock-crow, we keep it yet.

" Thou ! if thou wast He, who at mid-watch came,
By the starlight, naming a dubious name !
And if, too heavy with sleep—too rash
With fear—O thou, if that martyr-gash
Fell on Thee coming to take Thine own,
And we gave the Cross, when we owed the Throne—

" Thou art the Judge.   We are bruised thus.
But, the Judgment over, join sides with us !
Thine, too, is the cause ! and not more thine
Than ours, is the work of these dogs and swine,
Whose life laughs through and spits at their creed,
Who maintain Thee in word, and defy Thee in deed !

"We withstood Christ then?   Be mindful how
At least we withstand Barabbas now!
Was our outrage sore?   But the worst we spared,
To have called these—Christians, had we dared!
Let defiance to them pay mistrust of Thee,
And Rome make amends for Calvary!

"By the torture, prolonged from age to age,
By the infamy, Israel's heritage,
By the Ghetto's plague, by the garb's disgrace,
By the badge of shame, by the felon's place,
By the branding-tool, the bloody whip,
And the summons to Christian fellowship,—

"We boast our proof that at least the Jew
Would wrest Christ's name from the Devil's crew.
Thy face took never so deep a shade
But we fought them in it, God our aid!
A trophy to bear, as we march, thy band
South, East, and on to the Pleasant Land!"

A TOCCATA OF GALUPPI'S

Oh, Galuppi Baldassaro, this is very sad to find!
I can hardly misconceive you; it would prove me deaf
    and blind;
But although I take your meaning, 'tis with such a
    heavy mind!

Here you come with your old music, and here's all the
    good it brings.
What, they lived once thus at Venice, where the mer-
    chants were the kings,
Where St. Mark's is, where the Doges used to wed the
    sea with rings?

Ay, because the sea's the street there, and 'tis arched
    by . . . what you call
. . . Shylock's bridge with houses on it, where they kept
    the carnival :
I was never out of England—it's as if I saw it all.

Did young people take their pleasure when the sea was
    warm in May?
Balls and masks begun at midnight, burning ever to
    midday,
When they made up fresh adventures for the morrow,
    do you say?

Was a lady such a lady, cheeks so round and lips so
    red,—
On her neck the small face buoyant, like a bell-flower
    on its bed,
O'er the breast's superb abundance where a man might
    base his head?

Well, and it was graceful of them : they'd break talk off
    and afford
—She, to bite her mask's black velvet, he, to finger on
    his sword,
While you sat and played Toccatas, stately at the
    clavichord?

What? Those lesser thirds so plaintive, sixths diminished, sigh on sigh,
Told them something? Those suspensions, those solutions—" Must we die?"
Those commiserating sevenths—" Life might last! we can but try!"

" Were you happy?"—" Yes."—" And are you still as happy?"—" Yes. And you?"
—"Then, more kisses!"—" Did *I* stop them, when a million seemed so few?"
Hark, the dominant's persistence till it must be answered to!

So, an octave struck the answer. Oh, they praised you, I dare say!
" Brave Galuppi! that was music! good alike at grave and gay!
I can always leave off talking when I hear a master play!"

Then they left you for their pleasure, till in due time, one by one,
Some with lives that came to nothing, some with deeds as well undone,
Death stepped tacitly and took them where they never see the sun.

But when I sit down to reason, think to take my stand nor swerve,
While I triumph o'er a secret wrung from nature's close reserve,
In you come with your cold music till I creep thro' every nerve.

Yes, you, like a ghostly cricket, creaking where a house
    was burned ;
" Dust and ashes, dead and done with, Venice spent
    what Venice earned.
The soul, doubtless, is immortal—where a soul can be
    discerned.

" Yours, for instance : you know physics, something of
    geology,
Mathematics are your pastime ; souls shall rise in their
    degree ;
Butterflies may dread extinction—you'll not die, it can-
    not be !

" As for Venice and her people, merely born to bloom
    and drop,
Here on earth they bore their fruitage, mirth and folly
    were the crop :
What of soul was left, I wonder, when the kissing had
    to stop ?

" Dust and ashes ! " So you croak it, and I want the
    heart to scold.
Dear dead women, with such hair, too—what's become
    of all the gold
Used to hang and brush their bosoms ? I feel chilly
    and grown old.

W. M. THACKERAY. 1811–1863

FROM "THE CHRONICLE OF THE DRUM"

Hurrah! what a storm was a-brewing,
  The day of our vengeance was come;
Through scenes of what carnage and ruin
  Did I beat on the patriot drum.
Let's drink to the famed tenth of August,
  At midnight I beat the tattoo,
And woke up the pikemen of Paris
  To follow the bold Barbaroux.

With pikes, and with shouts, and with torches,
  Marched onward our dusty battalions,
And we girt the tall castle of Louis,
  A million of tatterdemalions!
We stormed the fair gardens where towered
  The walls of his heritage splendid,
Ah, shame on him, craven and coward,
  That had not the heart to defend it!

With the crown of his sires on his head,
  His nobles and knights by his side,
At the foot of his ancestors' palace,
  'Twere easy, methinks, to have died.
But no; when we burst through his barriers,
  'Mid heaps of the dying and dead,
In vain through the chambers we sought him,
  He had turned like a craven and fled.

.   .   .   .   .

The drummer now bared his old breast,
  And show'd us a plenty of scars,
Rude presents that Fortune had made him,
  In fifty victorious wars.

" This came when I followed bold Kleber,
   'Twas shot by a Mameluke gun ;
And this from an Austrian sabre,
   When the field of Marengo was won.

" My forehead has many deep furrows,
   But this is the deepest of all ;
A Brunswicker made it at Jena,
   Beside the fair river of Saal.
This cross, 'twas the Emperor gave it
   (God bless him), it covers a blow,
I had it at Austerlitz fight,
   As I beat on my drum in the snow."

AT THE CHURCH GATE

Although I enter not, Yet round about the spot
      Sometimes I hover ;
And at the sacred gate, With longing eyes I wait,
      Expectant of her.

The Minster bell tolls out, Above the city's rout
      And noise and humming ;
They've stopped the chiming bell, I hear the organ's
   swell ;
      She's coming—coming.

My lady comes at last, Timid and stepping fast,
      And hastening hither
With modest eyes downcast.   She comes—she's here—
   she's past,
      May heaven go with her.

Kneel undisturbed, fair Saint. Pour out your praise or
    plaint
        Meekly and duly ;
I will not enter there, To sully your pure prayer
        With thoughts unruly.

But suffer me to pace Round the forbidden place,
        Lingering a minute,
Like outcast spirits who wait And see through Heaven's
    gate
        Angels within it !

THOMAS DAVIS. 1814–1845

THE BATTLE-EVE OF THE BRIGADE

(From the "Nation")

The mess-tent is full, and the glasses are set,
And the gallant Count Thomond is president yet;
The vet'ran arose like an uplifted lance,
Crying, "Comrades, a health to the monarch of France!"
With bumpers and cheers they have done as he bade,
For King Louis is loved by the Irish Brigade.

"A health to King James," and they bent as they quaffed;
"Here's to George the Elector!" and fiercely they
        laughed;
"Good luck to the girls we wooed long ago,
Where Sionainn, and Bearbha, and Abhaindubh flow;"
"God prosper Old Ireland!" you'd think them afraid,
So pale grew the chiefs of the Irish Brigade.

"But surely, that light cannot come from our lamp—
And that noise—are they *all* getting drunk in the camp?"
"Hurrah! boys, the morning of battle is come,
And the *generale's* beating on many a drum."
So they rush from the revel to join the parade,
For the van is the right of the Irish Brigade.

They fought as they revelled, fast, fiery, and true,
And, though victors, they left on the field not a few;
And they who survived fought and drank as of yore,
But the land of their hearts' hope they never saw more
For in far, foreign fields from Dunkirk to Belgrade
Lie the soldiers and chiefs of the Irish Brigade.

F. W. FABER. 1814–1863

PREFACE

Blame not my verse if echoes of church bells
With every change of thought or dream are twining,
Fetching a murmuring sameness from the fells
And lakes and rivers with their inland shining.
And marvel not in these loose drifting times
If anchored spirits in their blythest motion
Dip to their anchors veiled within the ocean,
Catching too staid a measure for their rhymes.
An age comes on, which came three times of old,
When the enfeebled nations shall stand still
To be by Christian science shaped at will;
And Taste and Art, rejecting heathen mould,
Shall draw their types from Europe's middle night,
Well pleased if such good darkness be their light !

PAST FRIENDS

Are there such things as friends that pass away ?
When each fresh opening season of our life,
Through the dim struggling crowd and weary strife,
Brings kindred spirits nigh whom we would pray
Might live with us, and by our deathbed stay.
Do these, our chosen ones, sink down at last
Into the common grave of visions past ?
Ah ! there are few men in the world can say

They had a dream which they do not dream still;
Few fountains in the heart which cease to play,
When those whose touch evoked them at their will
Sit there no more : and I my dreams fulfil
When to high Heaven my tongue still nightly bears
Old names, like broken music, in my prayers.

WRITTEN IN CONWAY CASTLE

England! thy strifes are written on thy fields
In grim old characters, which studious time
Wears down to beauty, while green nature yields
Soft ivy-veils to clothe grey holds of crime,
And hides war's prints with spring flowers that might wave
Their pale sweet selves upon a martyr's grave.
Here hath the ploughshare of the Conquest worn
The furrowed moat around a cruel tower ;
There York's White Roses fringe in blameless scorn
The ledge of some Lancastrian lady's bower ;
Least, for my country's sake may I regret
The fruitful angers, and good blood that ran
So hot from Royalist and Puritan,
Which in our very soil is red and throbbing yet.

GENOA

I am where snowy mountains round me shine;
But in sweet vision truer than mine eyes
I see pale Genoa's marble crescent rise
Between the water and the Apennine.

On the sea-bank she couches like a deer,
A creature giving light with her soft sheen,
While the blue ocean and the mountain green
Pleased with the wonder always gaze on her.

And day and night the mild sea-murmur fills
The corridors of her cool palaces,
Taking the freshness from the orange trees,
A fragrant gift into the peaceful hills.

And from the balustrades into the street,
From time to time there are voluptuous showers,
Gentle descents, of shaken lemon flowers
Snapped by the echo of the passing feet.

And when the sun his noonday height hath gained,
How mute is all that slumbrous Apennine,
Upon whose base the streaks of green turf shine,
With the black olive-gardens interveined!

How fair it is when, in the purple bay,
Of the soft sea the clear edged moon is drinking,
Or the dark sky amid the shipmasts winking
With summer lightning over Corsica!

O Genoa! thou art a marvellous birth—
A clasp which joins the mountains and the sea:
And the two powers do homage unto thee
As to a matchless wonder of the earth.

Can life be common life in spots like these
Where they breathe breath from orange gardens wafted?
O joy and sorrow surely must be grafted
On stems apart for these bright Genoese.

The place is islanded amid her mirth,
The very girdle of her beauty thrown
About her in men's minds, a virgin zone,
Marks her a spot unmated on the earth.

I hear the deep coves of the Apennine,
Filled with a gentle trouble of sweet bells:
And the blue tongues of sea that pierce the dells,
As conscious of the Virgin's feast day shine.

For Genoa the Proud for many an age
Hath been pre-eminent as tributary
Unto the special service of St. Mary,
The sinless Virgin's chosen appanage.

I see the street with very stacks of flowers
Choked up, a wild and beautiful array,
And in my mind I thread my fragrant way
Once more amid the rich and cumbrous bowers.

And unforgotten beauty ! by the Bay,
I see the two boys and the little maiden
With crimson tulips for the Virgin laden,
Wending along the road from Spezzia.

TO A LAKE PARTY

We shall all meet again,
Not in the wood or plain,
Nor by the lake's green marge ;
But we shall meet once more
By a far greener shore,
With our souls set at large.

We all shall never stand
On Rothay's white-lipped strand,
And hear the far sheep-cries :
The Wansfell wind may blow,
But not to kindle now
The bright fire in our eyes.

The three cleft mountains stand
In their own treeless land,
Where we all stood and wondered.
The black cliffs are the same
Where the hundred echoes came
That dark day when it thundered.

The summer sun sinks nightly
Into the Solway brightly—
We are not there to see.
The mountain loophole seems
Full of the golden beams,
Full as it used to be.

Athwart the sunlit vale
The heavy ravens sail,
Each to his craggy dwelling;
While evening gathers brown
On thy stone-sprinkled down,
Thou desolate Helvellyn!

.　　　.　　　.　　　.　　　.

But vain to me the show;
My heart is weary now
Of all its holy places.
Oh! what are sun and shower,
Hill-path and forest-bower,
Where there are no friends' faces?

We shall all meet again,
Not in the wood or plain,
Nor by the lake's green marge;
The past shall be lived o'er
By a far greener shore,
With our souls set at large.

THERAPIA

The sunny wisdom of the Greeks
  All o'er the earth is strewed:
On every dark and awful place,
  Rude hill and haunted wood,
The beautiful bright people left
  A name of omen good.

They would not have an evil word
  Weigh heavy on the breeze,
They would not darken mountain side,
  Nor stain the shining seas
With names of some disastrous past,
  The unwise witnesses.

Here legendary Argo touched
  In this blue watered bay;
Here dark Medea in pursuit
  Her poisons cast away,
Polluting even the odorous shades
  Of pure Therapia.

Look how the interlacing trees
  Their glowing blossoms wreathe!
Is this a spot for poison plants,
  For crime, or savage death?
The Greeks endured not that on it
  Should pass so dire a breath.

Unlike the children of romance—
  From out whose spirit deep
The touch of gloom hath passed on fen
  And mountain, lake, and steep,
On Devil's Bridge and Raven's Tower,
  And love-lorn Maiden's Leap;

Who sought in cavern, wood, and dell
  Where'er they could lay bare
The path of ill, and localised
  Terrific legends there,
Leaving a hoarse and ponderous name
  To haunt the very air.

Not so the radiant-hearted Greeks,
  Who hesitated still
To offend the blessed Presences
  Which Earth and Ocean fill;
Whose tongues, elsewhere so eloquent,
  Stammered at words of ill.

All places where their presence was,
  Upon the fruitful earth,
By kindly law were clasped within
  The circle of their mirth,
And in their spirits had a new
  And consecrated birth.

O bless them for it, traveller!
  The fair-tongued ancients bless!
Who thus from land and sea trod out
  All footmarks of distress,
Illuminating Earth with their
  Own inward cheerfulness.

Unto the Axine Sea they sent
  A name of better feeling,
Dark powers into Eumenides,
  A gentle change! were stealing,
And poison-stained Therapia
  Became the Bay of Healing!

AGED CITIES

I have known cities with the strong-armed Rhine
Clasping their mouldered quays in lordly sweep;
And lingered where the Maine's low waters shine
Through Tyrian Frankfort; and been fain to weep
'Mid the green cliffs where pale Mosella laves
That Roman sepulchre, imperial Trèves.
Ghent boasts her street, and Bruges her moonlight
    square;
And holy Mechlin, Rome of Flanders, stands,
Like a queen-mother, on her spacious lands;
And Antwerp shoots her glowing spire in air.
Yet have I seen no place, by inland brook,
Hill-top, or plain, or trim arcaded bowers,
That carries age so nobly in its look
As Oxford with the sun upon her towers.

BAMBERG

There are who blame sensations of delight,
Born of our happy strength and cheerful health,
As though we could lay by no moral wealth
From the pulsations of mere joyous might.

How poor they make themselves who thus disown
The fresh and temperate body's right to wait
Upon the soul, and to exhilarate
The heart with life from animal spirits thrown!

For me a very weight of moral wealth
From the bright sun upon the ivy wall
And white clouds in the sky, doth gaily fall,
Making my days a thanksgiving for health.

The whetting of the mower's scythe at morn,
The odorous withering of the new-cut grass,
Breeding, I know not what enjoyment, pass
Like a new world into my spirit borne.

O there are harvests from the buoyant mirth
Which hath such power my nature to unbind,
Letting my spirits flow upon the wind,
As though I were resolved into the earth.

When I have bounded with elastic tread,
Or floated, without root, a frolic breeze
Waked by the sunlight on the fields or seas,
Moods of ripe thought have thence been harvested.

I stood upon the Michaelsberg ; below,
Into three cities cloven by the streams,
Was ancient Bamberg, and the morning beams
Had touched a thousand gables with their glow.

Around, a dull expanse, did cornfields shine,
The shallow Regnitz and the winding Maine
Were coiled in ruddy links upon the plain,
And lost beyond the pinewood's hard black line.

The radiance on the minster roof was poured,
And then above the convent's dusky bowers
Sprung all at once the four illumined towers,
As though St. Michael had unsheathed his sword.

I thought not, Bamberg ! of thy bishops old,
The rich Franconian church, or abbots gone
To beard the emperor at Ratisbon,
With saucy squires and Swabian barons bold.

But there I stood upon the dizzy edge,
And saw a sight worth all the barons bold,
A woven web of purple and of gold,
A living web thrown o'er the rocky ledge.

It was a cloud of rooks in morning's beam,
Which, rising from the neighbouring convent trees,
With all their pinions open to the breeze,
Swam down the steep in one majestic stream.

It was a purple cataract that flung
Its living self adown a rocky rent,
And midway in its clamorous descent
The rainbow-glancing morning o'er it hung.

Some were of gold, which in a moment shifted
Into a purple or a brilliant black,
And some had silver dewdrops on their back,
Changing as through the beams the creatures drifted.

Beneath, the multitudinous houses lay :
The living cataract one instant flashed
Through the bright air, then on the roofs was dashed
In seeming shower of gold and sable spray.

I watched with joy the noisy pageant leap
Into the quiet city ; and the thrill
Of health did so my glowing body fill,
That I would fain sail with it down the steep.

I was beside myself ; I could not think ;
A beauty is a thing entire, apart,
And may be flung into a passive heart,
And be a fountain there whence we may drink.

Ah me ! the morning was so cool and bright,
And I so strong, and it was such a mirth
To be so far away upon the earth,
That I was overflowed with sheer delight.

Away, like stocks and stones, went serious thought,
Now buried in the foamy inundation,
Now through the waves of exquisite sensation
From time to time unto the surface brought.

I rescued nothing, for I had no power;
And in the retrospect I dare to boast,—
I would not for a world of thought have lost
The animal enjoyment of that hour!

THE SHADOW OF THE ROCK

The Shadow of the Rock!
Stay, Pilgrim! Stay!
Night treads upon the heels of day;
There is no other resting-place this way.
The Rock is near,
The Well is clear,
Rest in the Shadow of the Rock.

The Shadow of the Rock!
The desert wide
Lies round thee like a trackless tide,
In waves of sand forlornly multiplied,
The Sun has gone,
Thou art alone,
Rest in the Shadow of the Rock.

The Shadow of the Rock!
All come alone,
All, ever since the sun hath shone,
Who travelled by this road have come alone.
Be of good cheer,
A home is here,
Rest in the Shadow of the Rock.

The Shadow of the Rock !
Night veils the land ;
How the palms whisper as they stand !
How the well tinkles faintly through the sand !
Cool water take
Thy thirst to slake,
Rest in the Shadow of the Rock.

The Shadow of the Rock !
Abide ! Abide !
This Rock moves ever at thy side,
Pausing to welcome thee at eventide.
Ages are laid
Beneath its shade,
Rest in the Shadow of the Rock.

The Shadow of the Rock !
Always at hand,
Unseen it cools the noontide land,
And quells the fire that flickers in the sand.
It comes in sight
Only at night,
Rest in the Shadow of the Rock.

The Shadow of the Rock !
'Mid skies storm-riven
It gathers shadows out of heaven,
And holds them o'er us all night cool and even.
Through the charmed air
Dew falls not there,
Rest in the Shadow of the Rock.

The Shadow of the Rock !
To angels' eyes
This Rock its shadow multiplies,
And at this hour in countless places lies.
One Rock, one shade,
O'er thousands laid,
Rest in the Shadow of the Rock.

The Shadow of the Rock !
To weary feet,
That have been diligent and fleet,
The sleep is deeper, and the shade more sweet.
O weary ! rest,
Thou art sore pressed,
Rest in the Shadow of the Rock.

The Shadow of the Rock !
Thy bed is made ;
Crowds of tired souls like thine are laid
This night beneath the self-same placid shade.
They who rest here
Wake with Heaven near,
Rest in the Shadow of the Rock.

The Shadow of the Rock !
Pilgrim ! sleep sound ;
In night's swift hours with silent bound
The Rock will put thee over leagues of ground,
Gaining more way
By night than day,
Rest in the Shadow of the Rock.

The Shadow of the Rock !
One day of pain
Thou scarce wilt hope the Rock to gain,
Yet there wilt sleep thy last sleep on the plain ;
And only wake
In Heaven's daybreak,
Rest in the Shadow of the Rock.

THE FLIGHT OF THE WILD SWANS

(*From " Prince Amadis "*)

But away and away, in the midnight blue,
That fleet of white creatures went steering through ;
And away and away through the sweet daybreak
From the white Alps flashed, their road they take

Through the tingling noon and the evening vapour,
Which Hesper lights with his little taper,
Through the tremulous smiles of moonlight mirth,
And the balmy descents of dew to the earth.

Through the calms, through the winds, when the hail-
stones ring,
The convoy passed with untiring wing,
And oft from their course for hours they drove,
As though they winnowed the air for love.

And now they would mount and now they would stoop,
And almost to earth or river droop,
And harshly would pipe through the sheer delight
Of their boisterous wings, and their strength of flight.

P

They saw the young Save in the next night's moon,
They were over Belgrade by the afternoon,
And ere the sun set their journey was o'er,
On a willow-isle by the Danube's shore.

DR. CHARLES MACKAY. 1814–1889

FROM "SISYPHUS"

Do not all Earth and Sea
Repeat eternally
  Th' unvarying strain?
The old and sad lament
With human voices blent,
  In vain, in vain!

Through the green forest arch
The wild winds in their march
  Sigh and complain;
The torrent on the hill
Moans to the midnight chill,
  In vain, in vain!

The hoarse monotonous waves
Attune from all their caves,
  Through storm and rain,
The melancholy cry
To listening Earth and Sky,
  In vain, in vain!

Love mourns its early dead;
Hope its illusions fled,
  Or rudely slain;
And Wealth and Power prolong
The same, th' eternal song,
  In vain, in vain!

Toil, Sisyphus, toil on!
Thou'rt many, though but one!
Toil heart and brain!
One—but the type of all
Rolling the dreadful ball,
In vain, in vain!

PRINCIPAL J. C. SHAIRP. 1815–1885

A REMEMBRANCE

Within the ancient College-gate I passed,
   Looked round once more upon the well-known
      square ;
Change had been busy since I saw it last,
   Replacing crumbled walls by new and fair ;
The old chapel gone—a roof of statelier show
Soared high—I wondered if it sees below
   As pure heart-worship, as confiding prayer.

But though walls, chapel, garden, all are changed,
   And through these courts quick generations fleet,
There are whom still I see round table ranged,
   In chapel snowy-stoled for matins meet ;
Though many faces since have come and gone,
Changeless in memory these still live on,
   A scholar brotherhood, high-souled and complete.

From old foundations where the nation rears
   Her darlings, came that flower of England's youth,
And here in latest teens, or riper years,
   Stood drinking in all nobleness and truth.
By streams of Isis 'twas a fervid time,
When zeal and young devotion held their prime,
   Whereof not unreceptive these in sooth.

The voice that weekly from St. Mary's spake,
   As from the unseen world oracular,
Strong as another Wesley, to rewake
   The sluggish heart of England, near and far,
Voice so intense to win men, or repel,
Piercing yet tender, on these spirits fell,
   Making them other, higher than they were.

Foremost one [1] stood, with forehead high and broad,—
  Sculptor ne'er moulded grander dome of thought,—
Beneath it, eyes dark-lustred rolled and glowed,
  Deep wells of feeling where the full soul wrought;
Yet lithe of limb, and strong as shepherd boy,
He roamed the wastes and drank the mountain joy,
  To cool a heart too cruelly distraught.

The voice that from St. Mary's thrilled the hour,
  He could not choose but let it in, though loth;
Yet a far other voice with earlier power
  Had touched his soul and won his first heart-troth,
In school-days heard, not far from Avon's stream:
Anon there dawned on him a wilder dream,
  Opening strange tracts of thought remote from both.

All travail pangs of thought too soon he knew,
  All currents felt, that shake these anxious years,
Striving to walk to tender conscience true,
  And bear his load alone, nor vex his peers.
From these, alas! too soon he moved apart;
Sorrowing they saw him go, with loyal heart,
  Such heart as greatly loves, but more reveres.

Away o'er Highland Bens and glens, away
  He roamed, rejoicing without let or bound.
And, yearning still to vast America,
  A simpler life, more freedom, sought, not found.
Now the world listens to his lone soul-songs;
But he, for all its miseries and wrongs
  Sad no more, sleeps beneath Italian ground.

[1] Clough.

Beside that elder scholar one [1] there stood,
  On Sunday mornings 'mid the band white-stoled,
As deep of thought, but chastened more of mood,
  Devout, affectionate, and humble-souled.
There, as he stood in chapel, week by week,
Lines of deep feeling furrowed down his cheek
  Lent him, even then, an aspect strangely old.

Not from the great foundations of the land,
  But from a wise and learnèd father's roof,
His place he won amid the scholar band,
  Where finest gifts of mind were put to proof;
And if some things he missed which great schools teach,
More precious traits he kept, beyond their reach,—
  Shy traits that rougher world had scared aloof.

Him early prophet souls of Oriel
  A boy companion to their converse drew,
And yet his thought was free, and pondered well
  All sides of truth, and gave to each its due.
O pure wise heart, and guileless as a child!
In thee, all jarring discords reconciled,
  Knowledge and reverence undivided grew.

Ah me! we dreamed it had been his to lead
  The world by power of deeply-pondered books,
And lure a rash and hasty age to heed
  Old truths set forth with fresh and winsome looks;
But he those heights forsook for the low vale
And sober shades, where dwells misfortune pale,
  And sorrow pines in unremembered nooks.

[1] Prichard.

Where'er a lone one lay and had no friend,
   A son of consolation there was he ;
And all life long there was no pain to tend,
   No grief to solace, but his heart was free ;
And then his years of pastoral service done,
And his long suffering meekly borne, he won
   A grave of peace by England's southern sea.

More than all arguments in deep books stored,
   Than any preacher's penetrative tone,
More than all music by rapt poet poured,
   To have seen thy life, thy converse to have known,
Was witness for thy Lord—that thus to be
Humble, and true, and loving like to thee—
   This was worth living for, and this alone.

Fair-haired and tall, slim, but of stately mien,
   Inheritor of a high poetic name,
Another,[1] in the bright bloom of nineteen,
   Fresh from the pleasant fields of Eton came :
Whate'er of beautiful or poet sung,
Or statesman uttered, round his memory clung ;
   Before him shone resplendent heights of fame.

With friends around the board, no wit so fine
   To wing the jest, the sparkling tale to tell ;
Yet oft-times listening in St. Mary's shrine,
   Profounder moods upon his spirit fell :
We heard him then, England has heard him since,
Uphold the fallen, make the guilty wince,
   And the hushed Senate have confessed the spell.

[1] J. D. Coleridge, later Lord Coleridge.

There too was one,[1] broad-browed, with open face,
  And fame for toil compacted—him with pride
A school of Devon from a rural place
  Had sent to stand these chosen ones beside;
From childhood trained all hardness to endure,
To love the things that noble are, and pure,
  And think and do the truth, whate'er betide.

With strength for labour, " as the strength of ten,"
  To ceaseless toil he girt him night and day;
A native king and ruler among men,
  Ploughman or Premier, born to bear true sway;
Small or great duty never known to shirk,
He bounded joyously to sternest work,
  Less buoyant others turn to sport and play.

Comes brightly back one day—he had performed
  Within the Schools some more than looked-for feat,
And friends and brother scholars round him swarmed
  To give the day to gladness that was meet:
Forth to the fields we fared,—among the young
Green leaves and grass, his laugh the loudest rung;
  Beyond the rest his bound flew far and fleet.

All afternoon o'er Shotover's breezy heath
  We ranged, through bush and brake instinct with
    Spring,
The vernal dream-lights o'er the plains beneath
  Trailed, overhead the skylarks carolling;
Then home through evening-shadowed fields we went,
And filled our College rooms with merriment,—
  Pure joys, whose memory contains no sting.

[1] F. Temple (Archbishop of Canterbury).

And thou [1] wast there that day, my earliest friend
　　In Oxford! sharer of that joy the while!
Ah me, with what delightsome memories blend
　　"Thy pale calm face, thy strangely soothing smile;"
What hours come back, when pacing College walks,
New knowledge dawned on us, or friendly talks,
　　Inserted, long night labours would beguile.

What strolls through meadows mown of fragrant hay,
　　On summer evenings by smooth Cherwell stream,
When Homer's song, or chaunt from Shelley's lay,
　　Added new splendour to the sunset gleam:
Or how, on calm of Sunday afternoon,
Keble's low sweet voice to devout commune,
　　And heavenward musings, would the hours redeem.

But when on crimson creeper o'er the wall
　　Autumn his finger beautifully impressed,
And came, the third time, at October's call,
　　Cheerily trooping to their rooms the rest,
Filling them with glad greetings and young glee,
His room alone was empty—henceforth we
　　By his sweet fellowship no more were blest.

Too soon, too quickly from our longing sight,
　　Fading he passed, and left us to deplore
From all our Oxford day a lovely light
　　Gone, which no after morning could restore.
Through his own meadows Cherwell still wound on,
And Thames by Eton fields as glorious shone—
　　He who so loved them would come back no more.

[1] Seymour.

Among that scholar band the youngest pair
　　In hall and chapel side by side were seen,
Each of high hopes and noble promise heir,
　　But far in thought apart—a world between.
The one,[1] wide-welcomed for a father's fame,
Entered with free bold step that seemed to claim
　　Fame for himself, nor on another lean.

So full of power, yet blithe and debonair,
　　Rallying his friends with pleasant banter gay,
Or half adream chaunting with jaunty air
　　Great words of Goethe, catch of Béranger.
We see the banter sparkle in his prose,
But knew not then the undertone that flows,
　　So calmly sad, through all his stately lay.

The other [2] of an ancient name, erst dear
　　To Border Hills, though thence too long exiled,
In lore of Hellas scholar without peer,
　　Reared in grey halls on banks of Severn piled :
Reserved he was, of few words and slow speech,
But dwelt strange power, that beyond words could
　　　　reach,
　　In that sweet face by no rude thought defiled.

Oft at the hour when round the board at wine
　　Friends met, and others' talk flowed fast and free,
His listening silence and grave look benign
　　More than all speech made sweet society.
But when the rowers, on their rivals gaining,
Close on the goal bent, every sinew straining—
　　Then who more stout, more resolute than he ?

---

[1] Matthew Arnold.　　　　　　[2] James Riddell.

With that dear memory come back most of all
　　Calm days in Holy Week together spent;
Then brightness of the Easter Festival
　　O'er all things streaming, as a-field we went
Up Hincksey Vale, where gleamed the young primroses,
And happy children gathered them in posies,
　　Of that glad season meet accompaniment.

Of that bright band already more than half
　　Have passed beyond earth's longing and regret;
The remnant, for grave thought or pleasant laugh,
　　Can meet no longer as of old they met:
Yet, O pure souls! there are who still retain
Deep in their hearts the high ideal strain
　　They heard with you, and never can forget.

To have passed with them the threshold of young life,
　　Where the man meets, nor yet absorbs the boy,
And, ere descending to the dusty strife,
　　Gazed from clear heights of intellectual joy,
That an undying image left enshrined,
A sense of nobleness in human kind
　　Experience cannot dim, nor time destroy.

Since then, through all the jars of life's routine,
　　All that down-drags the spirit's loftier mood,
I have been soothed by fellowship serene
　　Of single souls with Heaven's own light endued.
But look where'er I may—before, behind—
I have not found, nor now expect to find,
　　Another such high-hearted brotherhood.

THE BUSH ABOON TRAQUAIR

" Will ye gang wi' me and fare
    To the bush aboon Traquair?
Owre the high Minchmuir we'll up and awa',
    This bonny simmer noon,
    While the sun shines fair aboon,
And the licht sklents saftly doun on holm and ha'."

    " And what wad ye do there,
    At the bush aboon Traquair?
A lang dreich road, ye had better let it be;
    Save some auld scrunts o' birk
    I' the hill-side that lirk
There's nocht i' the world for man to see.

    " But the blythe lilt o' that air,
    ' The Bush aboon Traquair'
I need nae mair, it's eneuch for me;
    Owre my cradle its sweet chime
    Cam sughin' frae auld time,
Sae tide what may, I'll awa' and see."

    " And what saw ye there,
    At the bush aboon Traquair?
Or what did ye hear that was worth your heed?"
    " I heard the cushies croon
    Through the gowden afternoon,
And the Quair burn singing down to the Vale o' Tweed.

    " And birks saw I three or four,
    Wi' grey moss bearded owre,
The last that are left o' the birken shaw,
    Whar mony a simmer e'en
    Fond lovers did convene,
They bonny, bonny gloamings that are lang awa'.

" Fra mony a but and ben,
　　By muirland, holm and glen,
They came ane hour to spen' on the greenwood sward ;
　　But lang ha'e lad an' lass
　　Been lying 'neth the grass,
The green green grass o' Traquair Kirkyard.

" They were blest beyond compare,
　　When they held their trysting there,
Amang thae greenest hills shone on by the sun ;
　　And then they wan a rest,
　　The lonest and the best,
I' Traquair Kirkyard when a' was done.

" Now the birks to dust may rot,
　　Name o' luvers be forgot,
Nae lads and lasses there ony mair convene ;
　　But the blythe lilt o' yon air
　　Keps the bush aboon Traquair,
And the love that ance was there, aye fresh and green."

THE REV. THOMAS WHYTEHEAD.   1815–1843

THE SECOND DAY OF CREATION

This world I deem
But a beautiful dream
Of shadows that are not what they seem ;
Where visions rise
Giving dim surmise
Of the things that shall meet our waking eyes.

Arm of the Lord !
Creating Word !
Whose glory the silent skies record—
Where stands thy name
In scrolls of flame,
On the firmament's high-shadowing frame !

I gaze o'erhead,
Where thy hand hath spread
For the waters of Heaven that crystal bed ;
And stored the dew
In its deeps of blue,
Which the fires of the sun come tempered through.

Soft they shine
Through that pure shrine,
As beneath the veil of thy flesh divine
Beams forth the light
That were else too bright
For the feebleness of a sinner's sight.

And such I deem
This world will seem
When we waken from life's mysterious dream,
And burst the shell
Where our spirits dwell
In their wondrous antenatal cell.

I gaze aloof
On the tissued roof
Where time and space are the warp and woof,
Which the King of Kings
As a curtain flings
O'er the dreadfulness of eternal things.

A tapestried tent—
To shade us meant
From the bare everlasting firmament—
Where the blaze of the skies
Comes soft to our eyes
Through a veil of mystical imageries.

But could I see
As in truth they be,
The glories of heaven that encompass me,
I should lightly hold
The tissued fold
Of that marvellous curtain of blue and gold.

Soon the whole,
Like a parched scroll,
Shall before my amazed sight uproll;
And without a screen
At one burst be seen
The Presence wherein I have ever been.

O! who shall bear
The blinding glare
Of the Majesty that shall meet us there?
What eye may gaze
On the unveiled blaze
Of the light-girdled throne of the Ancient of Days?

Christ, us aid!
Himself be our shade,
That in that dread day we be not dismay'd

TO A SPIDER

Patient creature, sitting there,
Fisher of the deep-blue air,
    With thy net of filing twine,
    Stretch'd upon my cottage-vine,
    Sure a quiet heart is thine!

I have watched thee there this hour
In thy secret leafy bower;
    All the while a single fly
    Has not flown thy meshes by,—
    They are empty, night is nigh.

Yet thou lonesome thing, for thee
Few have thought or sympathy
    Where thy scanty food to get,
    Thou that weary watch dost set
    By thy solitary net.

Q

Thou, as God has given thee skill,
Dost thy humble task fulfil,
    Busy at thy lines outspread,
    Mending up each broken thread ;
    Thus thy little life is led.

Yet belike some idler's hand,
Who Nature cannot understand,
    As in pity for thy prey,
    All thy toil for many a day
    At one stroke will sweep away.

Shame upon the delicate sense
That at thee would take offence !
    Thus, some passing qualm to smother,
    Oft will man, too, treat his brother,
    Wronging one to right another.

Oh, how selfish and unsound
Such sensibility is found !
    Few there are of those, I trow,
    Who such tender hearts avow,
    Half as innocent as thou.

EMILY BRONTË. 1816–1855

REMEMBRANCE

Cold in the earth—and the deep snow piled above thee,
  Far, far removed, cold in the dreary grave!
Have I forgot, my only Love, to love Thee,
  Sever'd at last, by Time's all-severing wave?

Now, when alone, do my thoughts no longer hover
  Over the mountains, on that northern shore,
Resting their wings where heath and fern-leaves cover
  Thy noble heart for ever, ever more?

Cold in the earth—and fifteen wild Decembers
  From those brown hills have melted into Spring:
Faithful, indeed, is the spirit that remembers
  After such years of change and suffering!

Sweet love of youth, forgive, if I forget thee,
  While the world's tide is bearing me along;
Other desires and other hopes beset me,
  Hopes which obscure, but cannot do thee wrong!

No later light has lighten'd up my heaven,
  No second morn has ever shone for me;
All my life's bliss from thy dear life was given,
  All my life's bliss is in the grave with thee.

But when the days of golden dreams had perish'd,
  And even Despair was powerless to destroy,
Then did I learn how Existence could be cherish'd,
  Strengthen'd and fed without the aid of joy.

Then did I check the tears of useless passion—
    Wean'd my young soul from yearning after thine;
Sternly denied its burning wish to hasten
    Down to that tomb already more than mine.

And, even yet, I dare not let it languish,
    Dare not indulge in memory's rapturous pain;
Once drinking deep of that divinest anguish,
    How could I seek the empty world again?

G. SMYTHE (later VISCOUNT STRANGFORD).
1818–1857

FROM "THE ARISTOCRACY OF FRANCE"

Oh never yet was theme so meet for roundel or
romance
As the ancient aristocracy and chivalry of France ;—
As when they went for Palestine, with Louis at their
head,
And many a waving banner, and the Oriflamme out-
spread ;—
And many a burnished galley with its blaze of armour
shone
In the ports of sunny Cyprus and the Acre of St.
John ;—
And many a knight who signed the cross, as he saw
the burning sands
With a prayer for those whom he had left in green
and fairer lands.
God aid them all, God them assoil, for few shall see
again
Streams like their own, their azure Rhone, or swift
and silver Seine.
.   .   .   .

And they are far from their Navarre, and from their
soft Garonne,
The Lords of Foix and Grammont, and the Count of
Carcassonne ;
For they have left, those Southron knights, the clime
they loved so well—
The feasts of fair Montpellier and the Toulouse
Carousel,

And the chase in early morning, when the keen and
    pleasant breeze
Came cold to the cheek from many a peak of the
    snowy Pyrenees.

   .   .   .   .

Oh never yet was theme so meet for roundel or
    romance
As the ancient aristocracy and chivalry of France ;—
As when they lay before Tournay, and the Grand
    Monarque was there,
With the bravest of his warriors, and the fairest of his
    fair ;
And the sun that was his symbol, and on his army
    shone,
Was in lustre, and in splendour, and in light itself
    outdone,
For the lowland and the highland were gleaming as
    of old,
When England vied with France in pride, on the
    famous Field of Gold,
And morn, and noon, and evening, and all the live-
    long night,
Were the sound of ceaseless music and the echo of
    delight.
And but for Vauban's waving arm and the answering
    cannonade,
It might have been a festal scene in some Versailles
    arcade ;
For she was there, the beautiful, the daughter of
    Mortemart,
And her proud eyes flashed the prouder for the roaring
    of the war,

And many a dark-haired rival, who bound her lover's
arm
With a ribbon, or a ringlet, or a kerchief for a charm,
And with an air as dainty, and with a step as light,
As they moved among the masquers, they went into
the fight.

FROM "THE MERCHANTS OF OLD ENGLAND"

The Land, it boasts its titled hosts,—they could not vie
with these,
The Merchants of Old England, the Seigneurs of the
Seas,
In the days of Great Elizabeth, when they sought the
Western Main,
Maugre and spite the Cæsars' might, and the menaces
of Spain.
And the richly freighted argosy, and the good galleon
went forth,
With the bales of Leeds or Lincoln, and the broadcloths
of the North ;
And many a veteran mariner would speak 'midst glis-
tening eyes
Of the gain of some past voyage, and the hazards of
emprize ;
Or in the long night-watches the wondrous tale was told
Of isles of fruit and spices, and fields of waving gold.
And the young and buoyant-hearted would oft that tale
renew,
And dream their dearest dream should be, their wildest
hope come true.

So with brave hearts and dauntless, they sailed for the
    Unknown ;
For each he sought his inmost thought, and a secret of
    his own.

.   .   .   .

The land it boasts its titled hosts—they cannot vie with
    these,
The Merchants of Old England, the Seigneurs of the
    Seas,
In the days of Queen Victoria, for they have borne her
    sway
From the far Atlantic islands, to the islands of Cathay,
And o'er one-sixth of all the earth, and over all the
    main
Like some good Fairy, Freedom marks and blesses her
    domain.
And of the mighty empires that arose, and ruled, and
    died,
Since on the sea, his heritage, the Tyrian looked in
    pride,
Not Carthage, with her Hannibal, not Athens when she
    bore
Her bravest and her best to the Syracusan shore,
While the words of Alcibiades yet echoed wide and far,
" Where are corn-fields, and are olive-grounds, the
    Athenian's limits are."
And in each trireme was many a dream of the West and
    its unknown bliss ;
Of the maidens of Iberia, and the feasts of Sybaris—
Not in those younger ages, when St. Mark's fair city ran
Her race of fame and frailty,—each monarch's courtezan ;
Not Lusia in her palmier hour, in those commercial days
When Vasco sailed for Calicut, and Camöens sang his
    praise ;

Not Spain with all her Indies, the while she seemed to
    fling
Her fetters on the waters, like the Oriental king;
Not one among the conquerors that are or ever were,
In wealth, or fame, or grandeur with England may
    compare.

A. H. CLOUGH. 1819–1861

EASTER DAY

NAPLES, 1849

I

Through the great sinful streets of Naples as I passed,
  With fiercer heat than flamed above my head,
My heart was hot within me; till at last
  My brain was lightened when my tongue had said—
    Christ is not risen!

    Christ is not risen, no—
    He lies and moulders low;
    Christ is not risen!

What though the stone were rolled away, and though
    The grave found empty there?—
    If not there, then elsewhere;
If not where Joseph laid him first, why then
    Where other men
Translaid Him after, in some humbler clay.
    Long ere to-day
Corruption that sad perfect work hath done;
Which here she scarcely, lightly had begun:
    The foul engendered worm
Feeds on the flesh of the life-giving form
Of our most Holy and Anointed One.
    He is not risen, no—
    He lies and moulders low;
    Christ is not risen!

What if the women, ere the dawn was grey,
Saw one or more great angels, as they say
(Angels, or Him Himself)? Yet neither there, nor then,
Nor afterwards, nor elsewhere, nor at all,
Hath He appeared to Peter or the Ten ;
Nor, save in thunderous terror, to blind Saul ;
Save in an after Gospel and late Creed,
            He is not risen, indeed,—
                Christ is not risen !

Or, what if e'en, as runs a tale, the Ten
Saw, heard, and touched, again and yet again ?
What if at Emmaüs inn, and by Capernaum's Lake,
            Came One, the bread that brake—
Came One that spake as never mortal spake,
And with them ate, and drank, and stood, and walked
      about ?
            Ah ! "some" did well to "doubt" !
Ah ! the true Christ, while these things came to pass,
Nor heard, nor spake, nor walked, nor lived, alas !
            He was not risen, no—
            He lay and mouldered low ;
                Christ was not risen !

As circulates in some great city crowd
A rumour changeful, vague, importunate, and loud,
From no determined centre, or of fact
            Or authorship exact,
            Which no man can deny
                Nor verify ;
            So spread the wondrous fame ;
                He all the same
            Lay senseless, mouldering, low :
            He was not risen, no—
                Christ was not risen !

Ashes to ashes, dust to dust;
As of the unjust, also of the just—
　　Yea, of that Just One, too!
This is the one sad Gospel that is true—
　　Christ is not risen!

Is He not risen, and shall we not rise?
　　　Oh, we unwise!
What did we dream, what wake we to discover?
Ye hills, fall on us, and ye mountains cover!
　　In darkness and great gloom,
Come ere we thought it is *our* day of doom;
From the cursed world, which is one tomb,
　　　Christ is not risen!

Eat, drink, and play, and think that this is bliss:
　　There is no heaven but this;
　　　There is no hell,
Save earth, which serves the purpose doubly well,
　　Seeing it visits still
With equalest apportionment of ill
Both good and bad alike, and brings to one same dust
　　The unjust and the just
　　　With Christ who is not risen.

Eat, drink, and die, for we are souls bereaved:
Of all the creatures under heaven's wide cope
We are most hopeless, who had once most hope,
And most beliefless, that had most believed.
　　Ashes to ashes, dust to dust;
　　As of the unjust, also of the just—
　　　Yea, of that Just One, too!
　　It is the one sad Gospel that is true!
　　　Christ is not risen!

Weep not beside the tomb,
Ye women unto whom
He was great solace while ye tended Him;
Ye who with napkin o'er the head,
And folds of linen round each wounded limb,
Laid out the sacred Dead;
And thou that bar'st Him in thy wondering womb;
Yea, Daughters of Jerusalem, depart,
Bind up as best ye may your own sad bleeding heart:
Go to your homes, your living children tend,
Your earthly spouses love;
Set your affections *not* on things above,
Which moth and rust corrupt, which quickliest come to
   end:
Or pray, if pray ye must, and pray, if pray ye can,
For death; since dead is He whom you deemed more
   than man,
Who is not risen: no—
But lies and moulders low—
Who is not risen!

Ye men of Galilee!
Why stand ye looking up to heaven, where Him ye ne'er
   may see,
Neither ascending hence, nor returning hither again?
Ye ignorant and idle fishermen!
Hence to your huts and boats, and inland native shore,
And catch not men, but fish;
Whate'er things ye might wish,
Him neither here nor there ye e'er shall meet with more.
Ye poor deluded youths, go home,
Mend the old nets ye left to roam,
Tie the split oar, patch the torn sail:
It was indeed an idle tale,—
He was not risen!

And, oh! good men of ages yet to be,
Who shall believe *because* ye did not see—
    Oh, be ye warned, be wise!
    No more with pleading eyes,
    And sobs of strong desire,
    Unto the empty, vacant void aspire,
Seeking another and impossible birth
That is not of your own, and only mother earth.
But if there is no other life for you,
Sit down and be content, since this must even do:
    He is not risen!

    One look, and then depart,
    Ye humble and ye holy men of heart;
And ye! ye Ministers and Stewards of a Word
Which ye would preach, because another heard—
    Ye worshippers of that ye do not know,
    Take these things hence and go—
    He is not risen!

    Here on our Easter Day
We rise, we come, and lo! we find Him not,
Gardener, nor other, on the sacred spot:
Where they have laid Him there is none to say;
No sound, nor in, nor out—no word
Of where to seek the dead, or meet the living Lord.
There is no glistening of an angel's wings,
There is no voice of heavenly clear behest:
Let us go hence, and think upon these things
    In silence, which is best.
    Is He not risen? No—
    But lies and moulders low?
    Christ is not risen!

II

So in the sinful streets, abstracted and alone,
I with my secret self held communing of mine own.
So in the southern city spake the tongue
Of one that somewhat over-wildly sung,
But in a later hour I sat and heard
Another voice that spake—another graver word.
Weep not, it bade, whatever hath been said,
Though He be dead, He is not dead.
   In the true creed
   He is yet risen indeed ;
     Christ is yet risen.

   Weep not beside His tomb,
   Ye women unto whom
He was the great comfort and yet greater grief;
Nor ye, ye faithful few that wont with Him to roam,
Seek sadly what for Him ye left, go hopeless to your
  home ;
Nor ye despair, ye sharers yet to be of their belief;
   Though He be dead, He is not dead,
   Nor gone, though fled,
   Not lost though vanishèd.
   Though He return not, though
   He lies and moulders low ;
   In the true creed
   He is yet risen indeed ;
     Christ is yet risen !

Sit if ye will, sit down upon the ground,
Yet not to weep and wail, but calmly look around.
   Whate'er befell
   Earth is not hell ;

Now, too, as when it first began,
Life is yet life, and man is man.
For all that breathe beneath the heavens' high cope
Joy with grief mixes, with despondence hope.
Hope conquers cowardice, joy grief;
Or, at least, faith unbelief.

      Though dead, not dead;
      Not gone, though fled;
      Not lost, though vanishèd.
      In the great Gospel and true Creed,
      He is yet risen indeed;
           Christ is yet risen.

CLAUDE TO EUSTACE

Luther, they say, was unwise; like a half-taught German
    he could not
See that old follies were passing most tranquilly out of
    remembrance;
Leo the Tenth was employing all efforts to clear out
    abuses;
Jupiter, Juno, and Venus, Fine Arts, and Fine Letters,
    the Poets,
Scholars, and Sculptors, and Painters, were quietly
    clearing away the
Martyrs, and Virgins, and Saints, or at any rate, Thomas
    Aquinas:
He must forsooth make a fuss, and distend his huge
    Wittenberg lungs, and
Bring back Theology once yet again in a flood upon
    Europe:

Lo you, for forty days from the windows of heaven it
    fell; the
Waters prevail on the earth yet more for a hundred and
    fifty;
Are they abating at last? the doves that are sent to ex-
    plore are
Wearily fain to return, at the best with a leaflet of
    promise,—
Fain to return, as they went, to the wandering, wave-
    tost vessel,—
Fain to re-enter the roof which covers the clean and the
    unclean,—
Luther, they say, was unwise; he didn't see how things
    were going;
Luther was foolish,—but, O great God! what call you
    Ignatius?

Epilogue

So go forth to the world, to the good report and the evil!
Go, little book! thy tale, is it not evil and good?
Go, and if strangers revile, pass quietly by without
    answer;
Go, and if curious friends ask of thy rearing and age,
Say, "I am flitting about many years from brain unto
    brain of
Feeble and restless youths born to inglorious days:
But," so finish the word, "I was writ in a Roman chamber,
When from Janiculan heights thundered the cannon of
    France."

COME, POET, COME!

Come, Poet, come!
To give an utterance to the dumb,
And make vain babblers silent, come;
A thousand dupes point here and there,
Bewildered by the show and glare;
And wise men half have learned to doubt
Whether we are not best without.
Come, Poet: both but wait to see
Their error proved to them in thee.

Come, Poet, come!
In vain I seem to call.   And yet
Think not the living times forget.
Ages and heroes fought and fell
That Homer in the end might tell;
O'er grovelling generations past
Upstood the Doric fane at last;
And countless hearts on countless years
Had wasted thoughts, and hopes and fears,
Rude laughter and unmeaning tears,
Ere England Shakespeare saw, or Rome
The pure perfection of her dome.
Others, I doubt not, if not we,
The issue of our toils shall see;
Young children gather as their own
The harvest that the dead had sown,
The dead forgotten and unknown.

QUÂ CURSUM VENTUS

As ships becalmed at eve, that lay
  With canvas drooping, side by side,
Two towers of sail at dawn of day
  Are scarce long leagues apart descried;

When fell the night up sprung the breeze,
  And all the darkling hours they plied,
Nor dreamt but each the self-same seas
  By each was cleaving side by side.

E'en so—but why the tale reveal
  Of those, whom year by year unchanged,
Brief absence joined anew to feel
  Astounded, soul from soul estranged?

At dead of night their sails were filled,
  And onward each rejoicing steered—
Ah, neither blame, for neither willed,
  Or wist, what first with dawn appeared!

To veer, how vain! On onward strain,
  Brave barks, in light, in darkness too,
Through winds and tides one compass guides
  To that, and your own selves, be true.

But O blithe breeze! and O great seas,
  Though ne'er, that earliest parting past,
On your wide plain they join again,
  Together lead them home at last.

One port, methought, alike they sought,
  One purpose hold where'er they fare—
O bounding breeze, O rushing seas!
  At last, at last, unite them there!

SOME FUTURE DAY

Some future day when what is now is not,
When all old faults and follies are forgot,
And thoughts of difference passed like dreams away,
We'll meet again upon some future day.

When all that hindered, all that vexed our love,
As tall rank weeds will climb the blade above,
When all but it has yielded to decay,
We'll meet again upon some future day.

When we have proved, each on his course alone,
The wider world, and learnt what's now unknown,
Have made life clear, and worked out each a way,
We'll meet again,—we shall have much to say.

With happier mood, and feelings born anew,
Our boyhood's bygone fancies we'll review,
Talk o'er old talks, play as we used to play,
And meet again on many a future day.

Some day, which oft our hearts shall yearn to see,
In some far year, though distant yet to be,
Shall we indeed,—ye winds and waters, say !—
Meet yet again upon some future day?

WHERE LIES THE LAND?

Where lies the land to which the ship would go?
Far, far ahead is all her seamen know.
And where the land she travels from ?   Away,
Far, far behind, is all that they can say.

On sunny noons upon the deck's smooth face ;
Linked arm in arm, how pleasant here to pace ;
Or, o'er the stern reclining, watch below
The foaming wake far widening as we go.

On stormy nights when wild north-westers rave,
How proud a thing to fight with wind and wave !
The dripping sailor on the reeling mast
Exults to bear, and scorns to wish it past.

Where lies the land to which the ship would go ?
Far, far ahead, is all her seamen know.
And where the land she travels from ?   Away,
Far, far behind, is all that they can say.

SAY NOT THE STRUGGLE NOUGHT
AVAILETH

Say not the struggle nought availeth,
   The labour and the wounds are vain,
The enemy faints not, nor faileth,
   And as things have been they remain.

If hopes were dupes, fears may be liars ;
   It may be, in yon smoke concealed,
Your comrades chase e'en now the fliers,
   And, but for you, possess the field.

For while the tired waves, vainly breaking,
   Seem here no painful inch to gain,
Far back, through creeks and inlets making,
   Comes silent, flooding in, the main.

And not by eastern windows only,
　　When daylight comes, comes in the light,
In front, the sun climbs slow, how slowly,
　　But westward, look, the land is bright.

THE HIDDEN LOVE

O let me love my love unto myself alone,
And know my knowledge to the world unknown;
No witness to my vision call,
Beholding, unbeheld of all;
And worship Thee, with Thee withdrawn apart,
Whoe'er, whate'er Thou art,
Within the closest veil of mine own inmost heart.

What is it then to me
If others are inquisitive to see?
Why should I quit my place to go and ask
If other men are working at their task?
Leave my own buried roots to go
And see that brother plants shall grow;
And turn away from Thee, O Thou most Holy Light,
To look if other orbs their orbits keep aright
Around their proper sun,
Deserting Thee, and being undone.

O let me love my love unto myself alone,
And know my knowledge to the world unknown;
And worship Thee, O hid one, O much sought,
As but man can or ought,
Within the abstracted'st shrine of my least breathed-
　　on thought.

Better it were, thou sayest, to consent;
Feast while we may, and live ere life be spent;
Close up clear eyes, and call the unstable sure,
The unlovely lovely, and the filthy pure;
In self-belyings, self-deceivings roll,
And lose in Action, Passion, Talk, the soul.

Nay, better far to mark off thus much air,
And call it Heaven : place bliss and glory there;
Fix perfect homes in the unsubstantial sky,
And say, what is not, will be by-and-by.

J. W. BURGON. 1813–1888

PETRA

It seems no work of man's creative hand,
By labour wrought as wavering fancy plann'd,
But from the rock as if by magic grown,
Eternal, silent, beautiful, alone!
Not virgin-white like that old Doric shrine
Where erst Athena held her rites divine;
Not saintly-grey, like many a Minster fane,
That crowns the hill, and consecrates the plain;
But rosy-red as if the blush of dawn
That first beheld them were not yet withdrawn.
The hues of youth upon a brow of woe,
Which man deemed old two thousand years ago,
Match me such marvel save in Eastern clime,
A rose-red city half as old as Time.

CHARLES KINGSLEY.   1819–1875

THE SANDS OF DEE

"O Mary, go and call the cattle home,
  And call the cattle home,
  And call the cattle home,
  Across the sands of Dee."
The Western wind was wild and dank wi' foam,
  And all alone went she.

The creeping tide crept up along the sand,
  And o'er and o'er the sand,
  And round and round the sand,
  As far as eye could see.
The blinding mist came down, and hid the land—
  And never home came she.

"Oh! is it weed, or fish, or floating hair—
  A tress of golden hair,
  A drownèd maiden's hair,
  Above the nets at sea?
Was never salmon yet that shone so fair
  Among the stakes on Dee."

They rowed her in across the rolling foam,
  The cruel, crawling foam,
  The cruel, hungry foam,
  To her grave beside the sea:
But still the boatmen hear her call the cattle home
  Across the sands of Dee

FROM "HYPATIA"

That last drear mood
Of envious sloth, and proud decrepitude;
No faith, no art, no king, no priest, no God;
While round the freezing founts of life in snarling
    ring
Crouched on the bareworn sod,
Babbling about the unreturning spring,
And whining for dead gods, who cannot save,
The toothless systems shiver to their grave.

A FAREWELL

My fairest child, I have no song to give you;
    No lark could pipe to skies so dull and grey:
Yet, ere we part, one lesson I can leave you,
    For every day.

Be good, sweet maid, and let who will be clever;
    Do noble things, not dream them, all day long:
And so make Life, Death, and that vast For-Ever
    One grand sweet song.

JOHN RUSKIN. 1819–1900

THE MADONNA DELL' ACQUA

Around her shrine no earthly blossoms blow,
No footsteps fret the pathway to and fro,
No sign nor record of departed prayer,
Print of the stone, nor echo of the air,
Worn by the lip, nor wearied by the knee—
Only a deeper silence of the sea:
For there, in passing, pause the breezes bleak,
And the foam fades and all the waves are weak:
The pulse-like oars in softer fall succeed,
The black prow falters through the wild sea-weed,
Where twilight-borne the minute thunders reach
Of deep-mouthed surf that bays by Lido's beach.

MENELLA SMEDLEY. 1820-1877

BISHOP PATTESON

An Angel came and cried to him by night :
    "God needs a Martyr from your little band ;
    Name me the purest Soul, which, closely scanned,
Still overflows with sweetness and with light
    That find no limit till they reach the Land
Whence they first sprang !" Weeping for what must be,
    He named them all, with love adorning each ;

And still that Angel smiled upon his speech,
And, smiling still, went upward silently,
Not marking any name. Amazed he knelt,
    Pondering the silent choice. But when the stroke
    Fell, not an Angel, but the Master, spoke,
With voice so strong that nothing else was felt :
    "Thou art the man ! Belovèd, come to Me !"

W. E. AYTOUN.   1813–1865

JAMES IV. AT FLODDEN

No one failed him!   He is keeping
   Royal state and semblance still;
Knight and noble lie around him,
   Cold on Flodden's fatal hill.
Of the brave and gallant-hearted,
   Whom you sent with prayers away,
Not a single man departed
   From his Monarch yesterday.
Had you seen them, O my masters!
   When the night began to fall,
And the English spearmen gathered
   Round a grim and ghastly wall!
As the wolves in winter circle
   Round the leaguer on the heath,
So the greedy foe glared upward,
   Panting still for blood and death.
But a rampart rose before them,
   Which the boldest dared not scale;
Every stone a Scottish body,
   Every step a corpse in mail!
And behind it lay our Monarch,
   Clenching still his shivered sword;
By his side Montrose and Athole,
   At his feet a Southron lord.
All so thick they lay together,
   When the stars lit up the sky,
That I knew not who were stricken,
   Or who yet remained to die.

Few there were when Surrey halted,
　　And his wearied host withdrew;
None but dying men around me,
　　When the English trumpet blew.
Then I stooped, and took the banner,
　　As you see it, from his breast,
And I closed our hero's eyelids,
　　And I left him to his rest.

LOCKER-LAMPSON. 1821–1895

TO MY GRANDMOTHER

This Relative of mine,
Was she seventy-and-nine
      When she died?
By the canvas may be seen
How she look'd at seventeen,
      As a Bride.

Beneath a summer tree
Her maiden reverie
      Has a charm;
Her ringlets are in taste;
What an arm! and what a waist
      For an arm!

With her bridal wreath, bouquet,
Lace farthingale, and gay
      Falbala,—
If Romney's touch be true,
What a lucky dog were you,
      Grandpapa!

Her lips are sweet as love;
They are parting!   Do they move?
      Are they dumb?
Her eyes are blue, and beam
Beseechingly, and seem
      To say, "Come!"

What funny fancy slips
From atween these cherry lips?
      Whisper me,
Fair sorceress in paint,
What canon says I mayn't
      Marry thee?

That good-for-nothing Time
Has a confidence sublime !
    When I first
Saw this Lady, in my youth,
Her winters had, forsooth,
    Done their worst.

Her locks, as white as snow,
Once shamed the swarthy crow ;
    By-and-by
That fowl's avenging sprite
Set his cruel foot for spite
    Near her eye.

Her rounded form was lean,
And her silk was bombazine ;
    Well I wot
With her needles would she sit,
And for hours would she knit,—
    Would she not ?

Ah, perishable clay !
Her charms had dropt away
    One by one :
But if she heaved a sigh
With a burthen, it was, " Thy
    Will be done."

In travail, as in tears,
With the fardel of her years
    Overprest,
In mercy she was borne
Where the weary and the worn
    Are at rest.

O if you now are there
And sweet as once you were,
    Grandmamma,
This nether world agrees,
You'll all the better please
    Grandpapa.

THE ROSE AND THE RING

She smiles, but her heart is in sable,
    Ay, sad as her Christmas is chill:
She reads, and her book is the fable
    He penn'd for her while she was ill.
It is nine years ago since he wrought it,
    Where reedy old Tiber is king;
And chapter by chapter he brought it,
    And read her the Rose and the Ring.

And when it was printed, and gaining
    Renown with all lovers of glee,
He sent her this copy containing
    His comical little *croquis ;*
A sketch of a rather droll couple—
    She's pretty, he's quite t'other thing!
He begs (with a spine vastly supple)
    She will study the Rose and the Ring.

It pleased the kind Wizard to send her
    The last and the best of his toys;
He aye had a sentiment tender
    For innocent maidens and boys;

S

And though he was great as a scorner
  The guileless were safe from his sting;
Oh, how sad is past mirth to the mourner!—
  A tear on the Rose and the Ring!

She reads; I may vainly endeavour
  Her mirth-chequer'd grief to pursue,
For she knows she has lost, and for ever,
  The heart that was bared to so few;
But here, on the shrine of his glory,
  One poor little blossom I fling;
And you see there's a nice little story
  Attach'd to the Rose and the Ring.

MATTHEW ARNOLD. 1822–1888

THE TOMB IN THE CHURCH OF BROU

So rest, for ever, O princely Pair!
In your high church, 'mid the still mountain-air,
Where horn and hound and vassals never come,
Only the blessed Saints are smiling dumb,
From the rich painted windows of the nave,
On aisle and transept, and your marble grave;
Where thou, young Prince! shalt never more arise
From the fringed mattress where thy Duchess lies,
On autumn mornings, when the bugle sounds
To hunt the boar in the crisp woods till eve;
And thou, O Princess! shalt no more receive,
Thou and thy ladies, in the hall of state,
The jaded hunters with their bloody freight,
Coming benighted to the castle-gate.
So sleep, for ever sleep, O marble Pair!
Or, if ye wake, let it be then, when fair
On the carved western front a flood of light
Streams from the setting sun, and colours bright
Prophets, transfigured Saints, and Martyrs brave,
In the vast western window of the nave;
And on the pavement round the Tomb there glints
A chequer-work of glowing sapphire-tints,
And amethyst, and ruby—then unclose
Your eyelids on the stone where ye repose,
And from your broider'd pillows lift your heads,
And rise upon your cold white marble beds;
And, looking down on the warm rosy tints,
Which chequer, at your feet, the illumined flints,
Say: *What is this? we are in bliss—forgiven—*
Behold the pavement of the Courts of Heaven!

Or let it be on Autumn nights, when rain
Doth rustlingly above your heads complain
On the smooth leaden roof, and on the walls
Shedding her pensive light at intervals,
The moon through the clerestory windows shines,
And the wind washes through the mountain-pines,
Then, gazing up 'mid the dim pillars high,
The foliaged marble forest where ye lie,
Hush, ye will say, it is eternity !
This is the glimmering verge of Heaven, and these
The columns of the heavenly palaces !
And, in the sweeping of the wind, your ear
The passage of the Angels' wings will hear,
And on the lichen-crusted leads above
The rustle of the eternal rain of love.

STANZAS IN MEMORY OF THE AUTHOR
OF "OBERMANN"

(*November* 1849)

In front the awful Alpine track
    Crawls up its rocky stair ;
The Autumn storm-winds drive the wrack
    Close o'er it, in the air.

Behind are the abandon'd baths
    Mute in their meadows lone ;
The leaves are in the valley-paths,
    The mists are on the Rhone—

The white mists rolling like a sea !
  I hear the torrents roar.
—Yes, Obermann, all speaks of thee ;
  I feel thee near once more !

I turn thy leaves ! I feel their breath
  Once more upon me roll ;
That air of languor, cold and death,
  Which brooded o'er thy soul.

Fly hence, poor wretch, whoe'er thou art,
  Condemn'd to cast about,
All shipwreck in thy own weak heart,
  For comfort from without !

A fever in these pages burns
  Beneath the calm they feign ;
A wounded human spirit turns,
  Here, on its bed of pain.

Yes, though the virgin mountain air
  Fresh through these pages blows ;
Though to these leaves the glaciers spare
  The soul of their white snows ;

Though here a mountain-murmur swells
  Of many a dark-bough'd pine ;
Though, as you read, you hear the bells
  Of the high-pasturing kine.

Yet, through the hum of torrent lone,
  And brooding mountain-bee,
There sobs I know not what ground-tone
  Of human agony.

Is it for this, because the sound
  Is fraught too deep with pain,
That Obermann ! the world around
  So little loves thy strain ?

Some secrets may the poet tell,
  For the world loves new ways ;
To tell too deep ones is not well—
  It knows not what he says.

Yet, of the spirits who have reign'd
  In this our troubled day,
I know but two, who have attain'd,
  Save thee, to see their way.

By England's lakes, in grey old age,
  His quiet home one keeps ;
And one, the strong much-toiling sage,
  In German Weimar sleeps.

But Wordsworth's eyes avert their ken
  From half of human fate ;
And Goethe's course few sons of men
  May think to emulate.

For he pursued a lonely road,
  His eyes on Nature's plan ;
Neither made man too much a god,
  Nor God too much a man.

Strong was he, with a spirit free
  From mists, and sane, and clear ;
Clearer, how much ! than ours—yet we
  Have a worse course to steer.

For though his manhood bore the blast
    Of Europe's stormiest time,
Yet in a tranquil world was pass'd
    His tenderer youthful prime.

But we, brought forth and rear'd in hours
    Of change, alarm, surprise—
What shelter to grow ripe is ours?
    What leisure to grow wise?

Like children bathing on the shore,
    Buried a wave beneath,
The second wave succeeds, before
    We have had time to breathe.

Too fast we live, too much are tried,
    Too harass'd, to attain
Wordsworth's sweet calm, or Goethe's wide
    And luminous view to gain.

And then we turn, thou sadder sage,
    To thee! we feel thy spell!
—The hopeless tangle of our age,
    Thou too hast scann'd it well!

Immovable thou sittest, still
    As death, composed to bear!
Thy head is clear, thy feeling chill,
    And icy thy despair.

Yes, as the son of Thetis said,
    One hears thee saying now:
Greater by far than thou are dead:
    Strive not! Die also thou!

Ah! two desires toss about,
　　The poet's feverish blood.
One drives him to the world without,
　　And one to solitude.

The glow, he cries, *the thrill of life*,
　　Where, where do these abound?—
Not in the world, not in the strife
　　Of men shall they be found.

He who hath watch'd, not shared, the strife,
　　Knows how the day hath gone.
He only lives with the world's life,
　　Who hath renounced his own.

To thee we come, then! Clouds are roll'd
　　Where thou, O Seer! are set;
Thy realm of thought is drear and cold—
　　The world is colder yet!

And thou hast pleasures, too, to share
　　With those who come to thee—
Balms floating on thy mountain-air,
　　And healing sights to see.

How often, where the slopes are green
　　On Jaman, hast thou sate
By some high châlet-door and seen
　　The summer-day grow late;

And darkness steal o'er the wet grass
　　With the pale crocus starr'd,
And reach that glimmering sheet of glass
　　Beneath the piny sward.

Lake Leman's waters, far below!
   And watch'd the rosy light
Fade from the distant peaks of snow
   And on the air of night

Heard accents of the eternal tongue
   Through the pine branches play—
Listen'd, and felt thyself grow young
   Listen'd and wept—Away!

Away the dreams that but deceive!
   And thou, sad guide, adieu!
I go, fate drives me; but I leave
   Half of my life with you.

We, in some unknown Power's employ,
   Move on a rigorous line;
Can neither, when we will, enjoy,
   Nor, when we will, resign.

I in the world must live; but thou,
   Thou melancholy shade!
Wilt not, if thou canst see me now,
   Condemn me, nor upbraid.

For thou art gone away from earth,
   And place with those dost claim,
The children of the Second Birth,
   Whom the world could not tame;

And with that small, transfigured band,
   Whom many a different way
Conducted to their common land,
   Thou learn'st to think as they.

Christian and pagan, king and slave,
  Soldier and anchorite,
Distinctions we esteem so grave,
  Are nothing in their sight.

They do not ask, who pined unseen,
  Who was on action hurl'd,
Whose one bond is, that all have been
  Unspotted by the world.

There without anger thou wilt see
  Him who obeys thy spell
No more, so he but rest, like thee
  Unsoil'd!—and so, farewell.

Farewell!—whether thou now liest near
  That much-loved inland sea,
The ripples of whose blue waves cheer
  Vevey and Meillerie;

And in that gracious region bland,
  Where with clear-rustling wave
The scented pines of Switzerland
  Stand dark round thy green grave.

Between the dusty vineyard-walls
  Issuing on that green place
The early peasant still recalls
  The pensive stranger's face,

And stoops to clear thy moss-grown date
  Ere he plods on again;—
Or whether, by maligner fate,
  Among the swarms of men,

Where between granite terraces
  The blue Seine rolls her wave,
The Capital of Pleasure sees
  Thy hardly-heard-of grave ;—

Farewell !   Under the sky we part,
  In this stern Alpine dell.
O unstrung will !   O broken heart !
  A last, a last farewell !

REQUIESCAT

Strew on her roses, roses,
  And never a spray of yew !
In quiet she reposes ;
  Ah ! would that I did too.

Her mirth the world required ;
  She bathed it in smiles of glee.
But her heart was tired, tired,
  And now they let her be.

Her life was turning, turning,
  In mazes of heat and sound ;
But for peace her soul was yearning,
  And now peace laps her round.

Her cabin'd, ample spirit,
  It flutter'd and fail'd for breath ;
To-night it doth inherit
  The vasty hall of death.

STANZAS FROM THE GRANDE CHARTREUSE

Through Alpine meadows soft-suffused
   With rain, where thick the crocus blows,
Past the dark forges long disused,
   The mule-track from Saint-Laurent goes;
The bridge is cross'd, and slow we ride,
Through forest, up the mountain-side.

The Autumnal Evening darkens round,
   The wind is up, and drives the rain;
While hark! far down, with strangled sound
   Doth the Dead Guier's stream complain,
Where that wet smoke, among the woods,
Over his boiling cauldron broods.

Swift rush the spectral vapours white
   Past limestone scars with ragged pines,
Showing—then blotting from our sight!—
   Halt—through the cloud-drift something shines!
High in the valley, wet and drear,
The huts of Courrerie appear.

Strike leftward! cries our guide; and higher
   Mounts up the stony forest-way—
At last the encircling trees retire;
   Look! through the showery twilight grey
What pointed roofs are these advance?—
A palace of the Kings of France?

Approach, for what we seek is here!
   Alight, and sparely sup, and wait
For rest in this outbuilding near,
   Then cross the sward and reach that gate.
Knock; pass the wicket! Thou art come
To the Carthusians' world-famed home.

The silent courts, where night and day
　Into their stone-carved basins cold
The splashing icy fountains play—
　The humid corridors behold!
Where, ghost-like in the deepening night,
Cowl'd forms brush by in gleaming white.

The chapel where no organ's peal,
　Invests the stern and naked prayer—
With penitential cries they kneel
　And wrestle; rising then, with bare
And white uplifted faces stand,
Passing the host from hand to hand;

Each takes, and then his visage wan
　Is buried in his cowl once more.
The cells!—the suffering Son of Man
　Upon the wall—the knee-worn floor—
And where they sleep, that wooden bed,
Which shall their coffin be, when dead!

The library, where tract and tome
　Not to feed priestly pride are there,
To hymn the conquering march of Rome,
　Nor yet to amuse, as ours are!
They paint of souls the inner strife,
Their drops of blood, their death in life.

The garden, overgrown—yet mild,
　See, fragrant herbs are flowering there!
Strong children of the Alpine wild,
　Whose culture is the brethren's care;
Of human tasks their only one,
And cheerful works beneath the sun.

Those halls, too, destined to contain
    Each its own pilgrim-host of old,
From England, Germany, or Spain—
    All are before me!   I behold
The House, the Brotherhood austere!
—And what am I, that I am here?

For rigorous teachers seized my youth,
    And purged its faith, and trimm'd its fire,
Show'd me the high, white Star of Truth,
    There bade me gaze, and there aspire.
Even now their whispers pierce the gloom :
What dost thou in this living tomb ?

Forgive me, masters of the mind !
    At whose behest I long ago
So much unlearnt, so much resign'd—
    I come not here to be your foe !
I seek these anchorites, not in ruth,
To curse and to deny your truth ;

Not as their friend, or child, I speak !
    But as, on some far northern strand,
Thinking of his own gods, a Greek
    In pity and mournful awe might stand
Before some fallen Runic stone—
For both were faiths, and both are gone.

Wandering between two worlds, one dead
    The other powerless to be born,
With nowhere yet to rest my head,
    Like these, on earth I wait forlorn.
Their faith, my tears, the world deride—
I come to shed them at their side.

Oh, hide me in your gloom profound,
　　Ye solemn seats of holy pain!
Take me, cowl'd forms, and fence me round,
　　Till I possess my soul again;
Till free my thoughts before me roll,
Not chafed by hourly, false control!

For the world cries your faith is now
　　But a dead time's exploded dream;
My melancholy, sciolists say,
　　Is a pass'd mode, an outworn theme—
As if the world had ever had
A faith, or sciolists been sad!

Ah, if it *be* pass'd, take away,
　　At least, the restlessness, the pain;
Be man henceforth, no more a prey
　　To these out-dated stings again!
The nobleness of grief is gone—
Ah, leave us not the fret alone!

But—if you cannot give us ease—
　　Last of the race of them who grieve,
Here leave us to die out with these,
　　Last of the people who believe!
Silent, while years engrave the brow;
Silent—the best are silent now.

Achilles ponders in his tent,
　　The kings of modern thought are dumb;
Silent they are, though not content,
　　And wait to see the future come.
They have the grief men had of yore,
But they contend and cry no more.

The fathers water'd with their tears
   This sea of time whereon we sail,
Their voices were in all men's ears
   Who passed within their puissant hail.
Still the same ocean round us raves,
But we stand mute, and watch the waves.

For what avail'd it all the noise,
   And outcry of the former men?—
Say, have their sons achieved more joys,
   Say, is life lighter now than then?
The sufferers died, they left their pain—
The pangs which tortured them remain.

What helps it now that Byron bore,
   With haughty scorn which mock'd the smart,
Through Europe to the Ætolian shore,
   The pageant of his bleeding heart?
That thousands counted every groan,
And Europe made his woe her own?

What boots it, Shelley! that the breeze
   Carried thy lovely wail away,
Musical through Italian trees
   Which fringe thy soft blue Spezzian bay?
Inheritors of thy distress
Have restless hearts one throb the less?

Or are we easier to have read,
   O Obermann! the sad stern page,
Which tells us how thou hidd'st thy head
   From the fierce tempest of thine age
In the lone brakes of Fontainebleau,
Or châlets near the Alpine snow?

Ye slumber in your silent grave !—
   The world, which for an idle day
Grace to your mood of sadness gave,
   Long since hath flung her weeds away.
The eternal trifler breaks your spell ;
But we—we learnt your lore too well !

Years hence, perhaps, may dawn an age
   More fortunate, alas ! than we,
Which without hardness will be sage,
   And gay without frivolity.
Sons of the world, oh, speed those years ;
But, while we wait, allow our tears !

Allow them ! We admire with awe
   The exulting thunder of your race ;
You give the universe your law,
   You triumph over time and space !
Your pride of life, your tireless powers,
We laud them, but they are not ours.

We are like children rear'd in shade
   Beneath some old-world abbey wall,
Forgotten in a forest glade,
   And secret from the eyes of all.
Deep, deep the greenwood round them waves,
Their abbey, and its close of graves !

But, where the road runs near the stream,
   Oft through the trees they catch a glance
Of passing troops in the sun's beam—
   Pennon and plume, and flashing lance !
Forth to the world those soldiers fare,
To life, to cities, and to war !

T

And through the wood, another way,
   Faint bugle-notes from far are borne,
Where hunters gather, staghounds bay,
   Round some fair forest-lodge at morn.
Gay dames are there, in sylvan green ;
Laughter and cries—those notes between !

The banners flashing through the trees
   Make their blood dance and chain their eyes ;
That bugle-music on the breeze
   Arrests them with a charm'd surprise.
Banner by turns and bugle woo :
Ye shy recluses, follow too !

O children what do ye reply !—
   " Action and pleasure, will ye roam
Through these secluded dells to cry
   And call us ?—but too late ye come !
Too late for us your call ye blow,
Whose bent was taken long ago.

" Long since we pace this shadow'd nave
   We watch those yellow tapers shine,
Emblems of hope over the grave,
   In the high altar's depth divine :
The organ carries to our ear
   Its accents of another sphere.

" Fenced early in this cloistral round
   Of reverie, of shade, of prayer,
How should we grow in other ground ?
   How can we flower in foreign air ?
—Pass, banners, pass, and bugles, cease,
And leave our desert to its peace ! "

TRISTRAM AND ISEULT

I

TRISTRAM.

Is she not come? The messenger was sure.
Prop me upon the pillows once again—
Raise me, my page! this cannot long endure.
—Christ, what a night! how the sleet whips the pane!
What lights will those out to the northward be?

THE PAGE.

The lanterns of the fishing-boats at sea.

TRISTRAM.

Soft—who is that stands by the dying fire?

THE PAGE.

Iseult.

TRISTRAM

Ah! not the Iseult I desire.

.   .   .   .   .

What knight is this so weak and pale,
Though the locks are yet brown on his noble head.
Propt on pillows in his bed,
Gazing seaward for the light
Of some ship that fights the gale
On this wild December night?
Over the sick man's feet is spread
A dark green forest-dress;
A gold harp leans against the bed,
Ruddy in the fire's light.

I know him by his harp of gold,
Famous in Arthur's court of old.
I know him by his forest-dress—
The peerless hunter, harper, knight—
Tristram of Lyoness.

What Lady is this, whose silk attire
Gleams so rich in the light of the fire?
The ringlets on her shoulders lying
In their flitting lustre vying
With the clasp of burnish'd gold,
Which her heavy robe doth hold.
Her looks are sweet, her fingers slight,
As the driven snow are white;
But her cheeks are sunk and pale.
Is it that the bleak sea-gale
Beating from the Atlantic sea
On this coast of Brittany,
Nips too keenly the sweet flower?
Is it that a deep fatigue
Hath come on her, a chilly fear
Passing all her youthful hour
Spinning with her maidens here,
Listlessly through the window bars
Gazing seawards many a league
From her lonely shore-built tower,
While the knights are at the wars?
Or, perhaps, has her young heart
Felt already some deeper smart
Of those that in secret the heart-strings rive,
Leaving her sunk and pale, though fair?
Who is this snowdrop by the sea?—
I know her by her mildness rare,
Her snow-white hands, her golden hair;

I know her by her rich silk dress,
And her fragile loveliness—
The sweetest Christian soul alive,
Iseult of Brittany.

Iseult of Brittany?—but where
Is that other Iseult fair?
That proud, first Iseult, Cornwall's queen?
She, whom Tristram's ship of yore
From Ireland to Cornwall bore,
To Tyntagel, to the side
Of King Marc, to be his bride?
She who, as they voyaged, quaff'd
With Tristram that spiced magic draught,
Which since then for ever rolls
Through their blood, and binds their souls,
Working love, but working teen?—
There were two Iseults who did sway
Each her hour of Tristram's day;
But one possess'd his waning time,
The other his resplendent prime.
Behold her here, the patient flower,
Who possess'd his darker hour!
Iseult of the snow-white hand
Watches pale by Tristram's bed.
She is here who had his gloom,
Where art thou who hadst his bloom?
One such kiss as those of yore
Might thy dying knight restore!
Does the love-draught work no more?
Art thou cold, or false, or dead,
Iseult of Ireland?

Loud howls the wind, sharp patters the rain,
And the knight sinks back on his pillows again.
He is weak with fever and pain,

And his spirit is not clear;
Hark! he mutters in his sleep,
As he wanders far from here,
Changes place and time of year,
And his closèd eye doth sweep
O'er some fair unwintry sea,
Not this fierce Atlantic deep,
While he mutters brokenly:—

TRISTRAM.

The calm sea shines, loose hang the vessel's sails,
Before us are the sweet green fields of Wales,
And overhead the cloudless sky of May.—
" *Ah, would I were in those green fields at play,*
Not pent on ship-board this delicious day!
Tristram, I pray thee, of thy courtesy,
Reach me my golden cup that stands by thee,
But pledge me in it first for courtesy."—
Ha! dost thou start? are thy lips blanch'd like mine?
Child! 'tis no true draught this, 'tis poison'd wine!
Iseult! . . . .

　　　.　　　.　　　.　　　.　　　.

Ah, sweet angels, let him dream!
Keep his eyelids! let him seem
Not this fever-wasted wight
Thinn'd and paled before his time,
But the brilliant youthful knight
In the glory of his prime,
Sitting in the gilded barge,
At thy side, thou lovely charge,
Bending gaily o'er thy hand,
Iseult of Ireland!
And she too, that princess fair,
If her bloom be now less rare,

Let her have her youth again—
Let her be as she was then!
Let her have her proud dark eyes,
And her petulant quick replies—
Let her sweep her dazzling hand
With its gesture of command,
And shake back her raven hair
With the old imperious air!
As of old, so let her be,
That first Iseult, princess bright,
Chatting with her youthful knight
As he steers her o'er the sea,
Quitting at her father's will
The green isle where she was bred,
And her bower in Ireland,
For the surge-beat Cornish strand:
Where the prince whom she must wed
Dwells on loud Tyntagel's hill,
High above the sounding sea.
And that phial rare her mother
Gave her, that her future lord,
Gave her, that King Marc and she
Might drink it on their marriage-day,
And for ever love each other—
Let her, as she sits on board,
Ah, sweet saints, unwittingly!
See it shine, and take it up,
And to Tristram laughing say:
"Sir Tristram, of thy courtesy,
Pledge me in my golden cup!"
Let them drink it—let their hands
Tremble, and their cheeks be flame,
As they feel the fatal bands
Of a love they dare not name,

With a wild delicious pain,
Twine about their hearts again!
Let the early summer be
Once more round them, and the sea
Blue, and o'er its mirror kind
Let the breath of the May-wind,
Wandering through their drooping sails,
Die on the green fields of Wales!
Let a dream like this restore
What his eye must see no more!

TRISTRAM.

Chill blows the wind, the pleasaunce-walks are drear—
Madcap, what jest was this, to meet me here?
Were feet like those made for so wild a way?
The southern winter-parlour, by my fay,
Had been the likeliest trysting-place to-day!—
" *Tristram!—nay, nay—thou must not take my hand!—*
Tristram!—sweet love!—we are betrayed—out-plann'd.
Fly—save thyself—save me!—I dare not stay."—
One last kiss first!—"'*Tis vain—to horse—away!*"

.   .   .   .   .   .

Ah! sweet saints, his dream doth move
Faster surely than it should,
From the fever in his blood!
All the spring-time of his love
Is already gone and past,
And instead thereof is seen
Its winter, which endureth still—
Tyntagel on its surge-beat hill,
The pleasaunce-walks, the weeping queen,
The flying leaves, the straining blast,
And that long, wild kiss—their last.
And this rough December night,
And his burning fever-pain,

Mingle with his hurrying dream,
Till they rule it, till he seem
The press'd fugitive again,
The love-desperate banish'd knight
With a fire in his brain
Flying o'er the stormy main.
—Whither does he wander now?
Haply in his dreams the wind
Wafts him here, and lets him find
The lovely orphan child again
In her castle by the coast ;
The youngest, fairest chatelaine,
That this realm of France can boast,
Our snowdrop by the Atlantic sea,
Iseult of Brittany.
And—for through the haggard air,
The stain'd arms, the matted hair
Of that stranger-knight ill-starr'd,
There gleam'd something, which recall'd
The Tristram who in better days
Was Launcelot's guest at Joyous Gard—
Welcomed here, and here install'd,
Tended of his fever here.
Haply he seems again to move
His young guardian's heart with love ;
In his exiled loneliness,
In his stately, deep distress,
Without a word, without a tear.
—Ah ! 'tis well he should retrace
His tranquil life in this lone place ;
His gentle bearing at the side
Of his timid youthful bride,
His long rambles by the shore
On winter-evenings, when the roar

Of the near waves came, sadly grand,
Through the dark, up the drown'd sand ;
Or his endless reveries
In the woods, where the gleams play
On the grass under the trees,
Passing the long summer's day
Idle as a mossy stone
In the forest-depths alone,
The chase neglected, and his hound
Couch'd beside him on the ground.
—Ah ! what trouble's on his brow ?
Hither let him wander now ;
Hither, to the quiet hours
Pass'd among these heaths of ours
By the grey Atlantic sea ;
Hours, if not of ecstasy,
From violent anguish surely free !

TRISTRAM.

All red with blood the whirling river flows,
The wide plain rings, the dazed air throbs with blows.
Upon us are the chivalry of Rome !
Their spears are down, their steeds are bathed in foam.
"Up, Tristram, up," men cry, "thou moonstruck knight!
What foul fiend rides thee?   On into the fight!"
—Above the din her voice is in my ears ;
I see her form glide through the crossing spears.—
Iseult ! . . . .

.   .   .   .   .

Ah ! he wanders forth again ;
We cannot keep him ; now, as then,
There's a secret in his breast
Which will never let him rest.

These musing fits in the green wood,
They cloud the brain, they dull the blood!
—His sword is sharp, his horse is good;
Beyond the mountains will he see
The famous towns of Italy,
And label with the blessed sign
The heathen Saxons on the Rhine.
At Arthur's side he fights once more
With the Roman Emperor.
There's many a gay knight where he goes
Will help him to forget his care;
The march, the leaguer, Heaven's blithe air,
The neighing steeds, the ringing blows—
Sick pining comes not where these are.
—Ah! what boots it, that the jest
Lightens every other brow,
What, that every other breast
Dances as the trumpets blow,
If one's own heart beats not light
On the waves of the toss'd fight,
If oneself cannot get free
From the clog of misery?
Thy lovely youthful wife grows pale
Watching by the salt sea-tide
With her children at her side
For the gleam of thy white sail.
Home, Tristram, to thy halls again!
To our lonely sea complain,
To our forests tell thy pain!

TRISTRAM.

All round the forest sweeps off, black in shade;
But it is moonlight in the open glade.
And in the bottom of the glade shine clear
The forest-chapel and the fountain near.

—I think, I have a fever in my blood;
Come, let me leave the shadow of this wood,
Ride down, and bathe my hot brow in the flood.
—Mild shines the cold spring in the moon's clear
　　light.
God! 'tis *her* face plays in the waters bright.
" Fair love," she says, " canst you forget so soon,
At this soft hour, under this sweet moon?"
Iseult! . . . .

．　　　　．　　　　．　　　　．　　　　．

　　Ah, poor soul! if this be so,
　Only death can balm thy woe.
　The solitudes of the green wood
　Had no medicine for thy mood;
　The rushing battle clear'd thy blood
　As little as did solitude.
　—Ah! his eyelids slowly break
　Their hot seals, and let him wake;
　What new change shall we now see?
　A happier? Worse it cannot be.

TRISTRAM.

Is my page here? Come, turn me to the fire!
Upon the window panes the moon shines bright;
The wind is down—but she'll not come to-night.
Ah no! she is asleep in Cornwall now,
Far hence; her dreams are fair—smooth is her brow.
Of me she recks not, nor my vain desire.
—I have had dreams, I have had dreams, my page,
Would take a score years from a strong man's age;
And with a blood like mine, will leave, I fear,
Scant leisure for a second messenger.

—My princess, art thou there? Sweet, 'tis too late!
To bed, and sleep! my fever is gone by;
To-night my page shall keep me company.
Where do the children sleep? kiss them for me!
Poor child, thou art almost as pale as I;
This comes of nursing long and watching late,
To bed—good night!

    .   .   .   .   .

> She left the gleam-lit fireplace,
> She came to the bedside;
> She took his hands in hers—her tears
> Down on her slender fingers rain'd.
> She raised her eyes upon his face—
> Not with a look of wounded pride,
> A look as if the heart complain'd—
> Her look was like a sad embrace;
> The gaze of one who can divine
> A grief, and sympathise.
> Sweet flower! thy children's eyes
> Are not more innocent than thine.

> But they sleep in shelter'd rest,
> Like helpless birds in the warm nest,
> On the castle's southern side;
> Where feebly comes the mournful roar
> Of buffeting wind and surging tide
> Through many a room and corridor.
> —Full on their window the moon's ray
> Makes their chamber as bright as day;
> It shines upon the blank white walls,
> And on the snowy pillow falls,
> And on two angel-heads doth play
> Turn'd to each other—the eyes closed,
> The lashes on the cheeks reposed.

Round each sweet brow the cap close-set
Hardly lets peep the golden hair;
Through the soft-open'd lips the air
Scarcely moves the coverlet.
One little wandering arm is thrown
At random on the counterpane,
And often the fingers close in haste
As if their baby-owner chased
The butterflies again.
This stir they have, and this alone;
But else they are so still!
—Ah, tired madcaps! you lie still;
But were you at the window now,
To look forth on the fairy sight
Of your illumined haunts by night,
To see the park-glades where you play
Far lovelier than they are by day,
To see the sparkle on the eaves,
And upon every giant-bough
Of those old oaks, whose wet red leaves
Are jewell'd with bright drops of rain—
How would your voices run again!
And far beyond the sparkling trees
Of the castle-park one sees
The bare heaths spreading, clear as day,
Moor behind moor, far, far away,
Into the heart of Brittany.
And here and there, lock'd by the land,
Long inlets of smooth glittering sea,
And many a stretch of watery sand
All shining in the white moon-beams—
But you see fairer in your dreams!

What voices are these on the clear night air?
What lights in the court—what steps on the stair?

II

ISEULT OF IRELAND

TRISTRAM.

Raise the light, my page! that I may see her—
  Thou art come at last then, haughty Queen.
Long I've waited, long I've fought my fever;
  Late thou comest, cruel thou hast been.

ISEULT.

Blame me not, poor sufferer! that I tarried;
  Bound I was, I could not break the band.
Chide not with the past, but feel the present!
  I am here—we meet—I hold thy hand.

TRISTRAM.

Thou art come, indeed—thou hast rejoined me;
  Thou hast dared it—but too late to save.
Fear not now that men should tax thine honour!
  I am dying; build—(thou may'st)—my grave!

ISEULT.

Tristram, ah, for love of Heaven, speak kindly!
  What, I hear these bitter words from thee?
Sick with grief I am, and faint with travel—
  Take my hand—dear Tristram, look on me!

TRISTRAM.

I forgot, thou comest from thy voyage—
  Yes, the spray is on thy cloak and hair.
But thy dark eyes are not dimm'd, proud Iseult!
  And thy beauty never was more fair.

ISEULT.

Ah, harsh flatterer! let alone my beauty!
  I, like thee, have left my youth afar.
Take my hand, and touch these wasted fingers,
  See my cheek and lips, how white they are!

TRISTRAM.

Thou art paler—but thy sweet charm, Iseult!
  Would not fade with the dull years away.
Ah, how fair thou standest in the moonlight!
  I forgive thee, Iseult!—thou wilt stay?

ISEULT.

Fear me not, I will be always with thee;
  I will watch thee, tend thee, soothe thy pain;
Sing thee tales of true, long-parted lovers,
  Join'd at evening of their days again.

TRISTRAM.

No, thou shalt not speak! I should be finding
  Something altered in thy courtly tone.
Sit—sit by me! I will think, we've lived so
  In the green wood, all our lives, alone.

ISEULT.

Alter'd, Tristram? Not in courts, believe me,
  Love like mine is alter'd in the breast.
Courtly life is light and cannot reach it—
  Ah! it lives, because so deep-suppress'd!

What, thou think'st men speak in courtly chambers
  Words by which the wretched are consoled?
What, thou think'st this aching brow was cooler
  Circled, Tristram, by a band of gold?

Royal state with Marc, my deep-wrong'd husband—
  That was bliss to make my sorrows flee !
Silken courtiers whispering honied nothings—
  Those were friends to make me false to thee !

Ah, on which, if both our lots were balanced,
  Was indeed the heaviest burden thrown—
Thee, a pining exile in thy forest,
  Me, a smiling queen upon my throne ?

Vain and strange debate, where both have suffer'd,
  Both have pass'd a youth consumed and sad,
Both have brought their anxious day to evening,
  And have now short space for being glad !

Join'd we are henceforth ; nor will thy people,
  Nor thy younger Iseult take it ill,
That a former rival shares her office,
  When she sees her humbled, pale, and still.

I, a faded watcher by thy pillow,
  I, a statue on thy chapel-floor,
Pour'd in prayer before the Virgin-Mother,
  Rouse no anger, make no rivals more.

She will cry : " Is this the foe I dreaded ?
  This his idol ? this that royal bride ?
Ah, an hour of health would purge his eyesight !
  Stay, pale queen ! for ever by my side."

Hush, no words ! that smile, I see, forgives me.
  I am now thy nurse, I bid thee sleep.
Close thine eyes—this flooding moonlight blinds
    them !—
  Nay, all's well again ! thou must not weep.

U

TRISTRAM.

I am happy! yet, I feel, there's something
  Swells my heart, and takes my breath away—
Through a mist I see thee; near—come nearer!
  Bend—bend down!—I yet have much to say.

ISEULT.

Heaven! his head sinks back upon the pillow—
  Tristram! Tristram! let thy heart not fail!
Call on God and on the holy angels!
  What, love, courage!—Christ! he is so pale.

TRISTRAM.

Hush, 'tis vain, I feel my end approaching!
  This is what my mother said should be,
When the fierce pains took her in the forest,
  The deep draughts of death, in bearing me.

"Son," she said, "thy name shall be of sorrow;
  Tristram art thou call'd for my death's sake."
So she said, and died in the drear forest—
  Grief since then his home with me doth make.

I am dying.—Start not, nor look wildly!
  Me, thy living friend, thou canst not save.
But, since living we were ununited,
  Go not far, O Iseult! from my grave.

Close mine eyes, then seek the princess Iseult;
  Speak her fair, she is of royal blood!
Say, I charged her, that thou stay beside me—
  She will grant it; she is kind and good.

Now to sail the seas of death I leave thee—
One last kiss upon the living shore!

ISEULT.

Tristram!—Tristram!—stay—receive me with thee!
Iseult leaves thee, Tristram! never more.

.   .   .   .   .   .

You see them clear—the moon shines bright.
Slow, slow and softly, where she stood,
She sinks upon the ground; her hood
Had fallen back; her arms outspread
Still hold her lover's hands; her head
Is bow'd, half-buried, on the bed.
O'er the blanch'd sheet her raven hair
Lies in disorder'd streams; and there,
Strung like white stars, the pearls still are;
And the golden bracelets, heavy and rare,
Flash on her white arms still.
The very same which yesternight
Flash'd in the silver sconces' light,
When the feast was gay and the laughter loud
In Tyntagel's palace proud.
But then they deck'd a restless ghost
With hot-flush'd cheeks and brilliant eyes,
And quivering lips on which the tide
Of courtly speech abruptly died,
And a glance which over the crowded floor,
The dancers, and the festive host,
Flew ever to the door.
That the knights eyed her in surprise,
And the dames whispered scoffingly:
" Her moods, good lack, they pass like showers!

But yesternight and she would be
As pale and still as wither'd flowers,
And now to-night she laughs and speaks
And has a colour in her cheeks ;
Christ keep us from such fantasy ! "
Yes, now the longing is o'erpast,
Which, dogg'd by fear and fought by shame,
Shook her weak bosom day and night,
Consumed her beauty like a flame,
And dimm'd it like the desert-blast.
And though the curtains hide her face,
Yet were it lifted to the light,
The sweet expression of her brow
Would charm the gazer, till his thought
Erased the ravages of time,
Fill'd up the hollow cheek, and brought
A freshness back as of her prime—
So healing is her quiet now.
So perfectly the lines express
A tranquil, settled loveliness,
Her younger rival's purest grace.

The air of the December night
Steals coldly around the chamber bright,
Where those lifeless lovers be ;
Swinging with it, in the light
Flaps the ghost-like tapestry.
And on the arras wrought you see
A stately Huntsman clad in green,
And round him a fresh forest-scene.
On that clear forest-knoll he stays,
With his pack round him, and delays.
He stares and stares, with troubled face,
At this huge, gleam-lit fireplace,

At that bright, iron-figured door,
And those blown rushes on the floor.
He gazes down into the room
With heated cheeks and flurried air,
And to himself he seems to say :
" *What place is this, and who are they ?*
Who is that kneeling Lady fair ?
And on his pillows that pale Knight
Who seems of marble on a tomb ?
How comes it here, this chamber bright,
Through whose mullion'd windows clear
The castle-court all wet with rain,
The drawbridge and the moat appear,
And then the beach, and, mark'd with spray,
The sunken reefs, and far away
The unquiet bright Atlantic plain ?
—What, has some glamour made me sleep,
And sent me with my dogs to sweep,
By night, with boisterous bugle-peal,
Through some old, sea-side, knightly hall,
Not in the free green wood at all ?
That Knight's asleep, and at her prayer
That Lady by the bed doth kneel—
Then hush, thou boisterous bugle-peal ! "
—The wild boar rustles in his lair ;
The fierce hounds snuff the tainted air ;
But lord and hounds keep rooted there.

Cheer, cheer thy dogs into the brake,
O Hunter ! and without a fear
Thy golden-tassell'd bugle blow,
And through the glades thy pastime take—
For thou wilt rouse no sleepers here !
For these thou seest are unmoved ;
Cold, cold as those who lived and loved
A thousand years ago.

III

ISEULT OF BRITTANY

A year had flown, and o'er the sea away,
In Cornwall, Tristram and Queen Iseult lay;
In King Marc's chapel, in Tyntagel old—
There in a ship they bore those lovers cold.

The young surviving Iseult, one bright day,
Had wandered forth.   Her children were at play
In a green circular hollow in the heath
Which borders the sea-shore—a country path
Creeps over it from the till'd fields behind.
The hollow's grassy banks are soft-inclined,
And, to one standing on them, far and near
The lone unbroken view spreads bright and clear
Over the waste.   The cirque of open ground
Is light and green; the heather, which all round
Creeps thickly, grows not here; but the pale grass
Is strewn with rocks, and many a shiver'd mass
Of vein'd white-gleaming quartz, and here and there
Dotted with holly-trees and juniper.
In the smooth centre of the opening stood
Three hollies side by side, and made a screen,
Warm with the winter-sun, of burnish'd green
With scarlet berries gemm'd, the fell-fare's food.
Under the glittering hollies Iseult stands,
Watching her children play; their little hands
Are busy gathering spars of quartz, and streams
Of stagshorn for their hats; anon, with screams
Of mad delight they drop their spoils, and bound
Among the holly clumps and broken ground,
Racing full speed, and startling in their rush
The fell-fares and the speckled missel-thrush

Out of their glossy coverts ;—but when now
Their cheeks were flush'd, and over each hot brow
Under the feather'd hats of the sweet pair,
In blinding masses shower'd the golden hair—
Then Iseult call'd them to her, and the three
Clustered under the holly-screen, and she
Told them an old-world Breton history.

Warm in their mantles wrapt, the three stood there,
Under the hollies, in the clear still air—
Mantles with those rich furs deep glistening
Which Venice ships do from swart Egypt bring.
Long they stayed still,—then, pacing at their ease,
Moved up and down under the glossy trees ;
But still, as they pursued their warm dry road,
From Iseult's lips the unbroken story flow'd,
And still the children listen'd, their blue eyes
Fix'd on their mother's face in wide surprise ;
Nor did their looks stray once to the sea-side,
Nor to the brown heaths round them, bright and
    wide,
Nor to the snow, which, though 'twas all away
From the open heath, still by the hedgerows lay,
Nor to the shining sea-fowl, that with screams
Bore up from where the bright Atlantic gleams,
Swooping to landward ; nor to where, quite clear,
The fell-fares settled on the thickets near.
And they would still have listen'd, till dark night
Came keen and chill down on the heather bright ;
But, when the red glow on the sea grew cold,
And the grey turrets of the castle old
Look'd sternly through the frosty evening air,
Then Iseult took by the hand those children fair,
And brought her tale to an end, and found the path,
And led them home, over the darkening heath.

And is she happy? Does she see unmoved
The days in which she might have lived and loved
Slip without bringing bliss slowly away,
One after one, to-morrow like to-day?
Joy has not found her yet, nor ever will,—
Is it this thought which makes her mien so still,
Her features so fatigued, her eyes, though sweet,
So sunk, so rarely lifted save to meet
Her children's? She moves slow; her voice alone
Hath yet an infantine and silver tone,
But even that comes languidly; in truth,
She seems one dying in a mask of youth.
And now she will go home, and softly lay
Her laughing children in their beds, and play
Awhile with them before they sleep; and then
She'll light her silver lamp, which fishermen
Dragging their nets through the rough waves, afar,
Along this iron-coast, know like a star,
And take her broidery frame, and there she'll sit
Hour after hour, her gold curls sweeping it;
Lifting her soft-bent head only to mind
Her children, or to listen to the wind.
And when the clock peals midnight, she will move
Her work away, and let her fingers rove
Across the shaggy brows of Tristram's hound,
Who lies, guarding her feet, along the ground;
Or else she will fall musing, her blue eyes
Fix'd, her slight hands clasp'd on her lap; then rise,
And at her prie-dieu kneel, until she have told
Her rosary-beads of ebony tipp'd with gold;
Then to her soft sleep—and to-morrow'll be
To-day's exact repeated effigy.

Yes, it is lonely for her in her hall,
The children, and the grey-hair'd seneschal,

Her women, and Sir Tristram's aged hound,
Are there the sole companions to be found.
But these she loves ; and noisier life than this
She would find ill to bear, weak as she is.
She has her children too, and night and day
Is with them ; and the wide heaths where they play,
The hollies, and the cliff, and the sea-shore,
The sand, the sea-birds, and the distant sails,
These are to her dear as to them ; the tales
With which this day the children she beguiled
She gleaned from Breton grandames, when a child,
In every hut along this sea-coast wild ;
She herself loves them still, and, when they are told,
Can forget all to hear them, as of old.

.   .   .   .

CADMUS AND HARMONIA

Far, far from here,
The Adriatic breaks in a warm bay
Among the green Illyrian hills ; and there
The sunshine in the happy glens is fair,
And by the sea, and in the brakes,
The grass is cool, the sea-side air
Buoyant and fresh, the mountain flowers
More virginal and sweet than ours.
And there, they say, two bright and aged snakes,
Who once were Cadmus and Harmonia,
Bask in the glens or on the warm sea-shore,
In breathless quiet, after all their ills ;
Nor do they see their country, nor the place
Where the Sphinx lived among the frowning hills,
Nor the unhappy palace of their race,
Nor Thebes, nor the Ismenus, any more.

There those two live, far in the Illyrian brakes.
They had stay'd long enough to see,
In Thebes, the billow of calamity
Over their own dear children roll'd,
Curse upon curse, pang upon pang,
For years, they sitting helpless in their home,
A grey old man and woman ; yet of old
The Gods had to their marriage come,
And at the banquet all the Muses sang.

Therefore they did not end their days
In sight of blood ; but were rapt, far away,
To where the west wind plays,
And murmurs of the Adriatic come
To those untrodden mountain-lawns ; and there,
Placed safely in changed forms, the pair
Wholly forget their first sad life, and home,
And all that Theban woe, and stray
For ever through the glens, placid and dumb.

DOVER BEACH

The sea is calm to-night,
The tide is full, the moon lies fair
Upon the straits ; on the French coast the light
Gleams and is gone ; the cliffs of England stand
Glimmering and vast, out in the tranquil bay.
Come to the window, sweet is the night-air !
Only, from the long line of spray
Where the sea meets the moon-blanch'd land,

Listen ! You hear the grating roar
Of pebbles, which the waves draw back, and fling
At their return, up the high strand,
Begin and cease, and then again begin,
With tremulous cadence slow, and bring
The eternal note of sadness in.

Sophocles long ago
Heard it on the Ægean, and it brought
Into his mind the turbid ebb and flow
Of human misery ; we
Find also in the sound a thought,
Hearing it by this distant northern sea.

The Sea of Faith
Was once, too, at the full, and round earth's shore
Lay like the folds of a bright girdle furl'd,
But now I only hear
Its melancholy, long, withdrawing roar,
Retreating to the breath
Of the night-wind, down the vast edges drear
And naked shingles of the world.

Ah, love, let us be true
To one another ! for the world, which seems
To lie before us, like a land of dreams,
So various, so beautiful, so new,
Hath really neither joy, nor love, nor light,
Nor certitude, nor peace, nor help for pain ;
And we are here as in a darkling plain,
Swept with confused alarms of struggle and flight,
Where ignorant armies clash by night.

A SUMMER NIGHT

In the deserted, moon-blanch'd street,
How lonely rings the echo of my feet !
Those windows, which I gaze at, frown,
Silent and white, unopening down,
Repellent as the world ;—but see,
A break between the housetops shows
The moon ! and, lost behind her, fading dim
Into the dewy dark obscurity
Down at the far horizon's rim,
Doth a whole tract of heaven disclose !

And to my mind the thought
Is on a sudden brought
Of a past night, and a far different scene.
Headlands stood out into the moon-lit deep
As clearly as at noon ;
The spring-tide's brimming flow
Heaved dazzlingly between ;
Houses, with long white sweep,
Girdled the glistening bay ;
Behind, through the soft air,
The blue haze-cradled mountains spread away.
That night was far more fair—
But the same restless pacings to and fro,
And the same vainly throbbing heart was there,
And the same bright calm moon.

And the calm moonlight seems to say :
Hast thou then still the old unquiet breast,
Which neither deadens into rest,
Nor ever feels the fiery glow
That whirls the spirit from itself away.
But fluctuates to and fro,

Never by passion quite possess'd
And never quite benumb'd by the world's sway ?—
And I, I know not if to pray
Still to be what I am, or yield and be
Like all the other men I see.

For most men in a brazen prison live,
Where the sun's hot eye,
With heads bent o'er their toil, they languidly
Their lives to some unmeaning taskwork give,
Dreaming of nought beyond their prison-wall.
And as, year after year,
Fresh products of their barren labour fall
From their tired hands, and rest
Never yet comes more near,
Gloom settles slowly down over their breast ;
And while they try to stem
The waves of mournful thought by which they are
     prest,
Death in their prison reaches them,
Unfreed, having seen nothing, still unblest.

And the rest, a few,
Escape their prison and depart
On the wide ocean of life anew.
There the freed prisoner, where'er his heart
Listeth, will sail ;
Nor doth he know how there prevail,
Despotic on that sea,
Trade-winds which cross it from eternity.
Awhile he holds some false way, undebarr'd
By thwarting signs, and braves
The freshening wind and blackening waves.
And then the tempest strikes him ; and between
The lightning-bursts is seen

Only a driving wreck,
And the pale master on his spar strewn-deck
With anguish'd face and flying hair
Grasping the rudder hard,
Still bent to make some port he knows not where,
Still standing for some false, impossible shore.
And sterner comes the roar
Of sea and wind, and through the deepening gloom
Fainter and fainter wreck and helmsmen loom,
And he too disappears, and comes no more.

Is there no life, but these alone?
Madman or slave, must man be one?

Plainness and clearness without shadow or stain!
Clearness divine!
Ye heavens, whose pure dark regions have no sign
Of languor, though so calm, and though so great,
Are yet untroubled and unpassionate;
Who, though so noble, share in the world's toil,
And, though so mask'd, keep free from dust and soil!
I will not say that your mild deeps retain
A tinge, it may be, of their silent pain
Who have long'd deeply once, and long'd in vain—
But I will rather say that you remain
A world above man's head, to let him see
How boundless might his soul's horizons be,
How vast, yet of what clear transparency!
How it were good to live there, and breathe free;
How fair a lot to fill
Is left to each man still!

LINES WRITTEN IN KENSINGTON GARDENS

In this lone, open glade I lie,
Screen'd by deep boughs on either hand ;
And at its end, to stay the eye,
Those black-crown'd, red-boled pine-trees stand !

Birds here make song, each bird has his,
Across the girdling city's hum.
How green under the boughs it is !
How thick the tremulous sheep cries come !

Sometimes a child will cross the glade
To take his nurse his broken toy ;
Sometimes a thrush flit overhead
Deep in her unknown day's employ.

Here at my feet what wonders pass,
What endless, active life is here !
What blowing daisies, fragrant grass !
And air-stirr'd forest, fresh and clear.

Scarce fresher is the mountain-sod
Where the tired angler lies, stretch'd out,
And, eased of basket and of rod,
Counts his day's spoil, the spotted trout.

In the huge world, which roars hard by,
Be others happy if they can !
But in my helpless cradle I
Was breathed on by the rural Pan.

I, on men's impious uproar hurl'd,
Think often, as I hear them rave,
That peace has left the upper world
And now keeps only in the grave.

Yet here is peace for ever new!
When I who watch them am away,
Still all things in this glade go through
The changes of their quiet day.

Then to their happy rest they pass!
The flowers upclose, the birds are fed,
The night comes down upon the grass,
The child sleeps warmly in his bed.

Calm soul of all things! make it mine
To feel, amid the city's jar,
That there abides a peace of thine,
Man did not make, and cannot mar.

The will to neither strive nor cry,
The power to feel with others give!
Calm, calm me more! nor let me die
Before I have begun to live.

MEMORIAL VERSES

(*April* 1850)

Goethe in Weimar sleeps, and Greece,
Long since, saw Byron's struggle cease,
But one such death remain'd to come;
The last poetic voice is dumb—
We stand to-day by Wordsworth's tomb.

When Byron's eyes were shut in death,
We bow'd our head, and held our breath.
He taught us little ; but our soul
Had *felt* him like the thunder's roll.
With shivering heart the strife we saw
Of passion with eternal law ;
And yet with reverential awe
We watch'd the fount of fiery life
Which served for that Titanic strife.

When Goethe's death was told, we said :
Sunk, then, is Europe's sagest head.
Physician of the iron age,
Goethe has done his pilgrimage.
He took the suffering human race,
He read each wound, each weakness clear ;
And struck his finger on the place,
And said : *Thou ailest here, and here !*
He looked on Europe's dying hour
Of fitful dream and feverish power ;
His eye plunged down the weltering strife,
The turmoil of expiring life—
He said : *The end is everywhere,*
Art still has truth, take refuge there !
And he was happy if to know
Causes of things, and far below
His feet to see the lurid flow
Of terror, and insane distress,
And headlong fate, be happiness.

And Wordsworth !—Ah, pale ghosts, rejoice !
For never has such soothing voice
Been to your shadowy world convey'd,
Since erst, at morn, some wandering shade

x

Heard the clear song of Orpheus come
Through Hades, and the mournful gloom.
Wordsworth has gone from us—and ye.
Ah, may ye feel his voice as we !
He too upon a wintry clime
Had fallen—on this iron time
Of doubts, disputes, distractions, fears.

He found us when the age had bound
Our souls in its benumbing round ;
He spoke, and loosed our heart in tears.
He laid us as we lay at birth,
Smiles broke from us, and we had ease ;
The smiles were round us, and the breeze
On the cool flowery lap of earth,
Went o'er the sun-lit fields again ;
Our foreheads felt the wind and rain.
Our youth return'd ; for there was shed
On spirits that had long been dead,
Spirits dried up and closely furl'd,
The freshness of the early world.

Ah ! since dark days still bring to light
Man's prudence and man's fiery might,
Time may restore us in his course
Goethe's sage mind and Byron's force ;
But where will Europe's latter hour
Again find Wordsworth's healing power ?
Others will teach us how to dare,
And against fear our breast to steel ;
Others will strengthen us to bear—
But who, ah ! who, will make us feel ?
The cloud of mortal destiny,
Others will front it fearlessly—
But who, like him, will put it by ?

Keep fresh the grass upon his grave,
O Rotha, with thy living wave !
Sing him thy best ! for few or none
Hears thy voice right, now he is gone.

THE SCHOLAR-GIPSY

Go, for they call you, shepherd, from the hill ;
  Go, shepherd, and untie the wattled cotes !
    No longer leave thy wistful flock unfed,
  Nor let thy bawling-fellows rack their throats,
    Nor the cropp'd grasses shoot another head ;
      But when the fields are still,
  And the tired men and dogs all gone to rest,
    And only the white sheep are sometimes seen
    Cross and recross the strips of moon-blanched green,
  Come, shepherd, and again renew the quest.

Here, where the reaper was at work of late,
  In this high field's dark corner, where he leaves
    His coat, his basket, and his earthen cruse,
  And in the sun all morning binds the sheaves,
    Then here, at noon, comes back his stores to use—
      Here will I sit and wait.
  While to my ear from uplands far away
    The bleating of the folded flocks is borne,
    With distant cries of reapers in the corn—
  All the live murmur of a summer's day.

Screen'd is this nook o'er the high, half-reap'd field,
  And here till sun-down, shepherd ! will I be.
    Through the thick corn the scarlet poppies peep,
  And round green roots and yellowing stalks I see
    Pale pink convolvulus in tendrils creep ;
      And air-swept lindens yield

Their scent, and rustle down their perfumed showers
Of bloom on the bent grass where I am laid,
And bower me from the August sun with shade;
And the eye travels down to Oxford's towers.

And near me on the grass lies Glanvil's book—
Come, let me read the oft-read tale again!
The story of that Oxford scholar poor,
Of pregnant parts and quick inventive brain,
Who, tired of knocking at preferment's door,
One summer morn forsook
His friends, and went to learn the gipsy lore,
And roam'd the world with that wild brotherhood,
And came, as most men deem'd, to little good,
But came to Oxford and his friends no more.

But once, years after, in the country lanes,
Two scholars, whom at college erst he knew,
Met him, and of his way of life enquired;
Whereat he answer'd, that the gipsy-crew,
His mates, had arts to rule as they desired
The workings of men's brains,
And they can bind them to what thoughts they will.
"And I," he said, "the secret of their art,
When fully learn'd, will to the world impart;
But it needs heaven-sent moments for this skill."

This said, he left them, and return'd no more.—
But rumours hung about the country-side,
That the lost Scholar long was seen to stray,
Seen by rare glimpses, pensive and tongue-tied,
In hat of antique shape, and cloak of grey,
The same the gipsies wore.

Shepherds had met him on the Hurst in spring,
   At some lone alehouse in the Berkshire moors,
      On the warm ingle-bench, the smock-frock'd boors
Had found him seated at their entering.

But, 'mid their drink and clatter, he would fly.
   And I myself seem half to know thy looks,
      And put the shepherds, wanderer! on thy trace;
   And boys who in lone wheatfields scare the rooks
      I ask if thou hast pass'd their quiet place;
         Or in my boat I lie
Moor'd to the cool bank in the summer-heats,
      'Mid wide grass meadows which the sunshine fills,
      And watch the warm, green-muffled Cumnor hills,
And wonder if thou haunt'st their shy retreats.

For most, I know, thou lov'st retired ground!
   Thee at the ferry Oxford riders blithe,
      Returning home on summer nights, have met
   Crossing the stripling Thames at Bab-lock-hithe,
      Trailing in the cool stream thy fingers wet,
         As the punt's rope chops round;
   And leaning backward in a pensive dream,
      And fostering in thy lap a heap of flowers
      Pluck'd in shy fields and distant Wychwood bowers,
And thine eyes resting on the moonlit stream.

And then they land, and thou art seen no more!—
   Maidens, who from the distant hamlets come
      To dance around the Fyfield elm in May,
   Oft through the darkening fields have seen thee roam,
      Or cross a stile into the public way;
         Oft thou has given them store

Of flowers—the frail-leaf'd, white anemone,
　　Dark bluebells drench'd with dews of summer eves,
　　And purple orchises with spotted leaves—
But none hath words she can report of thee.

And, above Godstow Bridge, when hay-time's here
　　In June, and many a scythe in sunshine flames,
　　　Men who through those wide fields of breezy grass,
　　Where black-wing'd swallows haunt the glittering
　　　　Thames,
　　　To bathe in the abandon'd lasher pass,
　　　　Have often pass'd thee near
Sitting upon the river bank o'ergrown;
　　Mark'd thine outlandish garb, thy figure spare,
　　Thy dark vague eyes, and soft abstracted air—
But, when they came from bathing, thou wast gone!

At some lone homestead in the Cumnor hills,
　　Where at her open door the housewife darns,
　　　Thou hast been seen, or hanging on a gate
　　To watch the threshers in the mossy barns.
　　　Children, who early range these slopes and late
　　　　For cresses from the rills,
　　Have known thee eyeing, all an April day,
　　　The springing pastures and the feeding kine;
　　　And mark'd thee, when the stars come out and
　　　　shine,
Through the long dewy grass move slow away.

In autumn, on the skirts of Bagley Wood—
　　Where most the gipsies by the turf-edged way
　　　Pitch their smoked tents, and every bush you see
　　With scarlet patches tagg'd and shreds of grey,
　　　Above the forest-ground call'd Thessaly—
　　　　The blackbird picking food

Sees thee, nor stops his meal, nor fears at all ;
　So often has he known thee past him stray,
　Rapt, twirling in thy hand a wither'd spray,
And waiting for the spark from heaven to fall.

And once, in winter, on the causeway chill
　Where home through flooded fields foot-travellers go,
　Have I not pass'd thee on the wooden briuge,
　Wrapt in thy cloak and battling with the snow,
　　Thy face toward Hinksey and its wintry ridge ?
　　And thou hast climb'd the hill,
　And gain'd the white brow of the Cumnor range ;
　　Turn'd once to watch, while thick the snowflakes
　　　fall,
　　The line of festal light in Christ-Church hall—
Then sought thy straw in some sequester'd grange.

But what—I dream !　Two hundred years are flown
　Since first thy story ran through Oxford halls,
　And the grave Glanvil did the tale inscribe
That thou wert wander'd from the studious walls
　　To learn strange arts, and join a gipsy tribe ;
　　And thou from earth art gone
　Long since, and in some quiet churchyard laid—
　　Some country-nook, where o'er thy unknown grave
　　Tall grasses and white flowering nettles wave,
Under a dark, red-fruited yew-tree's shade.

—No, no, thou hast not felt the lapse of hours !
　For what wears out the life of mortal men ?
　　'Tis that from change to change their being rolls ;
　'Tis that repeated shocks, again, again,
　　Exhaust the energy of strongest souls,
　　　And numb the elastic powers.

Till having used our nerves with bliss and teen,
    And tired upon a thousand schemes our wit,
      To the just-pausing Genius we remit
Our well-worn life, and are—what we have been.

Thou hast not lived, why should'st thou perish, so?
    Thou hadst *one* aim, *one* business, *one* desire;
      Else wert thou long since number'd with the dead!
    Else hadst thou spent, like other men, thy fire!
      The generations of thy peers are fled,
        And we ourselves shall go;
    But thou possessest an immortal lot,
      And we imagine thee exempt from age,
      And living as thou liv'st on Glanvil's page,
Because thou hadst—what we, alas! have not.

For early didst thou leave the world, with powers
    Fresh, undiverted to the world without,
      Firm to their mark, not spent on other things:
    Free from the sick fatigue, the languid doubt,
      Which much to have tried, in much been baffled,
        brings.
        O life unlike to ours!
    Who fluctuate idly without term or scope,
      Of whom each strives, nor knows for what he strives,
      And each half lives a hundred different lives;
Who wait like thee, but not, like thee, in hope.

Thou waitest for the spark from heaven! and we,
    Light half-believers of our casual creeds,
      Who never deeply felt, nor clearly will'd,
    Whose insight never has borne fruit in deeds,
      Whose vague resolves never have been fulfill'd;
        For whom each year we see

Breeds new beginnings, disappointments new;
  Who hesitate and falter life away,
  And lose to-morrow the ground won to-day—
Ah! do not we, wanderer! await it too?

Yes, we await it!—but it still delays,
  And then we suffer! and amongst us one,
  Who most has suffer'd, takes dejectedly
His seat upon the intellectual throne;
  And all his store of sad experience he
    Lays bare of wretched days;
Tells us his misery's birth and growth and signs,
  And how the dying spark of hope was fed,
  And how the breast was soothed, and how the head
And all his hourly varied anodynes.

This for our wisest! and we others pine,
  And wish the long unhappy dream would end,
  And waive all claim to bliss, and try to bear;
With close-lipp'd patience for our only friend,
  Sad patience, too near neighbour to despair—
    But none has hope like thine!
Thou through the fields and through the wood dost stray,
  Roaming the country-side, a truant-boy,
  Nursing thy project in unclouded joy,
And every doubt long blown by time away.

O born in days when wits were fresh and clear,
  And life ran gaily as the sparkling Thames;
  Before this strange disease of modern life,
With its sick hurry, its divided aims,
  Its heads o'ertax'd, its palsied hearts, was rife—
    Fly hence, our contact fear!

Still fly, plunge deeper in the bowering wood!
　　Averse, as Dido did with gesture stern
　　From her false friend's approach in Hades turn,
Wave us away, and keep thy solitude!

Still nursing the unconquerable hope,
　　Still clutching the inviolable shade,
　　　With a free, onward impulse brushing through,
　　By night, the silver'd branches of the glade—
　　　Far on the forest-skirts, where none pursue,
　　　　On some mild pastoral slope
　　Emerge, and resting on the moonlit pales
　　　Freshen thy flowers as in former years
　　　With dew, or listen with enchanted ears,
From the dark dingles, to the nightingales!

But fly our paths, our feverish contact fly!
　　For strong the infection of our mental strife,
　　　Which, though it gives no bliss, yet spoils for rest;
　　And we should win thee from thy own fair life,
　　　Like us distracted, and like us unblest.
　　　　Soon, soon thy cheer would die,
　　Thy hopes grow timorous, and unfix'd thy powers,
　　　And thy clear aims be cross and shifting made;
　　And then thy glad perennial youth would fade,
Fade, and grow old at last, and die like ours.

Then fly our greetings, fly our speech and smiles!
　　—As some grave Tyrian trader, from the sea,
　　　Descried at sunrise an emerging prow
　　Lifting the cool-hair'd creepers stealthily,
　　　The fringes of a southward-facing brow
　　　　Among the Ægæan isles;

And saw the merry Grecian coaster come,
    Freighted with amber grapes, and Chian wine,
    Green, bursting figs, and tunnies steep'd in brine—
And knew the intruders on his ancient home,

The young light-hearted masters of the waves—
    And snatch'd his rudder, and shook out more sail,
    And day and night held on indignantly
O'er the blue Midland waters with the gale,
    Betwixt the Syrtes and soft Sicily,
        To where the Atlantic raves
Outside the western straits, and unbent sails
    There where down cloudy cliffs, through sheets of
        foam,
    Shy traffickers, the dark Iberians come ;
And on the beach undid his corded bales.

THE FORSAKEN MERMAN

Come, dear children, let us away ;
Down and away below !
Now my brothers call from the bay,
Now the great winds shoreward blow,
Now the salt tides seaward flow ;
Now the wild white horses play,
Champ and chafe and toss in the spray.
Children dear, let us away !
This way, this way !

Call her once before you go—
Call once yet !
In a voice that she will know :
" Margaret ! Margaret ! "

Children's voices should be dear
(Call once more) to a mother's ear;
Children's voices, wild with pain—
Surely she will come again!
Call her once and come away;
This way, this way!
"Mother dear, we cannot stay!
The wild white horses foam and fret."
Margaret! Margaret!

Come, dear children, come away down;
Call no more!
One last look at the white-wall'd town,
And the little grey church on the windy shore;
Then come down!
She will not come though you call all day!
Come away, come away!

Children dear, was it yesterday
We heard the sweet bells over the bay?
In the caverns where we lay,
Through the surf and through the swell,
The far-off sound of a silver bell?
Sand-strewn caverns, cool and deep,
Where the winds are all asleep;
Where the spent lights quiver and gleam,
Where the salt weed sways in the stream,
Where the sea-beasts, ranged all round,
Feed in the ooze of their pasture-ground;
Where the sea-snakes coil and twine,
Dry their mail and bask in the brine;
Where great whales come sailing by,
Sail and sail, with unshut eye,
Round the world for ever and aye?
When did music come this way?
Children dear, was it yesterday?

Children dear, was it yesterday
(Call yet once) that she went away?
Once she sate with you and me,
On a red gold throne in the heart of the sea,
And the youngest sate on her knee.
She comb'd its bright hair, and she tended it well,
When down swung the sound of a far-off bell.
She sigh'd, she look'd up through the clear green sea ;
She said : "I must go, for my kinsfolk pray
In the little grey church on the shore to-day.
'Twill be Easter-time in the world—ah me !
And I lose my poor soul, Merman ! here with thee."
I said : "Go up, dear heart, through the waves ;
Say thy prayer, and come back to the kind sea-caves !"
She smiled, she went up through the surf in the bay.
Children dear, was it yesterday?

Children dear, were we long alone?
"The sea grows stormy, the little ones moan ;
Long prayers," I said, "in the world they say ;
Come !" I said ; and we rose through the surf in the
          bay.
We went up the beach, by the sandy down
Where the sea-stocks bloom, to the white-wall'd town ;
Through the narrow paved streets, where all was still,
To the little grey church on the windy hill.
From the church came a murmur of folk at their prayers,
But we stood without in the cold blowing airs.
We climb'd on the graves, on the stones worn with rains,
And we gazed up the aisle through the small leaded
          panes.
She sate by the pillar ; we saw her clear :
"Margaret, hist ! come quick, we are here !
Dear heart," I said, "we are long alone ;
The sea grows stormy, the little ones moan."

But, ah, she gave me never a look,
For her eyes were seal'd to the holy book!
Loud prays the priest; shut stands the door.
Come away, children, call no more!
Come away, come down, call no more!

Down, down, down!
Down to the depths of the sea!
She sits at her wheel in the humming town,
Singing most joyfully.
Hark what she sings: "O joy, O joy,
For the humming street, and the child with its toy!
For the priest, and the bell, and the holy well;
For the wheel where I spun,
And the blessed light of the sun!"
And so she sings her fill,
Singing most joyfully,
Till the spindle drops from her hand,
And the whizzing wheel stands still.
She steals to the window, and looks at the sand,
And over the sand at the sea;
And her eyes are set in a stare;
And anon there breaks a sigh,
And anon there drops a tear,
From a sorrow-clouded eye,
And a heart sorrow-laden,
A long, long sigh;
For the cold strange eyes of a little Mermaiden,
And the gleam of her golden hair.

Come away, away, children;
Come children, come down!
The hoarse wind blows colder;
Lights shine in the town.

She will start from her slumber
When gusts shake the door;
She will hear the winds howling,
Will hear the waves roar.
We shall see, while above us
The waves roar and whirl,
A ceiling of amber,
A pavement of pearl.
Singing: "Here came a mortal,
But faithless was she!
And alone dwell for ever
The kings of the sea."

But, children, at midnight,
When soft the winds blow,
When clear falls the moonlight,
When spring-tides are low;
When sweet airs come seaward
From heaths starr'd with broom,
And high rocks throw mildly
On the blanch'd sands a gloom;
Up the still, glistening beaches,
Up the creeks we will hie,
Over banks of bright seaweed
The ebb-tide leaves dry.
We will gaze, from the sand-hills,
At the white, sleeping town;
At the church on the hill-side—
And then come back down.
Singing: "There dwells a loved one,
But cruel is she!
She left lonely for ever
The kings of the sea."

JOHN O'HAGAN. 1822–1890

THE OLD STORY

He came across the meadow-pass,
    That summer eve of eves;
The sunlight streamed along the grass
    And glanced amid the leaves;
And from the shrubbery below,
    And from the garden trees,
He heard the thrushes' music flow,
    And humming of the bees.
The garden-gate was swung apart—
    The space was brief between;
But there, for throbbing of his heart,
    He paused perforce to lean.

He leaned upon the garden-gate;
    He looked, and scarce he breathed;
Within the little porch she sate,
    With woodbine overwreathed;
Her eyes upon her work were bent
    Unconscious who was nigh;
But oft the needle slowly went,
    And oft did idle lie;
And ever to her lips arose
    Sweet fragments faintly sung,
But ever, ere the notes could close,
    She hushed them on her tongue.

Why should I ever leave this spot,
    But gaze until I die?
A moment from that bursting thought
    She felt his footsteps nigh.

One sudden lifted glance—but one,
  A tremor and a start,
So gently was their greeting done
  That who would guess their heart?

Long, long the sun had sunken down,
  And all his golden trail
Had died away to lines of brown,
  In duskier hues that fail.
That grasshopper was chirping shrill—
  No other living sound
Accompanied the tiny rill
  That gurgled underground—
No other living sound, unless
  Some spirit bent to hear
Low words of human tenderness
  And mingling whispers near.

The stars, like pallid gems at first,
  Deep in the liquid sky,
Now forth upon the darkness burst,
  Sole kings and lights on high
In splendour, myriad-fold, supreme—
  No rival moonlight strove,
Nor lovelier e'er was Hesper's beam,
  Nor more majestic Jove.
But what if hearts there beat that night
  That recked not of the skies,
Or only felt their imaged light
  In one another's eyes!

And if two worlds of hidden thought
  And fostered passion met,
Which, passing human language, sought
  And found an utterance yet;

Y

And if they trembled like to flowers
    That droop across a stream,
The while the silent starry hours
    Glide o'er them like a dream;
And if, when came the parting time,
    They faltered still and clung;
What is it all?—an ancient rhyme
    Ten thousand times besung—
That part of paradise which man
    Without the portal knows—
Which hath been since the world began,
    And shall be till its close.

SYDNEY DOBELL. 1824–1874

THE BALLAD OF KEITH OF RAVELSTON

The murmur of the mourning ghost
　That keeps the shadowy kine,
O Keith of Ravelston,
　The sorrows of thy line !

Ravelston, Ravelston,
　The merry path that leads
Down the golden morning hill,
　And thro' the silver meads ;

Ravelston, Ravelston,
　The stile beneath the tree,
The maid that kept her mother's kine,
　The song that sang she !

She sang her song, she kept her kine,
　She sat beneath the thorn,
When Andrew Keith of Ravelston
　Rode thro' the Monday morn.

His henchmen sing, his hawk-bells ring,
　His belted jewels shine ;
O Keith of Ravelston,
　The sorrows of thy line !

Year after year, where Andrew came,
　Comes evening down the glade,
And still there sits a moonshine ghost
　Where sat the sunshine maid.

Her misty hair is faint and fair,
  She keeps the shadowy kine;
O Keith of Ravelston,
  The sorrows of thy line!

I lay my hand upon the stile,
  The stile is lone and cold,
The burnie that goes babbling by
  Says naught that can be told.

Yet, stranger! here, from year to year,
  She keeps her shadowy kine;
O Keith of Ravelston,
  The sorrows of thy line!

Step out three steps, where Andrew stood—
  Why blanch thy cheeks for fear?
The ancient stile is not alone,
  'Tis not the burn I hear!

She makes her immemorial moan,
  She keeps her shadowy kine;
O Keith of Ravelston,
  The sorrows of thy line!

W. CORY (formerly JOHNSON). 1823–1892

FROM "CALLIMACHUS"

They told me, Heraclitus, they told me you were dead ;
They brought me bitter news to hear, and bitter tears to
    shed.
I wept as I remembered how often you and I
Had tired the sun with talking, and sent him down the
    sky.

And now that thou art lying, my dear old Carian guest,
A handful of grey ashes, long, long ago at rest,
Still are thy pleasant voices, thy nightingales, awake,
For Death, he taketh all away, but them he cannot take.

ADELAIDE PROCTER. 1825–1864

A LOST CHORD

Seated one day at the Organ,
I was weary and ill at ease,
And my fingers wandered idly
Over the noisy keys.

I do not know what I was playing,
Or what I was dreaming then ;
But I struck one chord of music,
Like the sound of a great Amen.

It flooded the crimson twilight
Like the close of an Angel's Psalm,
And it lay on my fevered spirit
With a touch of infinite calm.

It quieted pain and sorrow,
Like love overcoming strife ;
It seemed the harmonious echo
From our discordant life.

It linked all perplexed meanings
Into one perfect peace,
And trembled away into silence,
As if it were loth to cease.

I have sought, but I seek it vainly,
That one lost chord divine,
Which came from the soul of the Organ,
And entered into mine.

It may be that Death's bright angel
 Will speak in that chord again,—
It may be that only in Heaven
 I shall hear that grand Amen.

CANON BRIGHT. 1825–1901

CROWNED AND DISCROWNED

Wherefore thus 'mid foemen lurking, when my place is
far away,

Here's no room for feet of Stuarts on a Brunswick's
crowning day ;

Yet awhile I fain would linger—needless now this veiling
guise—

In an hour of regal joyance, safe 'mid unsuspecting eyes.

There be those within this presence, Lordships some,
perhaps a Grace,

Who, if questioned, might bethink them they have seen
Charles Stuart's face ;

But that face is changed and saddened, I am not what I
was then,

Foes, that thirsted for my life-blood, gaze on me with
harmless ken :

Let us watch this cursed pageant, high of heart and
calm of brow,

Oh, ye roofs of old St. Peter's, wot ye whom ye shelter
now ?

Ye beheld my martyred grandsire in his robes of boding
white,

Better ye were levin-blasted ere ye looked on this day's
rite !

Oh ! ye perjured English traitors, pledged to be our
liegemen true,

God that lives to judge the faithless judge between your
kings and you !

Ye are come with vows of homage—hold—there listens
    One on high—
"Life and limb and earthly worship, faith and truth to
    live or die."
We have heard such words aforetime, words by all but
    One forgot,
So they sware to us, the Exiles—oh, young king, believe
    them not!
Ha! 'tis brave to hear the traitors mouth the pledge of
    royal faith—
"Thou whom God hath throned above me, I am thine
    for life or death."
In our old imperial vestures they their man-made king
    enfold,
Kneeling to their own creation, as they knelt to us of old.
Why, ye speak as though He heard not—nay, ye shout
    as in His ear—
"We uptore what Thou hadst planted, lo, our goodlier
    plant is here."
I must see your May-game ritual, see you give the crown
    and globe,
I must see your German masquing in my Sire's Dalmatic
    robe.
For ye keep our sacred symbols, Edward's staff and
    Edward's crown,
Ye that build a throne for strangers, hurled your native
    monarchs down.
Why, what needs that priestly unction? have ye kings by
    grace of God,
Now the old and awful kingship 'neath the white steed's
    hoof is trod?
    Reverend lords in cope and rochet, clustering round
      St. Edward's chair,
Priests who wail for Charles the Martyr, where's your
    welcome for his heir?

Noble lords, the power of knighthood—knightly faith's
    a hollow thing,
Ye who hail a fifth usurper in the presence of your king!
All you had, my lords, we gave you, save one heirloom
    all your own,
Heirloom meet for noble houses, lying lips, and hearts
    of stone.
Oh, we know your inborn baseness, how it runs in cour-
    tiers' blood,
Ere we made ye knights and nobles ye were false to man
    and God;
But your creed reformed constrained you, but your pure
    faith made you vile.
There were others.   Hark! a Stuart knows, methinks,
    that ducal style—
One that bends before our altars lowlier stoops at Bruns-
    wick's shrine.
Norfolk?   Murray, I forgive thee! hell hath treasons
    worse than thine.
   Thou that tak'st that shameless homage, with my
      diadem on thy brow,
Proudly count thy kneeling lieges, I am truer king than
    thou;
Faithful hearts are all my kingdom, changing not with
    darkening years,
Holier than thine oil of gladness is the anointing of their
    tears.
I have been among my subjects proved in winter as in
    spring,
And their tears fell on my fingers as they whispered—
    Charles, my king.
Saw I ne'er such strong devotion, since the princely-
    hearted dame
Journeyed far with household treasures, as to Mersey's
    bank I came;

At my feet she laid her offerings, to my hands her white
    lips prest,
Strained her glassy eyes and murmured, "Royal Edward,
    be thou blest!
I have heard the voice of Stuart, let me now in peace
    depart."
Worth a realm of England's nobles was that blind one's
    peerless heart,
But her name recalls my vision, like a sunburst o'er the deep.
Oh! I see the summer morning on the shores of Moidart
    sleep,
And the Standard on Glenfinnan, and thy kindling
    glance, Lochiel,
And Macdonald's sudden rapture as his clansmen bared
    the steel ;
See the throng of lords and vassals round the gate of
    Holyrood,
Hark the burst of Scottish welcome when in Mary's halls
    I stood.
And our scattered foes at Preston, and the triumph at
    Carlisle,
And our bannered hose at Falkirk, bright with fortune's
    parting smile.
Ha ! 'tis past, that glorious vision, there's a wailing in
    mine ears,
Lo the field of red Culloden glooming through the mist
    of years ;
Oh, the faithful hearts that bore me scatheless to the
    Northern wave,
Oh, the more than friends and brothers sleeping now in
    felon's grave,
Traitor's doom and torturing scaffold—all they bore for
    Charles's sake.
Oh, it fires my brain to madness, tongue must hold or
    heart must break.

There are brave hearts yet in England, hearts as tender
　　and as true,

As when erst my loyal Cumbrians for the right their
　　broadswords drew ;

Though they lurk in upper chambers, though they boast
　　no Norman blood,

Still they hold their scorn of traitors, love of kings and
　　fear of God.

Oh, my lords that wait on fortune, watching how the tide
　　will turn,

Scorn them not, no peer has taught them all God's lessons
　　to unlearn ;

When they pledged them to Charles Edward, they had
　　counted honour's cost,

And they cleave to him that loves them, be the battle
　　won or lost.

All's not smooth to crowned usurpers, will your Guelphs
　　in trouble see

Peers of this day's vows as mindful as my friends of
　　theirs to me.

Then if these should fail you, prince, these in whom you
　　put your trust,

Think when darkest clouds are gathering, God remem-
　　bers the unjust ;

Think He reckons then with England for the scaffold of
　　Whitehall,

For the Stuart's wrongs and sorrows many a Guelphic
　　tear must fall.

So God show the right between us—here our paths for
　　ever part,

Know ye have not crushed your victim while he sways
　　one English heart.

'Tis a realm ye well might envy, one our House has held
　　of yore,

Fare you well and seek to win it,—Stuarts cross your
　　path no more.

MRS. CRAIK (née DINAH MARIA MULOCK).
1826–1887

FOUR YEARS

At the Midsummer, when the hay was down,
Said I mournful—Though my life be in its prime,
Bare lie my meadows all shorn before their time,
O'er my sere woodlands the leaves are turning brown ;
   It is the hot Midsummer, when the hay is down.

At the Midsummer, when the hay was down,
Stood she by the brooklet, young and very fair,
With the first white bindweed twisted in her hair—
Hair that drooped like birch-boughs, all in her simple
     gown—
   That eve in high Midsummer, when the hay was down.

At the Midsummer, when the hay was down,
Crept she a willing bride close into my breast ;
Low-piled the thunder-clouds had sunk into the west,
Red-eyed the sun out-glared like knight from leaguered
     town ;
   It was the high Midsummer, and the sun was down.

It is Midsummer—all the hay is down,
Close to her forehead press I dying eyes,
Praying God shield her till we meet in Paradise,
Bless her in love's name who was my joy and crown,
   And I go at Midsummer, when the hay is down.

MORTIMER COLLINS. 1827–1876

SHIRLEY CHASE

Cavalier Music ! Shirley Chase,
  Hidden deep amid oak-trees royal,
Is the noble home of a knightly race,
  Old as the oak-trees,—proud and loyal.
Snow has fallen on the White King's bier,—
  Cromwell lords it, late and early,
But as yet his troopers come not here ;
  At home in his hall sits Sir Everard Shirley.

Moonlight pours through the painted oriels,
  Firelight flickers on pictured walls,
Full of solemn and sad memorials
  Is the room where that mingled glimmer falls.
There is the banner of Arthur Shirley,
  Who died for Charles on a misty wold ;
There is his portrait—an infant curly,
  Whose corse in an unknown grave lies cold.

Hot and sudden swept Rupert's horse
  Down on the villainous Roundhead churls,
But they left young Arthur a mangled corse
  With the red mire clotting his chestnut curls :
Only son of an ancient race,
  As any that dwells in England's realm ;
Ah, a shadow sleeps on Sir Everard's face
  When he thinks of his soldier's snow-plumed helm.

Madrigal music fills the room
  With spring-like beauty and delicate grace ;
Vanishes half their weary gloom,
  As Harry St. Osyth's manly bass

And Maud's soprano and Amy in alt
  Mingle like streams on a verdurous shore ;
But memory sets them once at fault,
  As they think of the tenor that's heard no more.

After, a rare old English glee,
  Humorous, eloquent, daring, buoyant,
Rings through the chamber, strong and free,
  And shakes the mullioned panes flamboyant ;
Merry music of olden time,
  Gaily defying the Cromwell manacle,
Stoutly rebelling in hearty rhyme
  'Gainst cant and heresy puritanical.

Then Amy down to the organ sits,
  And a pleasant prelude sounds sonorous
As over the keys her white hand flits,
  And a Latin canon claims their chorus.
Not in the great cathedrals now
  Does saintly song as of yore find place ;
But it soothes awhile the furrowed brow
  Of the sad old Master of Shirley Chase.

DANTE GABRIEL ROSSETTI. 1828–1882

THE BLESSED DAMOZEL

The blessed damozel leaned out
　　From the gold bar of Heaven ;
Her eyes were deeper than the depth
　　Of waters stilled at even ;
She had three lilies in her hand,
　　And the stars in her hair were seven.

Her robe, ungirt from clasp to hem,
　　No wrought flowers did adorn,
But a white rose of Mary's gift
　　For service meetly worn ;
Her hair, that lay along her back,
　　Was yellow like ripe corn.

Her seemed she scarce had been a day
　　One of God's choristers ;
The wonder was not yet quite gone
　　From that still look of hers ;
Albeit, to them she left, her day
　　Had counted as ten years.

(To one it is ten years of years,
　　. . . Yet now, and in this place,
Surely she lean'd o'er me—her hair
　　Fell all about my face. . . .
Nothing : the autumn fall of leaves
　　The whole year sets apace.)

It was the rampart of God's house
  That she was standing on;
By God built over the sheer depth,
  The which is Space begun;
So high, that looking downward thence
  She scarce could see the sun.

It lies in Heaven, across the flood
  Of ether, as a bridge.
Beneath, the tides of day and night
  With flame of darkness ridge
The void, as low as where this earth
  Spins like a fretful midge.

Around her, lovers, newly met,
  'Mid deathless love's acclaims,
Spoke evermore among themselves
  Their heart-remembered names:
And the souls mounting up to God
  Went by her like thin flames.

And still she bowed herself and stooped
  Out of the circling charm;
Until her bosom must have made
  The bar she leaned on warm,
And the lilies lay as if asleep
  Along her bended arm.

From the fixed place of Heaven she saw
  Time like a pulse shake fierce
Through all the worlds.   Her gaze still strove
  Within the Gulf to pierce
Its path; and now she spoke, as when
  The stars sang in their spheres.

The sun was gone now; the curled moon
    Was like a little feather
Fluttering far down the Gulf; and now
    She spoke through the still weather.
Her voice was like the voice the stars
    Had when they sang together.

(Ah, sweet! even now, in that bird's song,
    Strove not her accents there,
Fain to be hearkened? When those bells
    Possessed the mid-day air,
Strove not her steps to reach my side
    Down all the echoing stair?)

" I wish that he were come to me,
    For he will come," she said;
" Have I not prayed in Heaven?—on earth,
    Lord, Lord, has he not prayed?
Are not two prayers a perfect strength?
    And shall I feel afraid?

" When round his head the aureole clings,
    And he is clothed in white,
I'll take his hand and go with him
    To the deep wells of light;
As unto a stream we will step down,
    And bathe there in God's sight.

" We two will stand beside that shrine,
    Occult, withheld, untrod,
Whose lamps are stirred continually
    With prayer sent up to God;
And see our old prayers, granted, melt
    Each like a little cloud.

" We two will lie i' the shadow of
  That living mystic tree,
Within whose secret growth the Dove
  Is sometimes felt to be,
While every leaf that His plumes touch
  Saith His Name audibly.

" And I myself will teach to him,
  I myself, lying so,
The songs I sing here; which his voice
  Shall pause in, hushed and slow,
And find some knowledge at each pause,
  Or some new thing to know."

(Alas! We two, we two, thou say'st!
  Yea, one wast thou with me
That once of old.   But shall God lift
  To endless unity
The soul whose likeness with thy soul
  Was but its love for thee?)

" We two," she said, " will seek the groves
  Where the Lady Mary is,
With her five handmaidens, whose names
  Are five sweet symphonies,
Cecily, Gertrude, Magdalen,
  Margaret, and Rosalys.

" Circlewise sit they, with bound locks
  And foreheads garlanded;
Into the fine cloth, white like flame,
  Weaving the golden thread,
To fashion the birth-robes for them
  Who are just born, being dead.

"He shall fear, haply, and be dumb;
　Then will I lay my cheek
To his, and tell about our love,
　Not once abashed or weak:
And the dear Mother will approve
　My pride, and let me speak.

"Herself shall bring us, hand in hand,
　To Him, round whom all souls
Kneel, the clear-ranged unnumbered heads
　Bowed with their aureoles:
And angels meeting us shall sing
　To their citherns and citoles.

"There will I ask of Christ the Lord
　Thus much for him and me:—
Only to live as once on earth
　With Love—only to be,
As then awhile, for ever now
　Together, I and he."

She gazed and listened and then said,
　Less sad of speech than mild,—
"All this is when he comes." She ceased.
　The light thrilled towards her, fill'd
With angels in strong level flight,
　Her eyes prayed, and she smil'd.

(I saw her smile.) But soon their path
　Was vague in distant spheres:
And then she cast her arms along
　The golden barriers,
And laid her face between her hands
　And wept. (I heard her tears.)

ELLEN MARY DOWNING (known as "MARY OF THE NATION"). 1828–1869

THE OLD CHURCH AT LISMORE

Old Church, thou still art Catholic !—e'en dream they
    as they may
That the new rites and worship have swept the old
    away ;
There is no form of beauty raised by Nature or by Art,
That preaches not God's saving truths to man's adoring
    heart !

In vain they tore the altar down ; in vain they flung
    aside
The mournful emblem of the death which our sweet
    Saviour died ;
In vain they left no single trace of saint or angel here—
Still Angel-spirits haunt the ground, and to the soul
    appear.

I marvel how, in scenes like these, so coldly they can
    pray,
Nor hold sweet commune with the dead who once knelt
    down as they ;
Yet not as they, in sad mistrust or sceptic doubt—
    for, oh,
They looked in hope to the blessed saints, these dead
    of long ago.

And then the churchyard, soft and calm, spread out
    beyond the scene,
With sunshine warm and soothing shade and trees upon
    the green ;

Ah! though their cruel Church forbid, are there no
    hearts will pray
For the poor souls that trembling left that cold and
    speechless clay?

My God! I am a Catholic! I grew into the ways
Of my dear Church since first my voice could lisp a
    word of praise;
But oft I think though my first youth were taught and
    trained awrong,
I still had learnt the one true faith from Nature and
    from Song!

For still, whenever dear friends die, it is such joy to
    know
They are not all beyond the care that healed their
    wounds below,
That we can pray them into peace, and speed them to
    the shore
Where clouds and cares and thorny griefs shall vex their
    hearts no more.

And the sweet saints, so meek below, so merciful above;
And the pure Angels, watching still with such untiring
    love;
And the kind Virgin, Queen of Heaven, with all her
    mother's care,
Who prays for earth, because She knows what breaking
    hearts are there!

Oh, let us lose no single link that our dear Church has
    bound
To keep our hearts more close to Heaven, on earth's
    ungenial ground;

But trust in Saint and Martyr yet, and o'er their hallowed
    clay,
Long after we have ceased to weep, kneel faithful down
    to pray.

So shall the land for us be still the Sainted Isle of old,
Where hymn and incense rise to Heaven, and holy beads
    are told;
And even the ground they tore from God, in years of
    crime and woe,
Instinctive with His truth and love, shall breathe of
    long ago!

CHRISTINA GEORGINA ROSSETTI. 1830–1894

UPHILL

Does the road wind uphill all the way?
    Yes, to the very end.
Will the day's journey take the whole long day?
    From morn to night, my friend.

But is there for the night a resting-place?
    A roof for when the slow, dark hours begin.
May not the darkness hide it from my face?
    You cannot miss that inn.

Shall I meet other wayfarers at night?
    Those who have gone before.
Then must I knock, or call when just in sight?
    They will not keep you waiting at that door.

Shall I find comfort, travel-sore and weak?
    Of labour you shall find the sum.
Will there be beds for me and all who seek?
    Yea, beds for all who come.

TOO LATE

Too late for love, too late for joy,
    Too late, too late!
You loitered on the road too long,
    You trifled at the gate.

The enchanted dove upon her branch
    Died without a mate;
The enchanted princess in her tower
    Slept, died, behind the grate;
Her heart was starving all this while
    You made it wait.

Ten years ago, five years ago,
    One year ago,
Even then you had arrived in time,
    Though somewhat slow;
Then you had known her living face
    Which now you cannot know;
The frozen fountain would have leaped,
    The buds gone on to blow,
The warm south wind would have awaked
    To melt the snow.

Is she fair now as she lies?
    Once she was fair;
Meet queen for any kingly king,
    With gold-dust on her hair.
Now there are poppies in her locks,
    White poppies she must wear;
Must wear a veil to shroud her face
    And the want graven there:
Or is the hunger fed at length,
    Cast off the care?

We never saw her with a smile
    Or with a frown;
Her bed seemed never soft to her,
    Though tossed of down;
She little heeded what she wore
    Kirtle or wreath or gown;

We think her white brows often ached
    Beneath her crown,
Till silvery hairs showed in her locks
    That used to be so brown.

We never heard her speak in haste :
    Her tones were sweet,
And modulated just so much
    As it was meet,
Her heart sat silent through the noise
    And concourse of the street ;
There was no hurry in her hands,
    No hurry in her feet ;
There was no bliss drew nigh to her,
    That she might run to greet.

You should have wept her yesterday,
    Wasting upon her bed :
But wherefore should you weep to-day
    That she is dead ?
Lo, we who love weep not to-day,
    But crown her royal head.
Let be these poppies that we strew,
    Your roses are too red :
Let be these poppies, not for you
    Cut down and spread.

JEAN INGELOW.   1830–1897

THE HIGH TIDE ON THE COAST OF
LINCOLNSHIRE

The Old Mayor climbed the belfry tower,
  The ringers rang by two, by three;
"Pull, if ye never pulled before;
  Good ringers, pull your best," quoth he.
"Play uppe, play uppe, O Boston bells!
Ply all your changes, all your swells,
  Play uppe 'The Brides of Enderby.'"

Men say it was a stolen tyde—
  The Lord that sent it, He knows all;
But in myne ears doth still abide
  The message that the bells let fall:
And there was nought of strange, beside
The flights of mews and peewits pied,
  By millions crouched on the old sea wall.

I sat and spun within the doore,
  My thread brake off, I raised myne eyes;
The level sun, like ruddy ore,
  Lay sinking in the barren skies;
And dark against day's golden death
She moved where Lindis wandereth,
  My sonne's faire wife, Elizabeth.

"Cusha! Cusha! Cusha!" calling,
For the dews will soone be falling;
"Leave your meadow grasses mellow,
    Mellow, mellow;
Quit your cowslips, cowslips yellow;

Come uppe Whitefoot, come uppe Lightfoot,
Quit the stalks of parsley hollow,
    Hollow, hollow ;
Come uppe Jetty, rise and follow,
From the clovers lift your head ;
Come uppe Whitefoot, come uppe Lightfoot,
Come up Jetty, rise and follow
Jetty to the milking shed ! "

If it be long, ay, long ago,
    When I beginne to think howe long,
Againe I hear the Lindis flow,
    Swift as an arrowe, sharpe and strong ;
And all the aire, it seemeth mee,
Bin full of floating bells (sayth shee)
That ring the tune of Enderby.

Alle fresh the level pasture lay,
    And not a shadowe mote be seene,
Save where full fyve good miles away
    The steeple tower'd from out the greene ;
And lo ! the great bell farre and wide
Was heard in all the country-side
That Saturday at eventide.

The swanherds where their sedges are
    Moved on in sunset's golden breath,
The shepherde lads I heard afarre,
    And my sonne's wife, Elizabeth ;
Till floating o'er the grassy sea
Came downe that kyndly message free,
The " Brides of Mavis Enderby."

Then some looked uppe into the sky,
    And all along where Lindis flows
To where the goodly vessels lie,
    And where the lordly steeple shows

They sayde, "And why should this thing be?
What danger lowers by land or sea?
They ring the tune of Enderby!

"For evil news from Mablethorpe,
    Of pyrate galleys warping down;
For shippes ashore beyonde the scorpe,
    They have not spared to wake the towne:
But while the west bin red to see,
And storms be none, and pyrates flee,
Why ring 'The Brides of Enderby'?"

I looked without, and lo! my sonne
    Came riding downe with might and main:
He raised a shout as he drew on,
    Till all the welkin rang again,
"Elizabeth! Elizabeth!"
(A sweeter woman ne'er drew breath
Than my sonne's wife, Elizabeth.)

"The olde sea wall (he cried) is downe,
    The rising tide comes on apace,
And boats adrift in yonder towne
    Go sailing uppe the market-place."
He shook as one that looks on death:
"God save you, mother!" straight he saith;
"Where is my wife, Elizabeth?"

"Good sonne, where Lindis winds away,
    With her two bairns I marked her long;
And ere yon bells beganne to play
    Afar I heard her milking song."
He looked across the grassy lea,
To right, to left, "Ho Enderby!"
They rang "The Brides of Enderby!"

With that he cried and beat his breast;
   For lo! along the river's bed
A mighty eygre reared his crest,
   And uppe the Lindis raging sped.
It swept with thunderous noises loud;
Shaped like a curling snow-white cloud,
Or like a demon in a shroud.

And rearing Lindis backward pressed
   Shook all her trembling bankes amaine;
Then madly at the eygre's breast
   Flung up her weltering walls again.
Then bankes came downe with ruin and rout—
Then beaten foam flew round about—
Then all the mighty floods were out.

So far, so fast the eygre drave,
   The heart had hardly time to beat,
Before a shallow seething wave
   Sobbed in the grasses at oure feet:
The feet had hardly time to flee
Before it brake against the knee,
And all the world was in the sea.

Upon the roofe we sat that night,
   The noise of bells went sweeping by;
I marked the lofty beacon light
   Stream from the church tower, red and high—
A lurid mark and dread to see;
And awesome bells they were to mee,
That in the dark rang "Enderby."

They rang the sailor lads to guide
   From roofe to roofe who fearless rowed;
And I—my sonne was at my side,
   And yet the ruddy beacon glowed;

And yet he moaned beneath his breath,
"O come in life, or come in death!
O lost! my love, Elizabeth."

And didst thou visit him no more?
　　Thou didst, thou didst, my daughter deare;
The waters laid thee at his doore,
　　Ere yet the early dawn was clear.
Thy pretty bairns in fast embrace,
The lifted sun shone on thy face,
Downe drifted to thy dwelling-place.

That flow strewed wrecks about the grass,
　　That ebbe swept out the flocks to sea;
A fatal ebbe and flow, alas!
　　To manye more than myne and mee:
But each will mourn his own (she saith),
And sweeter woman ne'er drew breath
Than my sonne's wife, Elizabeth.

I shall never hear her more,
By the reedy Lindis shore,
"Cusha! Cusha! Cusha!" calling
Ere the early dews be falling;
I shall never hear her song,
"Cusha! Cusha!" all along
Where the sunny Lindis floweth,
　　Goeth, floweth;
From the meads where melick groweth,
When the water winding down,
Onward floweth to the town.

I shall never see her more
Where the reeds and rushes quiver,
　　Shiver, quiver;
Stand beside the sobbing river,

Sobbing, throbbing in its falling
To the sandy lonesome shore;
I shall never hear her calling,
"Leave your meadow grasses mellow,
    Mellow, mellow;
Quit your cowslips, cowslips yellow;
Come uppe Whitefoot, come uppe Lightfoot;
Quit your pipes of parsley hollow,
    Hollow, hollow;
Come uppe Lightfoot, rise and follow;
    Lightfoot, Whitefoot,
From your clovers lift the head;
Come uppe Jetty, follow, follow,
Jetty to the milking shed."

THE FIRST EARL OF LYTTON. 1831–1892

FROM "THE WANDERER"

To-night she will dance at the Palace,
  With the diamonds in her hair;
And the Prince will praise her beauty—
  The loveliest lady there!

But tones, at times, in the music,
  Will bring back forgotten things;
And her heart will fail her sometimes,
  When her beauty is praised at the King's.

There sits in his silent chamber,
  A stern and sorrowful man;
But a strange, sweet dream comes to him,
  While the lamp is burning wan:

Of a sunset among the vineyards,
  In a lone and lovely land,
And a maiden standing near him,
  With fresh wild-flowers in her hand.

FROM "GOOD-NIGHT IN THE PORCH"

A little longer in the light, love, let me be.   The air is
  warm,
I hear the cuckoo's last good-night float from the copse
  below the farm;
A little longer, sister sweet—your hand in mine—on this
  old seat.

2 A

In yon red gable which the rose creeps round and o'er,
    your casement shines
Against the yellow west, o'er those forlorn and solitary
    pines;
The long, long day is nearly done.   How silent all the
    place is grown !

The stagnant levels, one and all, are burning in the
    distant marsh.
Hark ! 'twas the bittern's parting call.   The frogs are
    out, with murmurs harsh;
The low reeds vibrate.   See ! the sun catches the long
    pools one by one.

A moment, and those orange flats will turn dead grey
    or lurid white.
Look up o'erhead, the winnowing bats are come and
    gone, eluding sight;
The little worms are out.   The snails begin to move
    down shining trails,

With slow pink cones, and soft wet horns.   The garden
    bowers are dim with dew.
With sparkling drops the white-rose thorns are twinkling,
    where the sun slips through
Those reefs of coral buds hung free below the purple
    Judas-tree.

From the warm upland comes a gust made fragrant with
    the brown hay there.
The meek cows, with their white horns thrust above the
    hedge, stand still and stare ;
The steaming horses from the wains droop o'er the tank
    their plaited manes.

.   .   .   .

AUX ITALIENS

At Paris it was, at the Opera there ;—
    And she looked like a queen in a book that night,
With the wreath of pearl in her raven hair,
    And the brooch on her breast, so bright.

Of all the operas that Verdi wrote,
    The best, to my taste, is the "Trovatore";
And Mario can soothe with a tenor note
    The souls in Purgatory.

The moon on the tower slept soft as snow ;
    And who was not thrilled in the strangest way,
As we heard him sing, while the gas burn'd low,
    "*Non ti scordar di me*" ?

The Emperor there, in his box of state,
    Look'd grave, as if he had just then seen
The red flag wave from the city gate,
    Where his eagle in bronze had been.

The Empress, too, had a tear in her eye,
    You'd have said that her fancy had gone back again,
For one moment, under the old blue sky,
    To the old glad life in Spain.

Well ! there in our front-row box we sat,
    Together, my bride-betroth'd and I ;
My gaze was fix'd on my opera-hat,
    And hers on the stage hard by.

And both were silent, and both were sad ;
    Like a queen, she lean'd on her full white arm,
With that regal, indolent air she had ;
    So confident of her charm !

I have not a doubt she was thinking then
    Of her former lord, good soul that he was!
Who died the richest, and roundest of men,
    The Marquis of Carabas.

Meanwhile, I was thinking of my first love,
    As I had not been thinking of aught for years,
Till over my eyes there began to move
    Something that felt like tears.

I thought of the dress that she wore last time,
    When we stood, 'neath the cypress trees, together
In that lost land, in that soft clime,
    In the crimson evening weather:

Of that muslin dress (for the eve was hot),
    And her warm white neck in its golden chain,
And her full, soft hair, just tied in a knot,
    And falling loose again:

And the jasmin-flower in her fair young breast
    (Oh, the faint, sweet smell of that jasmin-flower),
And the one bird singing alone to his nest,
    And the one star over the tower.

I thought of our little quarrels and strife,
    And the letter that brought me back my ring;
And it all seem'd then, in the waste of life,
    Such a very little thing!

For I thought of her grave below the hill,
    Which the sentinel cypress tree stands over,
And I thought . . . "Were she only living still,
    How I could forgive her and love her!"

And, I swear, as I thought of her thus, in that hour,
    And of how, after all, old things were best,
That I smelt the smell of that jasmin-flower,
    Which she used to wear in her breast.

It smelt so faint, and it smelt so sweet,
  It made me creep, and it made me cold!
Like the scent that steals from the crumbling sheet
  Where a mummy is half unroll'd.

And I turn'd and look'd.   She was sitting there
  In a dim box, over the stage : and drest
In that muslin dress, with that full soft hair,
  And that jasmin in her breast!

I was here : and she was there :
  And the glittering horse-shoe curved between :—
From my bride-betroth'd, with her raven hair,
  And her sumptuous, scornful mien,

To my early love, with her eyes downcast,
  And over her primrose face the shade
(In short, from the Future back to the Past),
  There was but a step to be made

To my early love from my future bride
  One moment I look'd.   Then I stole to the door.
I traversed the passage ; and down at her side,
  I was sitting, a moment more.

My thinking of her, or the music's strain,
  Or something which never will be expressed,
Had brought her back from the grave again,
  With the jasmin in her breast.

She is not dead, and she is not wed!
  But she loves me now, and she loved me then!
And the very first word that her sweet lips said,
  My heart grew youthful again.

The Marchioness there, of Carabas,
  She is wealthy, and young, and handsome still,
And but for her . . . well, we'll let that pass,
  She may marry whomsoever she will.

But I will marry my own first love
   With her primrose face : for old things are best ;
And the flower in her bosom, I prize it above
   The brooch in my lady's breast.

The world is fill'd with folly and sin,
   And Love must cling where it can, I say :
For beauty is easy enough to win ;
   But one isn't loved every day.

And I think, in the lives of most women and men,
   There's a moment when all would go smooth and
      even,
If only the dead could find out when
   To come back and be forgiven.

But oh, the smell of that jasmin-flower !
   And oh, that music ! and oh, the way
That voice rang out from the donjon tower—
   " *Non ti scordar di me,*
      Non ti scordar di me ! "

LUCILE

(THE PARTING BEFORE SEBASTOPOL)

But she in response.   " Mark yon ship far away,
Asleep on the wave, in the last light of day,
With all its hushed thunders shut up ! Would you
   know
A thought which came to me a few days ago,
Whilst watching those ships ? . . . When the great Ship
   of Life,
Surviving, though shattered, the tumult and strife

Of earth's angry element—masts broken short,
Decks drench'd, bulwarks beaten—drives safe into port,
When the Pilot of Galilee, seen on the strand,
Stretches over the waters a welcoming hand;
When, heeding no longer the sea's baffled roar,
The mariner turns to his rest evermore.
What will then be the answer the helmsman must give?
Will it be, 'Lo, our log-book! Thus once did we live
In the zones of the South; thus we traversed the seas
Of the Orient; there dwelt with the Hesperides;
Thence follow'd the west wind; here, eastward we turn'd;
The stars failed us there; just here, land we discern'd
On our lee; there the storm overtook us at last;
That day went the bowsprit, the next day the mast;
There the mermen came round us, and there we saw bask
A siren.' The Captain of the Port, will he ask
Any one of such questions? I cannot think so!
But, 'What is the last Bill of Health you can show?'
Not 'How fared the soul through the trials she passed?'
But 'What is the state of that soul at the last?'"
"May it be so!" he sighed. "There, the sun drops,
        behold!"
And, indeed, whilst he spoke, all the purple and gold
In the West had turned ashen, save one fading strip
Of light that yet gleam'd from the dark nether lip
Of a long reef of clouds; and o'er sullen ravines
And ridges the raw damps were hanging white screens
Of melancholy mist.
                    "Nunc dimittis!" she said.
"O God of the living, whilst yet 'mid the dead
And the dying we stand here alive, and thy days
Returning, admit space for prayer and for praise.
In both these confirm us.
                    The helmsman, Eugène,
Needs the compass to steer by. Pray always. Again

We two part: each to work out Heaven's will: you, I trust,
In the world's ample witness; and I, as I must,
In secret and silence: you, love, fame await;
Me, sorrow and sickness. We meet at one gate
When all's over. The ways they are many and wide,
And seldom are two ways the same. Side by side
May we stand at the same little door when all's done!
The ways they are many, the end it is one.
He that knocketh shall enter; who asks shall obtain:
And who seeketh, he findeth. Remember, Eugène!"

C. S. CALVERLEY. 1831–1884

SHELTER

By the still lake margin I saw her lie,
The deep dark lake where the rushes sigh,
A fair young thing with a shy soft eye ;
And I deemed that her thoughts had flown
To her father and mother and sisters dear,
As she lay there watching the deep dark mere,
All motionless, all alone.
Then I heard a noise as of men and boys,
And a boisterous troop drew near.
Whither now shall escape those fairy feet ?
Where hide till the storm pass by ?
One glance—the wild glance of a hunted thing
She cast behind her, she gave one spring,
And I heard a splash and a widening ring
On the lake where the rushes sigh.
She has gone from the ken of ungentle men,
But scarce did I grieve for that,
For I knew she was safe in her own home, then,
And the danger o'er would appear again,
For she was a water rat.

A. LINDSAY GORDON. 1833–1870

FROM "THE SICK STOCKRIDER"

I've had my share of pastime, and I've done my share of
    toil,
  And life is short—the longest life a span ;
I care not now to tarry for the corn or for the oil,
  Or the wine that maketh glad the heart of man.
For good undone, and gifts misspent, and resolutions vain
  'Tis somewhat late to trouble.   This I know—
I should live the same life over, if I had to live again ;
  And the chances are I go where most men go.

HON. RODEN NOEL. 1834–1894

BYRON'S GRAVE

Nay ! Byron, nay ! not under where we tread,
Dumb weight of stone, lies thine imperial head !
Into no vault lethargic, dark and dank,
The splendid strength of thy swift spirit sank :
No narrow church in precincts cold and grey
Confines the plume, that loved to breast the day :
Thy self-consuming, scathing heart of flame
Was quenched to feed no silent coffin's shame !
A fierce, glad fire in buoyant hearts art thou,
A radiance in auroral spirits now ;
A stormy wind, an ever-sounding ocean,
A life, a power, a never-wearying motion !
Or deadly gloom, or terrible despair,
An earthquake mockery of strong Creeds that were
Assured possessions of calm earth and sky,
Where doom-distraught pale souls took sanctuary,
As in strong temples.   The same blocks shall build,
Iconoclast ! the edifice you spilled,
More durable, more fair : O scourge of God,
It was Himself who urged thee on thy road ;
And thou, Don Juan, Harold, Manfred, Cain,
Song-crowned within the world's young heart shall reign !
Where'er we hear embroiled lashed ocean roar,
Or thunder echoing among heights all hoar,
Brother ! thy mighty measure heightens theirs,
While Freedom on her rent red banner bears
The deathless names of many a victory won,
Inspired by thy death-shattering clarion !
In Love's immortal firmament are set
Twin stars of Romeo and Juliet,

And their companions young eyes discover
In Cycladean Haidee with her lover.
    May all the devastating force be spent?
Or all thy godlike energies lie shent?
Nay! thou art founded in the strength Divine;
The soul's immense eternity is thine!
Profound Beneficence absorbs thy power,
While ages tend the long-maturing flower:
Our Sun himself, one tempest of wild flame,
For source of joy, and very life men claim
In mellowing corn, in bird, and bloom of spring,
In leaping lambs, and lovers dallying.
Byron! the whirlwinds rended not in vain;
Aloof behold they nourish and sustain!
In the far end we shall account them gain.

JAMES THOMSON. 1834–1882

E. B. B. 1861

The white-rose garland at her feet,
  The crown of laurel at her head,
The noble life on earth complete,
  Lay her in the last low bed
For the slumber calm and deep:
"He giveth His beloved sleep."

Soldiers find their fittest grave
  In the field whereon they died;
So her spirit pure and brave
  Leaves the clay it glorified
To the land for which she fought
With such grand impassioned thought.

Keats and Shelley sleep at Rome,
  She in well-loved Tuscan earth;
Finding all their death's long home
  Far from their old home of birth.
Italy, you hold in trust
Very sacred English dust.

Therefore this one prayer I breathe,—
  That you yet may worthy prove
Of the heirlooms they bequeath
  Who have loved you with such love:
Fairest land while land of slaves
Yields their free souls no fit graves.

WILLIAM MORRIS.   1834–1899

THE EVE OF CREÇY

Gold on her head, and gold on her feet,
And gold where the hems of her kirtle meet,
And a golden girdle round my sweet ;—
   Ah ! quelle est belle La Marguerite.

Margaret's maids are fair to see,[1]
Freshly dress'd and pleasantly ;
Margaret's hair falls down to her knee ;—
   Ah ! quelle est belle La Marguerite.

If I were rich I would kiss her feet,
I would kiss the place where the gold hems meet,
And the golden girdle round my sweet—
   Ah ! quelle est belle La Marguerite.

Ah me ! I have never touch'd her hand ;
When the arrière-ban goes through the land
Six basnets under my pennon stand ;—
   Ah ! quelle est belle La Marguerite.

And many an one grins under his hood :
"Sir Lambert de Bois, with all his men good,
Has neither food nor firewood ; "—
   Ah ! quelle est belle La Marguerite.

If I were rich I would kiss her feet,
And the golden girdle of my sweet,
And thereabouts where the gold hems meet ;
   Ah ! quelle est belle La Marguerite.

Yet even now it is good to think,
While my few poor varlets grumble and drink
In my desolate hall where the fires sink,—
    Ah! quelle est belle La Marguerite.

Of Margaret sitting glorious there,
In glory of gold and glory of hair,
And glory of glorious face most fair;—
    Ah! quelle est belle La Marguerite.

Likewise to-night I make good cheer,
Because this battle draweth near:
For what have I to lose or fear?—
    Ah! quelle est belle La Marguerite.

For, look you, my horse is good to prance
A right fair measure in this war-dance,
Before the eyes of Philip of France;—
    Ah! quelle est belle La Marguerite.

And sometime it may hap, perdie,
While my new towers stand up three and three,
And my hall gets painted fair to see—
    Ah! quelle est belle La Marguerite.

That folks may say: "Times change by the rood,
For Lambert, banneret of the wood,
Has heaps of food and firewood;—
    Ah! quelle est belle La Marguerite.

"And wonderful eyes, too, under the hood
Of a damsel of right noble blood:"
St. Ives, for Lambert of the wood!—
    Ah! quelle est belle La Marguerite.

THE EARTHLY PARADISE

Of Heaven or Hell I have no power to sing,
I cannot ease the burden of your fears,
Or make quick-coming death a little thing,
Or bring again the pleasure of past years,
Nor for my words shall ye forget your tears,
Or hope again for aught that I can say,
The idle singer of an empty day.

But rather, when aweary of your mirth,
From full hearts still unsatisfied ye sigh,
And, feeling kindly unto all the earth,
Grudge every minute as it passes by,
Made the more mindful that the sweet days die—
—Remember me a little then, I pray,
The idle singer of an empty day.

The heavy trouble, the bewildering care
That weighs us down who live and earn our bread,
These idle verses have no power to bear;
So let me sing of names remembered,
Because they, living not, can ne'er be dead,
Or long time take their memory quite away
From us poor singers of an empty day.

Dreamer of dreams, born out of my due time,
Why should I strive to set the crooked straight?
Let it suffice me that my murmuring rhyme
Beats with light wing against the ivory gate,
Telling a tale not too importunate
To those who in the sleepy region stay,
Lulled by the singer of an empty day.

Folk say, a wizard to a northern king
At Christmas-tide such wondrous things did show,
That through one window men beheld the spring,
And through another saw the summer glow,
And through a third the fruited vines a-row;
While still, unheard, but in its wonted way,
Piped the drear wind of that December day.

So with this Earthly Paradise it is,
If ye will read aright and pardon me,
Who strive to build a shadowy isle of bliss
Midmost the beating of the steely sea,
Where tossed about all hearts of men must be;
Whose ravening monsters mighty men shall slay,
Not the poor singer of an empty day.

RIDING TOGETHER

For many, many days together
  The wind blew steady from the East;
For many days hot grew the weather,
  About the time of our Lady's feast.

For many days we rode together,
  Yet met we neither friend nor foe;
Hotter and clearer grew the weather,
  Steadily did the East wind blow.

We saw the trees in the hot, bright weather,
  Clear-cut with shadows very black,
As freely we rode on together
  With helms unlaced and bridles slack.

And often as we rode together,
   We, looking down the green-bank'd stream,
Saw flowers in the sunny weather,
   And saw the bubble-making bream.

And in the night lay down together,
   And hung above our heads the rood,
Or watch'd night-long in the dewy weather,
   The while the moon did watch the wood.

Our spears stood bright and thick together,
   Straight out the banners stream'd behind,
As we gallop'd on in the sunny weather,
   With faces turn'd towards the wind.

Down sank our threescore spears together,
   As thick we saw the pagans ride ;
His eager face in the clear fresh weather,
   Shone out that last time by my side.

Up the sweep of the bridge we dash'd together,
   It rock'd to the crash of the meeting spears,
Down rain'd the buds of the dear spring weather,
   The elm-tree flowers fell like tears.

There, as we roll'd and writhed together,
   I threw my arms above my head,
For close by my side, in the lovely weather,
   I saw him reel and fall back dead.

I and the slayer met together,
   He waited the death-stroke there in his place
With thoughts of death in the lovely weather,
   Gaspingly 'mazed at my madden'd face.

Madly I fought as we fought together ;
  In vain : the little Christian band
The pagans drown'd, as in stormy weather,
  The river drowns low-lying land.

They bound my blood-stain'd hands together,
  They bound his corpse to nod by my side :
Then on we rode, in the bright March weather,
  With clash of cymbals did we ride.

We ride no more, no more together ;
  My prison-bars are thick and strong,
I take no heed of any weather,
  The sweet Saints grant I live not long.

LORD DE TABLEY. 1835–1895

AT THE COUNCIL

I stood to-day in that great square of fountains,
    And heard the cannon of St. Angelo,
In many echoes towards the Alban mountains
    Boom over Tiber's flow.

I saw the nations throng thy burnished spaces,
    Cathedral of the Universe and Rome ;
One purpose held those earnest upturned faces
    Under the golden dome.

Tumult of light rolled on that human ocean ;
    Climax of sound replied in organ-storms,
And shook those altar Titans into motion
    Bernini's windy forms.

They seemed to toss their giant arms appealing
    Where Angelo with mighty hand has striven
To paint his angels on an earthly ceiling,
    Grander than those of heaven.

Mid-air among the columns seemed to hover
    Incense in clouds above the living tide.
Whence are these come who tread thy courts, Jehovah,
    In raiment deep and dyed ?

We are gathered thine elect among all races ;
    As at God's birth the Magian kings, afar
Thy whisper found us in our desert places,
    Where we beheld thy star.

Ninth Piety of Rome, with whom the Keys are,
    Regent to hold God's house, to feed His flock
Where Cæsar ruled ; and thou, supplanting Cæsar,
    Art firm on Peter's rock.

Nicæa's thunders yet are fresh as morning,
    Beams in whose light the Church has gone and goes ;
To-day Nicæa peals in Rome her warning,
    Pontiff, to curse thy foes.

We come, Armenia, Gaul, Missouri, Britain ;
    The chosen of the chosen priests are there :
To all men hath gone out his mandate written
    Who fills St. Peter's chair.

Grey heads have waves Atlantic wafted scathless,
    Weak feet have toiled o'er Libyan hills in fear ;
Old Bishops from the regions of the faithless
    Have crept on crutches here.

To far Canadian meres of ice-bound silence,
    To cities lost in continents of sand,
To shoaling belts around Pacific islands,
    The Pontiff raised his hand.

Then with one mind they came, the Bishop leaders,
    The outpost Captains of the Church at fight,
From uplands clothed with Lebanonian cedars,
    From realms of Arctic night.

Lo ! we are ready at thy summons, father ;
    Loose and we loosen, bind and we shall bind :
The conclave princes at thy blast shall gather,
    As red leaves after wind.

Thunder the doctrine of this last evangel;
　　Clear as the note of doom its accents sound!
While men regard thine aspect as an angel
　　In the sun's orb and crowned!

At thy reproof let nations quail in terror,
　　And tremble at the pealing of thy word;
For God hath made thy mouth His own, and error
　　In thy voice is not heard.

Let all be doomed on whom thy curses thunder;
　　Let none be righteous whom thou dost withstand;
The priesthood of a word, we kneel in wonder,
　　And kiss thy sacred hand.

Hear, shade of Calvin, ghost of Luther, hearken!
　　Ye renegades of Northern yesterday;
Infidel bones, which years of silence darken,
　　Turn and salute one ray!

Leave vain philosophies, old dreamer Teuton,
　　Great drowsy fly in webs of logic weak;
We silenced Galileo, menaced Newton,
　　And Darwin shall not speak.

Behold a sign, ye sceptic sons of evil!
　　The dogma; raising which, as Michael brave,
Our Pope confront their scientific devil
　　Over each unclosed grave;

Till Death and Doubt be thy tame sheep, O pastor,
　　Pontiff of souls and Vicar of God's choice—
Infallible, in whom the spirit-master
　　Hath breathed his spirit voice.

"Explain our faith ! all faithful hear thy mandate ;
  Emperors watch in dread our world debate ;
Thy fear is on all peoples ! " (but the bandit
  Who plunders at thy gate).

NUPTIAL SONG

Sigh, heart, and break not ; rest, lark, and wake not !
  Day I hear coming to draw my love away,
As mere-waves whisper and clouds grow crisper,
  Ah, like a rose he will waken up with day.

In moonlight lonely he is my love only,
  I share with none when Luna rides in grey.
As dawn-beams quicken, my rivals thicken
  The light and deed and turmoil of the day.

To watch my sleeper to me is sweeter
  Than any waking words my love can say ;
In dream he finds me and closer winds me !
  Let him rest by me a little more and stay.

Ah, mine eyes, close not ; and though he knows not,
  My lips, on his be tender while you may ;
Ere leaves are shaken, and ring-doves waken,
  And infant buds begin to scent new day.

Fair darkness measure thine hours, as treasure
  Shed each one slowly from thine urn, I pray ;
Hoard in and cover each from my lover ;
  I cannot lose him yet ; dear night, delay.

Each moment dearer, true-love lie nearer;
　My hair shall blind thee lest thou see the ray;
My locks encumber thine ears in slumber,
　Lest any bird dare give thee note of day.

He rests so calmly; we lie so warmly;
　Hand within hand, as children after play;
In shafted amber on roof and chamber
　Dawn enters; my love wakens; here is day.

A HYMN TO APHRODITE

Uranian Aphrodite, fair
　From ripples of the ocean spray:
Sweet as the sea-blooms in thy hair,
　Rosed with the blush of early day,
O hear us from thy temple steep,
Where Eryx crowns the Dorian deep.

Unfold the rapture of thy face,
　No more thy lustrous eyes conceal;
But from the rivers of thy grace
　The rich abundant joys reveal.
Give us the treasures of thy rest;
Take us as children to thy breast.

Desired of all the ages long,
　As Morning young, as old as Fate;
The kneeling world with choral song
　Has crowded round thy altar gate.
Thine are the seasons past and dumb,
And thine the unborn years to come.

We are not worthy to endure
   The fervour of thy burning eyes,
Thy perfect lips, thy bosom pure,
   Thy radiant aspect, sweetly wise.
Breathe balm upon our span of breath,
For thou art almost Queen of death.

To thee, enwreathed with passion flowers,
   Our unreluctant prayers are given :
Thou art so near, when other powers
   Seem worlds away in frigid heaven :
They know not, for they live apart,
The craving tumult of the heart.

Thy altar needs no victim slain ;
   It reeks not with the bleeding steer ;
Thy kingdom is no realm of pain,
   Thy worship is no creature's fear.
Yet art thou trebly more divine,
Needing no hecatombs of kine.

The empires wane, the empires grow ;
   They prosper or they are dismayed :
Time lays their wrangling voices low ;
   The victors and the vanquished fade.
The foam-wreath on the crested spray
Lasts but an instant less than they.

But thou abidest, in thy might
   Eternal, and a rainbow beam
Is round thy head ; and clusters bright
   Of orbs among thy tresses gleam :
Clothed in the garment of the sun,
Sweet as the star of day begun.

Parent of Nature, lovely Queen,
    Awake the frozen land's repose,
Until the perfumed buds are seen
    With promise of the myriad rose.
Descend, and on thy halcyon wing
Unlock the fountains of the Spring.

MISREPRESENTATION

Peace! there is nothing more for men to speak;
    A larger wisdom than our lips decrees.
Of that dumb mouth no longer reason seek,
    No censure reaches that eternal peace,
        And that immortal ease.

Believe them not that would disturb the end
    With earth's invidious comment, idly meant.
Speak and have done thy evil; for my friend
    Is gone beyond all human discontent,
        And wisely went.

Say what you will, and have your sneer and go,
    You see the specks, we only heed the fruit
Of a great life, whose truth—men hate truth so—
    No lukewarm age of compromise could suit.
        Laugh and be mute.

CHARLES, LORD BOWEN. 1835–1894

GOOD-NIGHT, GOOD-MORNING

The Sun, a shining orb, descends
   Behind the mountain wold ;
Gloom gathers fast, the daylight ends ;
   Sheep journey to the fold.
Peace and farewell, ye torrent rills—
   Good-night to earth and sky ;
So homeward from the silent hills
   We went, my love and I.
Come, sweet night.   Day, take thy flight :
My love will make the darkness light.

Rest to the earth—the weary earth—
   Sweet rest : till far away
Upon the hills we saw the birth
   And triumph of the day.
Again the mighty sun arose,
   And on each mountain lawn
Began the million golden glows
   That usher in the dawn.
Go, dear night.   Come, purple light ;
Rise, love, and make the morning bright.

At noon I found these violets blue
   Where early morning lies,
And brought them fresh with light and dew—
   Not purer than her eyes.
To her who was my morning flower,
   As is my flower of noon,
Soon comes a duskier twilight hour,
   And night will follow soon.
Sweet face, stay : life ebbs away ;
Be thou thy lover's evening ray.

AUGUSTA WEBSTER. 1837–1894

THE BROOK RHINE

Small current of the wilds afar from men,
    Changing and sudden as a baby's mood;
    Now a green babbling rivulet in the wood,
Now loitering broad and shallow through the glen,
Or threading 'mid the naked shoals, and then
    Brattling against the stones, half mist, half flood,
    Between the mountains where the storm-clouds
        brood,
And each change but to wake or sleep again.

Pass on, young stream, the world has need of thee;
    Far hence a mighty river on its breast
Bears the deep-laden vessels to the sea;
Far hence wide waters feed the vines and corn.
Pass on, small stream, to so great purpose born,
    On to the distant toil, the distant rest.

FREDERICK MYERS. 1843–1900

SAINT PAUL

Hark ! what a sound, and too divine for-hearing
   Stirs on the earth, and trembles in the air !
Is it the thunder of the Lord's appearing ?
   Is it the music of His people's prayer ?

Surely He cometh, and a thousand voices
   Shout to the saints, and to the deaf are dumb ;
Surely He cometh, and the earth rejoices,
   Glad in His coming who hath sworn, I come.

This hath He done, and shall we not adore Him ?
   This shall He do, and can we still despair ?
Come, let us quickly fling ourselves before Him,
   Cast at His feet the burthen of our care.

Yea thro' life, death, thro' sorrow and thro' sinning,
   He shall suffice me, for He hath sufficed :
Christ is the end, for Christ was the beginning,
   Christ the beginning, for the end is Christ.

JOHN ADDINGTON SYMONDS.   1840–1893

THE JEWS' CEMETERY ON THE LIDO

A tract of land swept by the salt sea-foam,
   Fringed with acacia flowers and billowy deep,
   In meadow-grasses, where tall poppies sleep,
And bees athirst for wilding honey roam.
How many a bleeding heart hath found its home,
   Under these hillocks which the sea-mews sweep!
   Here knelt an outcast race to curse and weep,
Age after age, 'neath heaven's unanswering dome.

Sad is the place and solemn.   Grave by grave,
   Lost in the dunes, with rank weeds overgrown,
   Pines in abandonment; as though unknown,
Uncared for, lay the dead, whose records pave
   This path neglected; each forgotten stone
Wept by no mourner but the moaning wave.

EDWARD BOWEN. 1837–1901

FORTY YEARS ON

Forty years on, when afar and asunder
   Parted are those who are singing to-day,
When you look back, and forgetfully wonder
   What you were like in your work and your play ;
Then it may be, there will often come o'er you
   Glimpses of notes like the catch of a song—
Visions of boyhood shall float them before you,
   Echoes of dreamland shall bear them along.
    Follow up ! Follow up ! Follow up ! Follow up !
     Till the field ring again and again,
      With the tramp of the twenty-two men,
       Follow up ! Follow up !

Routs and discomfitures, rushes and rallies,
   Bases attempted, and rescued, and won,
Strife without anger, and art without malice,—
   How will it seem to you forty years on ?
Then, you will say, not a feverish minute
   Strained the weak heart, and the wavering knee,
Never the battle raged hottest, but in it
   Neither the last nor the faintest were we !
       Follow up ! Follow up !

O the great days, in the distance enchanted,
   Days of fresh air, in the rain and the sun,
How we rejoiced as we struggled and panted—
   Hardly believable, forty years on !
How we discoursed of them, one with another,
   Auguring triumph, or balancing fate,
Loved the ally with the heart of a brother,
   Hated the foe with a playing at hate !
       Follow up ! Follow up !

Forty years on, growing older and older,
   Shorter in wind, and in memory long,
Feeble of foot and rheumatic of shoulder,
   What will it help you that once you were strong ?
God give us bases to guard or beleaguer,
   Games to play out, whether earnest or fun,
Fights for the fearless, and goals for the eager,
   Twenty, and thirty, and forty years on !
       Follow up ! Follow up !

SHEMUEL

Shemuel, the Bethlehemite,
Watched a fevered guest at night
All his fellows fared afield
Saw the angel host revealed ;
He nor caught the mystic story,
Heard the song, nor saw the glory.

Through the night they gazing stood,
Heard the holy multitude ;
Back they came in wonder home,
Knew the Christmas kingdom come,
Eyes aflame, and hearts elated ;
Shemuel sat alone, and waited.

Works of mercy now, as then,
Hide the angel host from men ;
Hearts attune to earthly love
Miss the angel notes above ;
Deeds at which the world rejoices,
Quench the sound of angel voices.

So they thought, nor deemed from whence
His celestial recompense.
Shemuel, by the fever bed,
Touched by beckoning hands that led,
Died, and saw the Uncreated ;
All his fellows lived, and waited.

COSMO MONKHOUSE.   1840–1901

THE NIGHT EXPRESS

With three great snorts of strength,
Stretching my mighty length,
Like some long dragon stirring in his sleep,
Out from the glare of gas
Into the night I pass,
And plunge alone into the silence deep.

Little I know or care
What be the load I bear,
Why thus compell'd, I seek not to divine;
At man's command I stir,
I, his stern messenger!
Does he his duty well as I do mine?

Straight on my silent road,
Flank'd by no man's abode,
No foe I parley with, no friend I greet;
On like a bolt I fly
Under the starry sky,
Scorning the current of the sluggish street.

Onward from South to North,
Onward from Thames to Forth,
On—like a comet—on, unceasingly,
Faster and faster yet.
On—where far boughs of jet
Stretch their wild woof against the pearly sky.

Faster and faster still—
Dive I through rock and hill,
Starting the echoes with my shrill alarms;
Swiftly I curve and bend;
While, like an eager friend,
The distance runs to clasp me in its arms.

Ne'er from my path I swerve
Rattling around a curve
Not vainly trusting to my trusty bars;
On through the hollow night,
While, or to left or right,
A city glistens like a clump of stars.

On through the night I steer;
Never a sound I hear
Save the strong beating of my steady stroke—
Save when the circling owl
Hoots, or the screaming fowl
Rise from the marshes like a sudden smoke.

Now o'er a gulf I go:
Dark in the depth below
Smites the slant beam the shoulder of the height—
Now through a lane of trees—
Past sleeping villages,
Their white walls whiter in the silver light.

Be the night foul or fair,
Little I reck or care,
Bandy with storms, and with the tempests jest;
Little I care or know
What winds may rage or blow,
But charge the whirlwind with a dauntless breast.

Now, through the level plain,
While, like a mighty main,
Stretches my endless breath in cloudy miles ;
Now, o'er a dull lagoon,
While the broad-beamed moon
Lights up its sadness into sickly smiles.

Oh, 'tis a race sublime !
I, neck and neck with Time,—
I, with my thews of iron and heart of fire,
Run without pause for breath ;
While all the earth beneath
Shakes with the shocks of my tremendous ire.

On—till the race be won ;
On—till the coming sun
Blinds moon and stars with his excessive light ;
On—till the earth be green
And the first lark be seen
Shaking away with songs the dews of night.

Sudden my speed I slack—
Sudden all force I lack—
Without a struggle yield I up my breath ;
Numb'd are my thews of steel,
Wearily rolls each wheel,
My heart cools slowly to the sleep of death.

Why for so brief a length
Dower'd with such mighty strength ?
Man is my God—I seek not to divine :
At his command I stir,
I, his stern messenger ;—
Does he his duty well as I do mine ?

R. L. STEVENSON. 1850–1894

A REQUIEM

Under the wide and starry sky
Dig the grave and let me lie :
Glad did I live and gladly die,
    And I laid me down with a will.
This be the verse you 'grave for me :
" Here he is where he long'd to be ;
Home is the sailor, home from sea,
    And the hunter home from the hill."

JAMES KENNETH STEPHEN. 1859–1892

ELEGY ON DE MARSAY

Come cats and kittens everywhere,
　Whate'er of cat the world contains,
From tabby on the kitchen stair
To tiger burning in his lair,
　Unite your melancholy strains.

Weep, likewise, kindred dogs, and weep
　Domestic fowls, and pigs, and goats ;
Weep horses, oxen, poultry, sheep,
Weep finny monsters of the deep,
　Weep foxes, weasels, badgers, stoats.

Weep more than all, exalted man,
　And hardly less exalted maid ;
Outweep creation if you can,
Which never yet, since time began,
　Such creditable grief displayed.

It little profiteth that we
　Go proudly up and down the land,
And drive our ships across the sea,
And babble of Eternity,
　And hold the Universe in hand,

If, when our pride is at its height,
　And glory sits upon our head,
A sudden mist can dim the light,
A voice be heard in pride's despite,
　A voice which cries, " De Marsay's dead."

De Marsay dead ! and never more
　Shall I behold that silky form
Lie curled upon the conscious floor
With sinuous limbs and placid snore,
　As one who sleeps through calm and storm ?

De Marsay dead ! De Marsay dead !
　And are you dead, De Marsay, you ?
The sun is shining overhead
With glory undiminishèd,
　And you are dead ; let me die too !

Then birds and beasts and fishes come,
　And people come, of all degrees ;
Beat, sadly beat the funeral drum,
And let the gloomy organ hum
　With dark mysterious melodies.

And (when we have adequately moaned)
　For all the world to wonder at,
Let this great sentence be intoned :
No cat so sweet a mistress owned ;
　No mistress owned so sweet a cat.

PART III

PART II

INTRODUCTORY NOTES

The third part of this selection, which includes only authors who are still alive, and many of whom have, I hope, long years of good work still before them, cannot be biographical, and must be of the briefest. A word or two to attract notice to each name in the text is all that would be appropriate.

In the older generation, the name of Sir FRANKLIN LUSHINGTON *is very conspicuous, and with him I have coupled his brother* HENRY, *although he died early, for they published their poems in the same volume, and it is impossible to think of them apart. It is the fashion now to say that the Crimean War was " a mistake from beginning to end," but few, I imagine, who lived at that time, and remember the attitude assumed in Europe by the Emperor Nicholas from* 1848 *onwards, will quite take that view. Those who do, however, and those who do not, will, I trust, acknowledge the extraordinary merit of the pieces by the Lushingtons which I have extracted. If there are finer patriotic poems in our literature, I do not know where to find them.*

Sir EDWIN ARNOLD, *so successful as an interpreter between the East and the West, has influenced his generation in many ways, but most as a poet.* Sir Lewis Morris *will be long remembered, not only by his works, but by the admiration which they excited in the mind of Mr. Bright, the greatest orator of his country in the reign of Queen Victoria.*

Mr. Pember *is best known to the world as one of the leaders of the Parliamentary Bar, and to his friends as one of the best talkers in London; but he has printed for private circulation a number of volumes of poetry, all full of striking things, but in which, to my thinking, the lines I quote are perhaps the most beautiful.*

Mr. Austin Dobson *has long ago won for himself an unique position.* *In some ways he resembles Praed, but it may be well doubted whether, even if Praed had lived much longer, he would have done anything as a poet better than what he did, and he remains a very long way behind his pupil.*

Dr. Richard Garnett, *famous for his services to the public at the British Museum, and for his vast erudition, is also a poet of no mean order, as the poem I have selected will show.*

Dr. Alexander, *Archbishop of Armagh and Primate of all Ireland, won a high place as a poet by a single effort—his poem on the University of Oxford and the death of the Duke of Wellington, delivered at the installation of the Earl of Derby as Chancellor in* 1853. *The late Lord De Tabley, who listened to it as an undergraduate, described to me the curious silence with which the first part of it was heard, which passed gradually, from the verse about Rupert's cavaliers I have quoted below, into wild enthusiasm. Dr. Alexander has published much that is excellent since this, witness the two beautiful epitaphs I have quoted, but somehow he seems always to receive an additional afflatus when he approaches his old university. The lines written in 1885 about the Oxford of 1845, mirror it to perfection.*

Father RYDER of the Birmingham Oratory is the author of the little but very perfect poem which some, I fancy, will copy into their photographic albums.

Mr. EDMUND GOSSE is well known not only by his poems, but also as an author of widely popular works on literature and criticism. I have chosen his " Charcoal-burner " because I particularly like the subject, but there is a great deal more among his poems which is quite as good.

Mr. JOHNSTONE, a master in the Edinburgh Academy, is the author of the short piece I have placed next to it as being similar in tone, and of much else which he has brought together in a privately printed book called " Echoes and Afterthoughts," full of grace and charm.

Mr. WADDINGTON, who, like Mr. Gosse and Mr. Dobson, has spent many years in the Board of Trade, has written many poems in various styles, but has given perhaps most attention to the sonnet. I have quoted one on " Beatrice."

Mr. LECKY *had done enough and more than enough for his own and future generations by his admirable contributions to history and philosophy; but the poem, which he has kindly allowed me to print, seems also, in its own way, altogether excellent.*

Mr. GEORGE MEREDITH, *the favourite novelist of a section of our contemporaries, has also a considerable following of admirers who delight in his poetry, of which I give a brief but characteristic specimen.*

Mr. AUBREY DE VERE *has led the ideal poetical life longer and more consistently than any man of our times, and all his work, even when it lacks the qualities which commend verse to most readers, has a certain* cachet *of elevation not always attained by poets who are more widely read. We all regret deeply that his first volume of "Reminiscences" was not followed by another which promised to be even more interesting.*

The name of Sir FREDERICK POLLOCK *is familiar to many as that of a great jurist and a man of profound learning, but to comparatively few as that of a poet.*

Mr. CHARLES KEGAN PAUL, *once widely welcomed in Oxford, London, and many other places, has been prevented by bad health, of late years, from appearing in his old haunts, but he retains the power which in a long past time enabled him to produce the fascinating little poem I have cited under his name.*

Mr. HERMAN MERIVALE *is the son of a father, who, first at the Colonial and then at the India Office, had an immense influence in the government of the Empire. Possessing the strongest powers of mind and vast knowledge, he had the disadvantages as well as the advantages of a member of the Civil Service; but no one was more highly thought of by those who came across him either as superiors or as colleagues. He was the Permanent while I was the Political Under-Secretary of State for India during five years, so that I had ample opportunities of knowing his real worth and importance. I have been permitted to publish two poems by his son, in different styles, but both of which appear to me to be worthy of his descent from a family which for several generations has been distinguished in letters. The first piece cited belongs to a very high class indeed.*

Mr. COURTHOPE, *who till recently was Professor of Poetry at Oxford, is best known as a critic and as the erudite and judicious historian of the art in which he excels. The piece which I have chosen is the account in Spenserian language of Canon Swayne of Salisbury and the unique garden which he formed at that place. It is supposed to be a fragment of the Elizabethan poet's third canto of Mutability.*

Passing over two striking poems which are anonymous, I come to the very beautiful lines, not half enough known, entitled "In the Jacquerie," by Mr. SIMCOX.

Sir ALFRED LYALL *has taken a most important part in the government of India. While resident in that country, he filled among other great offices those of Foreign Secretary and Lieutenant-Governor of the North-West, and since his return home he has been for many years a Member of the Council of the Secretary of State. That a man who has had such a career should also have published under the modest title of* "Verses written in India," *some poems which are in their kind simply unequalled, and should have put himself thereby at the head of all the writers of the two great Indian services through three hundred years, is a wonderful achievement.*

The very graceful poem by Mrs. EARL, *on the death of Mrs. Holland, was originally published in the collection of her letters which appeared under the editorship of her son, Mr. Bernard Holland, one of the most delightful books of recent years.*

Mr. WATSON'S *tribute to Matthew Arnold is worthy of its subject, and so are the lines on the* "Death of Tennyson," *by the President of Magdalen, which immediately follow it.*

Miss HICKEY'S *delightful stanzas, entitled* "Harebells," *were published in a magazine a few years ago, but the lines which follow them, written in memory of one of the best and wisest men who has lived in our days, appeared in a volume as far back as* 1889, *and was preceded by another collection of poems dating as far back as* 1881.

These are followed by a poem from the pen of Mrs. MEYNELL, *and that by the* "Christmas Carol" *of* Miss MAY PROBYN, *which has the merits of a picture by the most graceful of early Italian artists. Her volume entitled* "Pansies" *is full of exquisite things.*

After some beautiful verses by the wife of the present British Ambassador at Rome, known in literature by her nom de plume *of* VIOLET FANE, *come some by* Mr. BOURDILLON, *the work of a poet who speaks only to a small audience, and then an anonymous poem taken from the* "Child World," *published more than thirty years ago.*

No one can say whether the attempt to create a new school of Irish literature will succeed, but the poem which I cite from Mr. YEATS *is certainly not commonplace, any more than is the older and very different work of* Mr. GRAVES, *while the* "Songs of the Glens of Antrim," *by* MOIRA O'NEILL, *seem to me quite delicious.*

Mr. NEWBOLT *sprang into fame by his ballads on the naval glories of England, from which I select one in no way superior to several others in the same small but admirable collection.*

Mr. LE GALLIENNE *turns as naturally to themes of love as Mr. Newbolt to themes of war.*

2 D

Mr. RUDYARD KIPLING *counts his admirers by hundreds of thousands on either side of the Atlantic. The first of the two pieces I have selected is a State paper in the dress of a very vigorous poem.   It was called forth by a silly resolution, passed at an " Indian Congress," calling on the Government to allow every one to carry arms !   The line about the East in the second will live at least as long as our Eastern Empire.*

Mr. PHILLIPS *has made his mark, both as a poet and as a dramatist.*

Mr. SWINBURNE'S *fame has spread over all the English-speaking world, but I do not know that a better criticism has ever been passed upon him than that which was passed long years ago by Henry Smith, well known to Oxford men as the Admirable Crichton of his time, who was a tutor at Balliol when Swinburne was an undergraduate.   " Swinburne," he said, " has brought into English poetry something it never had before."*

The EARL OF CREWE *has inherited a good deal of his father's poetical gift, a gift which but rarely passes by descent.*

I conclude with some specimens of the work of several young men, who will perhaps be one day described as poets of the Edwardian age, but who all won their spurs before the death of Queen Victoria : Mr. ARTHUR LEGGE, Mr. WALTER WILSON GREG, Mr. LAURENCE BINYON, *and* Mr. DOUGLAS AINSLIE.

PART III

SIR FRANKLIN LUSHINGTON

THE FLEET UNDER SAIL

1854

They are gone from their own green shore !
Our armies sally forth to the East and to the North,
By the Lion of Gibraltar and the steep of Elsinore ;
And the long line of sail on the verge is low and pale,
And the dun smoke-track fades amid the cloudy wrack ;
    And we fade, as they look toward the shore.

    Many will come back no more ;
Whether they shall sleep twenty fathoms deep
'Neath the Black Sea's surge or the Baltic's icy floor,
Or whether they shall lie with their faces to the sky,
Till the mound upon the plain is heap'd above the slain ;
    Many shall come back no more.

    Did you scan those steady faces o'er ?
Which of all the troop that cheered from prow and
    poop,
As the signal to weigh anchor flew aloft at the fore—
When the sudden trumpet blares through the squadrons
    and the squares,
Shall be stricken by the breath of the messenger of
    death ?
    Which are they that shall come home no more ?

Did you mark what a frank air they wore,
The sea's hardy sons, that will stand beside their guns,
'Spite of batteries afloat and of bristling forts ashore ?
Stript bare to the waist, with their strong loins braced,
As fearless and as frank they will tread the ruddy plank,
    Where the boarder slips to rise no more.

    Hush, brothers, cheer no more !—
Let the low prayer rise in witness to the skies
Of our hope and our trust in His hand that rules the
   war ;
And the self-willed man, who has forced us to the van—
On his head be all the guilt of the blood that shall be
   spilt
    Of the many that come home no more.

    By the blood of those who come no more !
At the sword's point and edge we will seize a heavy
   pledge,
(Let us swear an oath and keep it in our true heart's
   core)
We will baulk his avid eyes, and win back the stolen
   prize,
And the ransom he shall yield is the world's peace,
   sealed
    In the blood that flows to ebb no more.

    Boom, great guns, along the shore !—
Let the giant hearts of oak puff out the wreathèd smoke
From their grim broad sides with a loud prophetic roar :
For the truer points your aim, and the quicker fits your
   flame,
The less shall be the list of the voices that are missed
    From our muster when the battle-day is o'er.

Let the echoes roll along the shore.
The sword shall not be sheathed, nor the word
  "Enough!" be breathed,
Till the battered bird of prey can no longer swoop or
  soar;
And the flags that are unfurled for the quiet of the world
Shall be free alike to sweep o'er the broad and narrow
  deep
    For ever and for evermore.

ALMA

Grey, grey morn o'er the hollow dark is creeping;
Call the men to arms, be they waking, be they sleeping:
From their cold beds of earth, 'neath the canopy of
  sky,
Fifty thousand men rise up to do or die:
For the fires we saw last night were the foe's upon the
  height,
The heights by the Alma river, where none but the brave
  may climb.

Broad daylight upon dewy morn is growing;
Hark to the tramp of the steady columns going:
Far along the sea-line sails of battle gleam,
Slowly pressing onwards amid the cloud of steam:
Yes, brothers of the fleet, you shall watch the armies
  meet
On the heights by the Alma river, for there we will die
  or climb.

High noontide glows hot upon the vines;
Lie down awhile till the cannon sweeps their lines:
Though the shells in angry answer plunge tearing
through the rank,
Lie down awhile till the French are on their flank:
Then forward to the fight, and God defend the right
On the heights by the Alma river—His aid is our heart
to climb.

Charge! through the foam-lashed river;—charge! up
the steep hill-side;
Close up to your grey head leaders, as calm in the
front they ride:
Charge! through sheets of leaden hail;—charge!
through the bellow of doom—
Charge! up to the belching muzzles;—charge! drive
the bayonet home:
Oh God, do we live or die? What's Death, what
Life, in the cry,
As we reel to the gory summit, all fire with the murderous
climb?

Grey, grey dusk is before the dark retiring:
Sound the recall-note; cease the random firing;
For the broken masses scurry from the whistle of the
balls
Till they find a safer shelter behind their city walls:
And the watch-fires to-night are ours upon the height,
The heights by the Alma river, the goal of our terrible
climb.

Oh, the gallant hearts that are lying cold and still
On the slopes below the summit, on the plateau of
the hill!

Oh, the gallant hearts that are sobbing out their souls,
As the chilly night wind searches through the burning
 bullet holes !
Oh, the writhing mass of pain, close packed with the
 tranquil slain,
When the grey morn breaks again o'er the heights that
 we dared to climb.

Will the bloody day of Alma be the bloodiest to be
 won ?
Will the mighty fortress crumble before the battering
 gun ?
God knows the end before us : God's hand is over all,
To-day, to-morrow, yesterday, to bid us stand or fall ;
God's peace with the free and the brave, who are left
 in the soldier's grave
On the heights by the Alma river, their own to the end
 of time.

HENRY LUSHINGTON

THE MORN OF INKERMAN

In the hour when coldest
   Night is mixed with morn,
Came I from the trenches
   Utterly outworn.

Thought alike and feeling
   In weary watching drowned,
As I was, I flung me
   On my bed, the ground.

Instantly before me,
   Real as in life,
Dearest, dead or living,
   Stood my darling wife.

As in dreams we lose not
   All our waking pain;
She was dead, I knew it,
   Yet she lived again.

And I said, "Oh, Lucy,
   Broken was my heart,
Thou art come, stay with me,
   Never will we part."

Came the answer, spoken
   In the voice so sweet—
"Not to-day, belovèd,
   Not to-day we meet.

" Thee shall pass the Angel,
   Chooser of the slain ;
Thou shalt see our children,
   Thine and mine again.

" Not for thy sake, dearest,
   Would thou wert with me—
But for theirs I prayed it,
   And it so shall be.

" One more kiss, a spirit's,
   On thy brow I lay :
Thus I mark thee scatheless
   For the coming day."

Into light she faded
   Where the morning beamed ;
I still sadly dreaming
   Thought, " I have but dreamed."

Sudden up I started,
   And as day began,
Roared the Russian cannon
   Over Inkerman.

INKERMAN

Come listen, you new comers,
You boys from the depot ;
You broke my tale of Alma
With many a loud bravo :—
But could I tell you truly
What Inkerman was like,
You'd clench your teeth in silence,
As men before they strike.

I came through, by God's mercy,
With this scratch above the knee;
So first to last I saw it,
All that one man might see.
Oh, the bloody laurels,
The slaughter and the woe!
Dreadful was the battle,
Five to one the foe.
What?   You call him coward?
Curse upon him—no.
Stubborn were the vanquished,
Loath and slow to yield:
Never wearied victors
Stood on sterner field.
Long before the morning
O'er the dim cold down
Came the sound of church-bells,
That rang in all the town;
Came there, too, half-muffled
By the ringing loud,
Tramp and hush and murmur
Of a moving crowd;
But night work in the trenches
Held down our heavy eyes,
And the dim dank morning
Made for a surprise.
Through the dim dank morning
O'er soppy ground and still,
Thousands, thousands, thousands
Are creeping round the hill:
Thousands, thousands, thousands
Are crossing by the bridge;
Sections, lines, divisions
Crown and crowd the ridge.
Ha!—the foe is on us—

Hark, the rifle shot
From our warning pickets,
Ringing clear and hot.
Louder, quicker, nearer—
'Tis in force they come—
Call to arms the sleepers—
Wake them with the drum.
So close they came and silent
Through the morning dank
Their shells our tents were tearing
Before we stood in rank.
'Twas a rough reveillée;
Some, too, never woke,
In their slumber stricken
By the sudden stroke.
Down to Balaklava
Went the mighty din;
Fighting till they reached us
Came our pickets in.
Which attack is real?
Where and what the foes?
Sudden through the rain-mist
There we saw them close.
Stealthy through the brushwood,
Hidden to the breast,
Crowds of points and helmets,
Up the hill they prest:
Misty columns looming
Far and near all round,
Cannon, ready planted,
Sweeping all our ground.
Thought I, "The devil surely
With one scoop of his hand
Has moved them, guns and army,
And set them where they stand."

Then as their great grey masses
Closed on our lines of red,
The rush, the roar, the wrestling,
The growing heaps of dead ;
On the stony hummock,
In the brushwood glen,
Backwards, forwards struggled
Fiercely-fighting men.
Eye to eye we saw them,
Hand to hand we came ;
In their very faces
Sent our volleying flame ;
Time was none for loading—
One crashing musket peal :
The bullet for the foremost,
For the next the steel,
Till with our savage struggle,
Our blood and our best strength,
Not victory, but a moment
Of rest we won at length.

Short the pause—make ready—
Here again they come—
Ah, how many of us
Thought just then of home.
England !—well we know it,
This November day,
Kept with bells and bonfires,
And with boys at play.
Mighty England, lying
Far beyond the night,
Thy suspense were anguish,
Didst thou dream our plight.
Ah, she thinks not on us !

Yet she shall not say
We, her children, shamed her
In our death to-day.

Once more closed their columns
On our line of red ;
Once again we met them,
Cathcart at our head.
Ah, 'twas noble error,
The daring cast he tried ;
Well it boots not grieving :
Like himself he died.
On " Cathcart's Hill " our Generals
Fill a famous grave ;
Braver died not any,
Many more as brave.
Then, as past and round us
Pressed their surging throng,
What a yell ran ringing,
Near and far and long !
Seemed as all their army
Howled from hill to hill—
" Now they cannot 'scape us—
They are ours to kill."
Little then could aid us,
Bugle or command ;
Most was native manhood,
And your own right hand.
Back to back, each fighting
For himself and all,
Broken, yet together,
Like a shattered wall,
In our ranks no bayonet
Lacked its stain of gore,

As through ten times our number
Our bloody path we tore.

Once more with weightier masses
They pressed us back—'twas then
In that redoubt they hemmed us,
That slaughter-house of men.
Thrice their flood swept through it,
Thrice 'twas ours again ;
Still in its embrasures
Grew the stacks of slain ;
Still in the combat's pauses
Yelled their myriads round,
Packs of wolves, all baying,
The hunters run to ground.
Long the battle agony
Swayed in that redoubt ;
Fifteen hundred corpses
In it and about.
Had it but had cannon !
'Twas a point of strength.
Well, it cost them dearly :
But 'twas theirs at length.
Ha, they kill our wounded !
Hark that bitter cry !
O great God, revenge it ;
Give us victory !
The low skies cleft no splendour,
No loud voice shook the air—
Yet He heard and sent us
Answer to our prayer.
Lo the Zouaves' bayonets
Rushing past our right ;
Scarce had sworded angels
Been a dearer sight ;

As with a shriek of cheering
Dashed they to the fight,
All the battle's glory
Made their faces bright.
Short the space we needed
To rally and reform ;
Then side by side with Frenchmen
We met again the storm.
Oh, battle-friends—oh, brethren
Across the chalky strait !
Oh, never more between us
Be spoken word of hate !
By treaty and fair promise
Our states are well allied.
But this the nations' compact
At Inkerman was tied.
French blood was given for English ;
They mingled on the field ;
And holy be the alliance
So for our children sealed.

Fiends, you have lost the battle ;
Aye, charge and charge again :
One has matched your utmost ;
You cannot beat the twain.
No, they could not conquer ;
Savagely they strove ;
Column after column,
Many a stubborn drove.
Up they came in order,
Dashed on us and broke,
Waves of war confusion
Backward rolled in smoke.
Hushed the crash of muskets,
Woke their cannonade ;

Fiercely intermittent
War's dread pulses played.
Yet the day turns westward,
And they still are there.
On them French and English !
Break their stern despair !
Pour upon their masses
The leaden acorn's hail ;
Stab and shoot and thrust them ;
Dash them down the vale.
As the sheaves in autumn
Fall before the mower,
Fell they, lines and sections,
By the Minié's shower.
Tens of theirs and twenties
Are falling to our one ;
Yet they turn and struggle,
Yet will not be gone ;
Yet their staggering masses
Scarcely seem to thin,
Though their corpses cumber
Every step we win.
Murderers of the wounded !
Wolfish stubborn slaves !
From contempt your courage
Not from hatred saves.
With bullet, bayonet, gunstock—
All at need avail—
Mightily we threshed them
With war's bloody flail.
So with shocks of slaughter,
Blood and toil untold,
We the burden from us
Of their battle rolled.
Westward, westward, ever

Sank the winter sun;
Nine hours of day and fighting,
And Inkerman was won.
Sullenly and slowly,
From the plateau down
Drew their beaten masses,
Towards the camp and town;
Gloomily retiring,
Though within our range,
Stepping slow, reluctant,
Leaving their revenge.
How their march in spreading
Filled the lower plains!
How our round shot smote them,
Cutting thorough lanes!
Far we could not follow,
All outworn and few:
Fiercest of avengers,
Lancaster, pursue.
Where men, guns, and tumbrils,
Cumbered columns showed
Closest packed and crowded
On a stretch of road,
Rushed the mighty iron
Screaming through the air;
Right and left it flung them,
Furrowing like a share.
Ha! beyond the thicket,
Near the watercourse,
See yon tall plumes moving
'Mid a rush of horse?
Aye, ride for the Tchernaya
Lest others choke the way;
Aye, cross at speed where slowly
You crossed before to-day.

2 E

Make way there for the Princes
The children of the Czar,
Whom his haughty cunning
Sent forth to end the war.
Aye, let fawning captains
Welcome you again :
Demi-gods of serfdom !
You are beaten men.
Write your Sire no letter
Full of princely lies ;
Say, immense the numbers,
Perfect the surprise :
Praise his servants' courage,
Praise his generals' skill ;
Add, eight thousand English
Held, and hold the hill ;
And till came the Zouaves
(Ah, the time was long)
Stood against his bravest
Sixty thousand strong.
Bishop ! thou that madest
Of the blood that saves
Draughts of frenzied passion
For the soldier-slaves ;
In the solemn midnight
Gav'st th' Incarnate Lord,
Cursing for thy Balak
Us, the Czar's abhorred ;
All thy priests around thee
Lifting battle psalms,
Failed they, thou mock Moses,
To uphold thy palms ?
Thou, whose lying promise
Fired thy savage fold,
Blasphemously mixing

Paradise and gold.
Shepherd, from the mountains
Come thy lambs in throng;
Some are lost—How many?
Count!   'Twill take thee long.

Ah, our thoughts were bitter
With the murderous fight,
We who round the watchfires
Bivouacked that night.
All our hearts were savage,
All our limbs were sore,
All our ears still ringing
With the battle's roar;
As our thoughts were bitter,
So our words that night
Were not glad nor thankful,
But hard and fierce and light.
Next morning in a temper
Other and less ill,
With a burying party
Stood I on the hill.
Ah! how still this morning
Where 'twas late so loud;
Conquerors come we hither,
Yet more sad than proud.
What an Aceldama!
What a hideous sight!
What a crime were battle,
Save for truth and right!
Sorely thinned our numbers,
Officers and men;
Yet of ours we find not
More than one in ten.
On the open hill-side,

In the tufts of wood,
Where they fell we find them,
Hardening in their blood.
Have you searched in bushes
For a wounded hare ?
'Twill be easier searching
In the slain men's lair.
In yon patch of brushwood
Find me if you can
Yard of ground where lies not
Dead or wounded man.
Lift our dead with honour ;
Know them, one by one ;
Bear them to be buried
On the field they won.
On the hill of battle
Dig a mighty trench,
Lay them there like brethren,
The English and the French.
Where they fought and conquered,
Brother-like allied,
Shoulder unto shoulder,
Lay them as they died.
Now for Russian bodies
Search the bloody down ;
Where you find but wounded
Tend them as our own.
But not on the same stretcher
Bear them to the tomb ;
Lay not slain by slayer :
On the hill is room.
On the hill of battle
Dig a larger trench,
Lay them there like soldiers ;
Men that did not blench.

Many a sad serf-mother
Yearns for these at home;
Yet she thinks, " My children
Never more shall come.
Few, alas, of many
Come back from the wars—
There they die fulfilling
God's will and the Czar's."
Think of her and leave them—
Why should we condemn?
Judge, O God, in mercy,
Judge both us and them.
These poor heaps of corpses,
Twisted, gashed, and scarred,
Are the tyrant's counters
Staked on Thy award.
Terrible the process,
But our cause is good;
Knowing all, Thou knowest
Whose the guilt of blood.
And, for him who sent them
To be slain and slay,
Judge, O God, between us
Justly, as to-day.

THE ROAD TO THE TRENCHES

" Leave me, comrades, here I drop;
    No, sir, take them on;
All are wanted, none should stop;
    Duty must be done.

Those whose guard you take will find me,
        As they pass below."
So the soldier spoke, and staggering,
        Fell amid the snow.
And ever on the dreary heights
        Down came the snow.

"Men, it must be as he asks;
        Duty must be done;
Far too few for half our tasks;
        We can spare not one.
Wrap him in this; I need it less;
        Fear not; they shall know;
Mark the place, yon stunted larch,
        Forward!"   On they go.
And silent on their silent march
        Down sank the snow.

O'er his features, as he lies,
        Calms the wrench of pain;
Close, faint eyes; pass, cruel skies,
        Freezing mountain plain.
With far soft sounds the stillness teems—
        Church bells, voices low;
Passing into English dreams
        There amid the snow,
And darkening, thickening o'er the heights,
        Down fell the snow.

Looking, looking for the mark
        Down the others came;
Struggling through the snowdrifts stark;
        Calling out his name:

" Here or there the drifts are deep ;
    Have we passed him ? "   No.
Look a little growing heap,
    Snow above the snow,
Where, heavy on his heavy sleep,
    Down fell the snow.

Strong hands raised him ; voices strong
    Spoke within his ears :
Ah, his dreams had softer tongues ;
    Neither now he hears.
One more gone for England's sake,
    Where so many go ;
Lying down, without complaint ;
    Dying in the snow ;
Starving, striving, for her sake ;
    Dying in the snow.

Simply done his soldier's part
    Through long months of woe ;
All endured with soldier heart—
    Battle, famine, snow ;
Noble, nameless, English heart,
    Snow-cold, in snow.

*To the Memory of Pietro D'Alessandro, Secretary to the
Provisional Government of Sicily in* 1848, *who died
in exile at Malta in January* 1855.

Beside the covered grave
Linger the exiles, though their task is done,
Yes, brethren, from your band once more is gone,
A good man and a brave.

Scanty the rites and train ;
How many of all the storied marbles, set
In all thy churches, City of La Valette,
Hide nobler heart and brain ?

Ah ! had his soul been cold ;
Tempered to make a sycophant or spy ;
To love hard truth less than an easy lie ;
His country less than gold,—

Then, not the spirit's strife,
Nor sickening pangs at sight of conquering crime,
Nor anxious watching of an evil time,
Had worn his chords of life.

Nor here, nor thus with tears
Untimely shed, but there, whence o'er the sea
The great volcano looks, his rest might be,—
The close of prosperous years.

No different hearts are bribed ;
And, therefore, in his cause's sad eclipse,
Here died he, with Palermo on his lips,
A poor man and proscribed.

Wrecked of all thy hopes, O friend—
Hopes for thyself, thine Italy, thine own,
High gifts defeated of their due renown,—
Long toil, and this the end.

The end ?   Not ours to scan ;
Yet grieve not, children, for your father's worth.
Oh ! never wish that in his native earth
He lay, a baser man.

What to the dead avail
The chance success, the blundering praise of fame?
Oh! rather trust, somewhere the noble aim
Is crowned, though here it fail.

Kind, generous, true wert thou;
This meed, at least, to goodness must belong,
That such it was; farewell; the world's great wrong
Is righted for thee now.

Rest in thy foreign grave,
Sicilian! whom our English hearts have loved,
Italian! such as Dante had approved,
An exile—not a slave.

EDWIN ARNOLD.

FROM "THE LIGHT OF ASIA"

.   .   .   .   .   .

We are the voices of the wandering wind,
Which moan for rest and rest can never find;
Lo! as the wind is so is mortal life—
A moan, a sigh, a sob, a storm, a strife.

Wherefore and whence we are ye cannot know;
Nor where life springs nor whither life doth go.
We are as ye are, ghosts from the inane;
What pleasure have we of our changeful pain?

What pleasure hast thou of thy changeless bliss?
Nay, if love lasted, there were joy in this;
But life's way is the wind's way, all these things
Are but brief voices breathed on shifting strings.

O Maya's son! because we roam the earth
Moan we upon these strings; we make no mirth,
So many woes we see in many lands',
So many streaming eyes and wringing hands.

Yet mock we while we wail, for could they know,
This life they cling to is but empty show;
'Twere all as well to bid a cloud to stand,
Or hold a running river with the hand.

But thou that art to save, thine hour is nigh!
The sad world waiteth in its misery;
The blind world stumbleth on its round of pain;
Rise, Maya's child! wake! slumber not again!

We are the voices of the wandering wind;
Wander thou, too, O Prince, thy rest to find;
Leave love for love of lovers, for woe's sake
Quit state for sorrow, and deliverance make.

So sigh we, passing o'er the silver strings,
To thee who know'st not yet of earthly things;
So say we; mocking, as we pass away,
These lovely shadows wherewith thou dost play.

ADELAIDE ANNE PROCTER

In Roman households, when their dear ones died,
   Thrice by his name the living called the dead;
And silence only answering as they cried,
   Ilicet—" go thou then!"—the mourners said.

Ilicet! let her part! the Poet's child,
   Herself a mistress of the lyric song:
Ilicet!—to a world so sad and wild
   To wish her back were far less love than wrong.

Ilicet! hard the word for those to say
   Who know what gentleness is gone from earth;
Harder for those whose dwelling day by day,
   Shone with her presence—echoed to her mirth.

Yet, if He wills it—whom she soars to meet,
   The Lord of this world's vineyard—shall *we* ask,
Who toil on, in the burden and the heat,
   A later wage for her—a longer task?

Ilicet! let her go! though it were brave,—
  In the hot vintage, where the strongest fail,
Weeding God's grapes from thistles—still to have,
  Her silver hymns o'er weariness prevail!

To hear her gentle, certain spirit of ruth
  Share its great sureties with less happy brothers,
And—from eyes bright with Heav'n's light—teach the truth
  Of "little children pleading for their mothers."

Ilicet! otherwhere they need those strains,
  Sounding so true for men—albeit low;
A throne was vacant (though its steps were pains)
  For a soul, tried, pure, perfect—let her go!

Sigh not "so young!"—"such promise!"—"ah! a flower
  That longer life had sunned to fruit of gold."
Be still and see!—God's year, and day, and hour,
  By lapse of mortal minutes is not told.

Who go are called—*ilicet!* let her go!
  Though a sweet harp is silent in the land,
A soft voice hushed—and, never more below,
  Poet and poet's child join song and hand.

Ilicet! ilicet! nos abimus!—
  To that divinest region of the skies,
Whence with clear sight she sees, knows, pities us,
  We shall attain!—Vex not the dead with sighs.

BERLIN—THE SIXTEENTH OF MARCH

Thunder of Funeral Guns!
  Deep sad Bells! with your boom;
Sorrowful voices of Soldiers and Folk!
  Whom lay ye here in the Tomb?

"Whom?" the cannons reply—
  Baying like dogs of War,
Whose master is gone on a path unknown—
  "Our Glory, and Lord, and Star!"

"William, Kaiser and King,
  For him our iron throats yell;
Victor we hailed him on many a field,
  We make to his soul farewell!"

"Whom?" say the slow-swinging bells—
  "William, pious and dear!
Oft-times he knelt to the King of Kings
  Where now he lies on his bier!

"He took from his God alone
  The Crown of the Fatherland;
And now he hath given it back undimmed
  To Death's all-masterful hand!"

"Whom?" shout the serried ranks—
  Guardsmen and Jägers and all—
"The lordliest Lord and the kingliest King
  That ever raised battle-call!"

At his word we thronged to the Field,
  Sure of success to betide;
Sure that the Kaiser would fight for peace;
  Sure of Heaven on our side!"

"Whom?" sigh women and men,
  And fair-haired Germany boys,
And girls, with eyes of his cornflower's hue.
  "For our Father we raise our voice!"

"William the Emperor dead!
  Lo! he made us the Land!
Thanks to him and his chosen chiefs,
  Strong and secure we stand!

"Steadfast from birth to death,
  Whatso was Right he wrought!
Duty he loved, and his people and home!
  Now to dust he is brought!"

Thunder of Funeral Guns!
  We hear you with English ears;
In English breasts it echoes—and bells!
  This tiding your tolling bears!

Warriors, stalwart and fierce!
  We see you are tender and true;
We are come of a kindred blood; we share
  This sorrow, to-day, with you!

Folk of the Fatherland!
  Our hearts for your grief are fain!
God guard you, Kaiser Frederick,
  And give ye good days again!

SIR LEWIS MORRIS.

THE EPIC OF HADES

APHRODITE

                    And then there came
Beauty and Joy in one, bearing the form
Of woman.   How to reach with halting words
That infinite perfection?   All have known
The breathing marbles which the Greek has left
Who saw her near, and strove to fix her charms,
And exquisitely failed, or those fair forms
The Painter offered at a later shrine,
And failed.   Nay, what are words—he knows it well
Who loves or who has loved.

                              She with a smile
Playing around her rosy lips, as plays
The sunbeam on a stream:

                              Shall I complain
Men kneel to me no longer, taking to them
Some graver, sterner worship; grown too wise
For fleeting joys of Love?   Nay, Love is youth,
And still the world is young.   Still shall I reign
Within the hearts of men, while Time shall last
And Life renews itself.   All Life that is,
From the weak things of earth or sea or air,
Which creep or float for an hour, to godlike man—
All know me and are mine.   I am the source
And mother of all, both gods and men; the spring
Of Force and Joy, which penetrating all
Within the hidden depths of the Unknown,
Sets the blind seed of Being, and from the bond
Of incomplete and dual Essences

Evolves the harmony which is Life.   The world
Were dead without my rays, who am the Light
Which vivifies the world.   Nay, but for me,
The universal order which attracts
Sphere unto sphere, and keeps them in their paths
For ever, were no more.   All things are bound
Within my golden chains, whose name is Love.

And if there be, indeed, some sterner souls,
Or sunk in too much learning, or hedged round
By care and greed, or haply too much rapt
By pale ascetic fervours, to delight
To kneel to me, the universal voice
Scorns them as those who, missing willingly
The good that Nature offers, dwelt unblest
Who might be blest, but would not.   Every voice
Of bard in every age has hymned me.   All
The breathing marbles, all the heavenly hues
Of painting, praise me.   Even the loveless shades
Of dim monastic cloisters show some gleam,
Tho' faint, of me.   Amid the busy throngs
Of cities reign I, and o'er lonely plains,
Beyond the ice-fields of the frozen North,
And the warm waves of undiscovered seas.

For I was born out of the sparkling foam
Which lights the crest of the blue mystic wave,
Stirred by the wandering breath of Life's pure dawn
From a young soul's calm depths.   There, without voice,
Stretched on the breathing curve of a young breast,
Fluttering a little, fresh from the great deep
Of life, and creamy as the opening rose,
Naked I lie, naked yet unashamed,
While youth's warm tide steals round me with a kiss,
And floods each limb with fairness.   Shame I know not.
Shame is for wrong, and not for innocence—

The veil which error grasps to hide itself
From the awful Eye.   But I, I lie unveiled
And unashamed—the livelong day I lie,
The warm wave murmuring to me; and all night,
Hidden in the moonlit caves of happy Sleep,
I dream until the morning, and am glad.
    Why should I seek to clothe myself, and hide
The treasure of my Beauty?
The venal charm, the simulated flush
Of fleshly passion, they are none of mine,
Only corruptions of me.   Yet I know
The counterfeit the stronger, since gross souls
And brutish sway the earth; and yet I hold
That sense itself is sacred, and I deem
'Twere better to grow soft and sink in sense
Than gloat o'er blood and wrong.
                                        My kingdom is
Over infinite grades of being.   All breathing things,
From the least crawling insect to the brute,
From brute to man, confess me.   Yet in man
I find my worthiest worship.   Where man is,
A youth and a maid, a youth and a maid, nought else
Is wanting for my temple.   Every clime
Kneels to me—the long breaker swells and falls
Under the palms, mixed with the merry noise
Of savage bridals, and the straight brown limbs
Know me, and over all the endless plains
I reign, and by the tents on the hot sand
And sea-girt isles am queen, and on the side
Of silent mountains, where the white cots gleam
Upon the green hill pastures, and no sound
But the thunder of the avalanche is borne
To the listening rocks around; and in fair lands
Where all is peace; where thro' the happy hush
Of tranquil summer evenings, 'mid the corn,

2 F

Or thro' cool arches of the gadding vines,
The lovers stray together hand in hand,
Hymning my praise; and by the stately streets
Of echoing cities—over all the earth,
Palace and cot, mountain and plain and sea,
The burning South, the icy North, the old
And immemorial East, the unbounded West,
No new God comes to spoil me utterly—
All worship and are mine.
                              With a sweet smile
Upon her rosy mouth, the goddess ceased;
And when she spoke no more, the silence weighed
As heavy on my soul as when it takes
Some gracious melody, and leaves the ear
Unsatisfied and longing, till the fount
Of sweetness springs again.

ON A BIRTHDAY

(LORD ABERDARE'S)

What shall be written of the man
    Who through life's mingled hopes and fears
Touches to-day our little span
        Of seventy years.

Who, with force undiminished still,
    A Nestor stands among his peers,
Full of youth's fire and dauntless will
        At seventy years.

Who knows no creeping chill of age,
    But, rich in all which life endears,
Keeps still the patriot's noble rage
        Through seventy years.

The form unbent, the flashing eye,
   The curious lore, the wit that cheers,
The scorn of wrong which can defy
      His seventy years;

To whom no wound which mars the state,
   No humblest neighbour's grief nor tears,
Appeal in vain for love or hate
      These seventy years;

For whom home's happy radiance yet
   A steadfast beacon-fire appears,
Bright through the storms, the stress, the fret
      Of seventy years;—

What else but this?   "Brave heart, be strong,
   Be of good hope; life holds no fears,
Nor death, for him who strives with wrong
      For seventy years.

Live, labour, spread that sacred light
   Of knowledge, which thy soul reveres;
Fight still the old victorious fight
      Of seventy years.

Live, labour, ripen to fourscore,
   While still the listening Senate hears;
Live till new summers blossom o'er
      These seventy years.

Or if a brighter, briefer lot
   Withdraw thee from thy country's tears,
Be sure there is where change is not,
      Nor age, nor years."

E. C. PEMBER, K.C.

PER GL' OCCH' ALMENO NON V'È CLAÜSURA

Perugia holds a picture wrought by one
   Whose cunning hand, rich heart, and master eyes
Have drawn their mellow forces from the sun
   That ripens all things 'neath Etruscan skies;
A convent wall it is that tells his tale,
   Crag-built, breast-high; a grey nun leans on it,
Gazing across a sweet home-teeming vale;
   And underneath for keynote has he writ—
     Per gl' Occh' almeno non v'è Claüsura.

We gaze with her, but know not whence we gaze—
   Some terraced perch perchance of Apennine—
For o'er his scene he spreads a studious haze
   That leaves mysterious what he found divine;
Nor may we raise the lappet of her veil
   To note if the clipped locks be gold or grey;
Nor ask whose spirit 'tis that thus breaks pale
   In one sad whisper to the summer day—
     Per gl' Occh' almeno non v'è Claüsura.

Her eyes are messengers that go and come
   To guild her soul with guesses; to make fair
The chambers of her mind, grown void and numb
   With painless penance and with prayerless prayer;
So may some manacled forgotten wretch
   Watch o'er his head chance swallow-shadows flit,
Blurring the shafts of light that faintly stretch
   Athwart the roof of his dark dungeon pit—
     Per gl' Occh' almeno non v'è Claüsura.

Life in those glancing shapes doth visit him,
　　Life of the fields, the air, the sunny sky,
Warm eaves, the clay-built nest, the homestead trim,
　　Byres, and the dovecote's burnished colony ;
No longer rots he in his oubliette,
　　But basks at large in sunshine, painless, free ;
One glimpse ; it flashed, and died, but leaves him yet
　　A horde of happy dreams for progeny—
　　　　Per gl' Occh' almeno non v'è Claùsura.

She straineth still her gaze across the plain
　　That nought but a replete confusion seems
Of meads and tufted trees and sheeted grain,
　　Now swathed in shade, now basking in the beams.
So long, so motionless, she scanneth there
　　All that divining love hath made her own,
That timid garden mice peep forth and stare,
　　And lizards gambol near her on the stone—
　　　　Per gl' Occh' almeno non v'è Claùsura.

She counts the huddled hamlets one by one,
　　Whose campanili top their clustering pines,
Marks every quivering stream that takes the sun,
　　Orchards, and olive-gardens looped with vines ;
And spiny locust-trees along a road
　　That threads the little bourg where she was born,
Then last, the whitewashed farm where once abode
　　Hopes that her vows forbid her e'en to mourn—
　　　　Per gl' Occh' almeno non v'è Claùsura.

O patient eyes, what if your halting sweep
　　Of eager search down from that mountain cage
Match but the fingers of the blind that creep,
　　And falter, labouring o'er their fretted page !

And what, O fasting soul, if, sore in need,
　　Thy faith to thine own feigning thou hast lent,
Like shipwrecked starvelings who are driven to feed
　　On husk and herb that bear no nutriment!—
　　　　Per gl' Occh' almeno non v'è Claüsura.

Too like to us thou art, O soul fast hemmed,
　　And ye too like to us, ye patient eyes,
We too are famine stricken, and condemned
　　To cheat our cravings with sweet forgeries :
Pent up in life and time, with Death's high pale
　　Between us and our lost ones, we are fain
To soothe our souls with dreams that less avail
　　E'en than your musings o'er your Tuscan plain—
　　　　Per gl' Occh' almeno non v'è Claüsura.

Like you we murmur, "Where and what are they?"
　　And are they happy?　Do they love us yet?
Do their plumes ever take our earthward way?
　　Or is our cell indeed an oubliette
Wherein we lie forgotten in our night,
　　While they in effortless effulgence float
From marvel unto marvel, with the light
　　Of their pure will for steed and chariot—
　　　　Per gl' Occh' almeno non v'è Claüsura.

We can but dream of them as once they were,
　　Our visions are but symbols of their change ;
White robes, steed, chariot, pinions, golden hair,
　　Are but wild phantoms which our visual range
Compounds from mortal loveliness and power,
　　Whereunder gleams the essence we adore ;
We can but ransack earth their forms to dower
　　With all we see, and puny is our store—
　　　　Per gl' Occh' almeno non v'è Claüsura.

Who from its nest—who never knew a bird—
  Could dream of eagle's glance or swallow's flight,
Or how the nightingale with songs unheard
  Doth sanctify the silence of the night?
Who from a seed could hint the towering pine,
  Or guess the pendant fruitage of the palm,
The wine-stored clusters of the stooping vine,
  The blushing rose's lips and mystic balm?—
    Per gl' Occh' almeno non v'è Claüsura.

Yet not, monastic Comrade, not in vain,
  We beat with baffled souls at prison bars;
Thou yearning for thy home in yonder plain,
  We tracking our lost treasure through the stars;
'Tis sweet to cheat ourselves a little while,
  And something gained it is for us and thee,
An hour or two of longing to beguile
  In blindly murmuring, "We see, we see!"—
    Per gl' Occh' almeno non v'è Claüsura.

AUSTIN DOBSON.

BEFORE SEDAN

Here, in this leafy place
   Quiet he lies,
Cold, with his sightless face
   Turned to the skies :
'Tis but another dead ;
All you can say is said

Carry his body hence,—
   Kings must have slaves ;
Kings climb to eminence
   Over men's graves :
So this man's eye is dim ;—
Throw the earth over him.

What was the white you touched
   There, at his side ?
Paper his hand had clutched
   Tight ere he died ;—
Message or wish, may be ;—
Smooth the folds out and see.

Hardly the worst of us
   Here could have smiled !
Only the tremulous
   Words of a child ;—
Prattle, that has for stops
Just a few ruddy drops.

Look! She is sad to miss,
   Morning and night,
His—her dead father's—kiss;
   Tries to be bright,
Good to mamma, and sweet.
That is all. "Marguerite."

Ah, if beside the dead
   Slumbered the pain!
Ah, if the hearts that bled
   Slept with the slain!
If the grief died;—But no;—
Death will not have it so.

THE BALLAD OF "BEAU BROCADE"

Seventeen hundred and thirty-nine:—
That was the date of this tale of mine.

First great George was buried and gone;
George the Second was plodding on.

London then, as the "Guides" aver,
Shared its glories with Westminster;

And people of rank, to correct their "tone,"
Went out of town to Marybone.

Those were the days of the war with Spain,
Porto-Bello would soon be ta'en;

Whitefield preached to the colliers grim,
Bishops in lawn sleeves preached at him;

Walpole talked "of a man and his price";
Nobody's virtue was over nice:

Those, in fine, were the brave days when
Coaches were stopped by . . . Highwaymen!

And of all the knights of the gentle trade
Nobody bolder than "Beau Brocade."

This they knew on the whole way down;
Best,—may be,—at the "*Oak and Crown.*"

(For timorous cits on their pilgrimage
Would "club" for a "Guard" to ride the stage;

And the Guard that rode on more than one
Was the Host of this hostel's son.)

Open we here on a March day fine,
Under the oak with the hanging sign.

There was Barber Dick with his basin by;
Cobbler Joe with the patch on his eye;

Portly product of Beef and Beer,
John the host, he was standing near.

Straining and creaking, with wheels awry,
Lumbering came the "*Plymouth Fly,*"

Lumbering up from Bagshot Heath,
Guard in the basket armed to the teeth;

Passengers heavily armed inside ;
Not the less surely the coach had been tried !

Tried !—but a couple of miles away,
By a well-dressed man !—in the open day !

Tried successfully, never a doubt,—
Pockets of passengers all turned out !

Cloak-bags rifled, and cushions ripped,
Even our Ensign's wallet stripped !

Even a Methodist hosier's wife
Offered the choice of her Money or Life !

Highwayman's manners no less polite,
Hoped that their coppers (returned) were right ;

Sorry to find the company poor,
Hoped next time they'd travel with more ;

Plucked them all at his ease, in short—
Such was the " *Plymouth Fly's* " report.

Sympathy ! horror ! and wonderment !
" Catch the villain ! "—but nobody went.

Hosier's wife led into the Bar ;
(That's where the best strong waters are !)

Followed the tale of the hundred-and-one
Things that somebody ought to have done.

Ensign (of Bragg's) made a terrible clangour ;
But for the Ladies had drawn his hanger !

Robber, of course, was " Beau Brocade,"
Outspoke Dolly the Chambermaid.

Devonshire Dolly, plump and red,
Spoke from the gallery overhead ;—

Spoke it out boldly, staring hard :—
"Why didn't you shoot then, George the Guard ? "

Spoke it out bolder, seeing him mute :—
"George the Guard, why didn't you shoot ? "

Portly John grew pale and red
(John was afraid of her, people said) ;

Gasped that " Dolly was surely cracked,"
(John was afraid of her—that's a fact !)

George the Guard grew red and pale,
Slowly finished his quart of ale ;—

" Shoot ? Why—Rabbit him !—didn't he shoot ? "
Muttered—" The Baggage was far too 'cute ! "

" Shoot ? Why he'd flashed the pan in his eye ! "
Muttered—" She'd pay for it by and by ! "
Further than this made no reply.

Nor could a further reply be made,
For George *was in league with* " Beau Brocade " !

And John the Host, in his wakefullest state,
Was not—on the whole—immaculate.

But nobody's virtue was over-nice
When Walpole talked " of a man and his price " ;

And wherever Purity found abode,
'Twas certainly *not* on a posting road.

" Forty " followed to " Thirty-nine."
Glorious days of the *Hanover* line !

Princes were born, and drums were banged ;
Now and then batches of Highwaymen hanged.

"Glorious news ! "—from the *Spanish Main ;*
Porto-Bello at last was ta'en.

"Glorious news ! "—for the liquor trade ;
Nobody dreamed of "Beau Brocade."

People were thinking of *Spanish Crowns ;*
Money was coming from seaport towns !

Nobody dreamed of "Beau Brocade"
(Only Dolly the Chambermaid !)

Blessings on Vernon !   Fill up the cans ;
Money was coming in " *Flys* " and "*Vans.*"

Possibly, John the Host had heard ;
Also, certainly, George the Guard.

And Dolly had possibly tidings, too,
That made her rise from her bed anew,

Plump as ever, but stern of eye,
With a fixed intention to warn the " *Fly.*"

Lingering only at John his door,
Just to make sure of a jerky snore ;

Saddling the grey mare, *Dumpling Star ;*
Fetching the pistol out of the bar ;

(The old horse-pistol, that, they say,
Came from the battle of Malplaquet) ;

Loading with powder that maids would use,
Even in " Forty " to clear the flues ;

And a couple of silver buttons, the Squire
Gave her, away in *Devonshire*.

These she wadded—for want of better—
With the B–sh–p of L–nd–n's " Pastoral Letter " ;

Looked to the flint, and hung the whole,
Ready to use, at her pocket-hole.

Thus equipped and accoutred, Dolly
Clattered away to " *Exciseman's Folly* " ;—

Such was the name of a ruined abode,
Just on the edge of the *London* road.

Thence she thought she might safely try,
As soon as she saw it, to warn the " *Fly*."

But as chance fell out, her rein she drew,
As the Beau came cantering into view.

By the light of the moon she could see him drest
In his famous gold-sprigged tambour vest ;

And under his silver-grey surtout,
The laced, historical coat of blue,

That he wore when he went to *London-Spaw*,
And robbed Sir Mungo Mucklethraw.

Out spoke Dolly the Chambermaid,
(Trembling a little, but not afraid),
" Stand and deliver, O ' Beau Brocade ! ' "

But the Beau rode nearer, and would not speak,
For he saw by the moonlight a rosy cheek;

And a spavined mare with a rusty hide;
And a girl with her hand at her pocket-side.

So never a word he spoke as yet,
For he thought 'twas a freak of Meg or Bet;—
A freak of the "Rose" or the "Rummer" set.

Out spoke Dolly the Chambermaid,
(Tremulous now, and sore afraid),
"Stand and deliver, O 'Beau Brocade'!"

Firing then, out of sheer alarm,
Hit the Beau in the bridle-arm.

Button the first went none knows where,
But it carried away his *solitaire*;

Button the second a circuit made,
Glanced in under the shoulder-blade;—
Down from the saddle fell "Beau Brocade"!

Down from the saddle and never stirred!
Dolly grew white as a *Windsor* curd.

Slipped not less from the mare, and bound
Strips of her kirtle about his wound.

Then, lest his Worship should rise and flee,
Fettered his ankles—tenderly.

Jumped on his chestnut, Bet the fleet
(Called after Bet of *Portugal Street*);

Came like the wind to the old inn-door;—
Roused fat John from a three-fold snore;—

Vowed she'd 'peach if he misbelieved . . .
Briefly, the "*Plymouth Fly*" was saved!

Staines and *Windsor* were all on fire ;—
Dolly was wed to a Yorkshire Squire ;
Went to Town at the K—g's desire !

But whether His M—j—sty saw her or not,
Hogarth jotted her down on the spot ;

And something of Dolly one still may trace
In the fresh contours of his *Milkmaid's* face.

George the Guard fled over the sea :
John had a fit—of perplexity ;

Turned King's evidence, sad to state ;—
But John was never immaculate.

As for the Beau, he was duly tried,
When his wound was healed, at Whitsuntide ;

Served—for a day—as the last of " sights,"
To the world of *St. James's Street* and " *White's*,"

Went on his way to Tyburn Tree
With a pomp befitting his high degree.

Every privilege rank confers :—
Bouquet of pinks at St. Sepulchre's ;

Flagon of ale at *Holborn Bar ;*
Friends (in mourning) to follow his Car—
(" t " is omitted where Heroes are !)

Every one knows the speech he made ;
Swore that he "rather admired the jade !"—

Waved to the crowd with his gold-laced hat :
Talked to the Chaplain after that ;

Turned to the Topsman undismayed . . .
This was the finish of " Beau Brocade " !

And this is the Ballad that seemed to hide
In leaves of a dusty " Londoner's Guide " ;
" *Humbly Inscrib'd* (*with curls and tails*)
By the Author to Frederick, *Prince of* Wales :
Published by Francis *and* Oliver Pine ;
Ludgate-Hill, at the Blackmoor Sign,
Seventeen-hundred-and-thirty-nine."

A FANCY FROM FONTENELLE

" *De Mémoires de Roses on n'a point vu Mourir le*
Jardinier."

The Rose in the garden slipped her bud,
And she laughed in the pride of her youthful blood,
As she thought of the Gardener standing by—
" He is old—so old ! And he soon must die ! "

The full Rose waxed in the warm June air,
And she spread and spread till her heart lay bare ;
And she laughed once more as she heard his tread—
" He is older now ! He will soon be dead ! "

But the breeze of the morning blew, and found
That the leaves of the blown Rose strewed the ground ;
And he came at noon, that Gardener old,
And he raked them softly under the mould.

And I wove the thing to a random rhyme,
For the Rose is Beauty, the Gardener, Time.

2 G

"GOOD-NIGHT, BABETTE!"
"*Si vieillesse pouvait!*"

Monsieur Vieuxbois.　　Babette.

M. Vieuxbois (*turning querulously*).

Day of my life! Where can she get?
Babette! I say! Babette!—Babette!

Babette (*entering hurriedly*).

Coming M'sieu'! If M'sieu' speaks
So loud, he won't be well for weeks!

M. Vieuxbois.

Where have you been?

Babette.

　　　　　　Why M'sieu' knows :—
April!... Ville d'Avray!... Ma'am'selle Rose!

M. Vieuxbois.

Ah! I am old,—and I forget.
Was the place growing green, Babette?

Babette.

But of a greenness!—yes, M'sieu'!
And then the sky so blue!—so blue!
And when I dropped my *immortelle*,
How the birds sang!

(*Lifting her apron to her eyes.*)

　　　　　　This poor Ma'am'selle!

M. VIEUXBOIS.

You're a good girl, Babette, but she,—
She was an Angel, verily.
Sometimes I think I see her yet
Stand smiling by the cabinet;
And once, I know, she peeped and laughed
Betwixt the curtains . . .

Where's the draught?

(*She gives him a cup.*)

Now I shall sleep, I think, Babette:—
Sing me your Norman chansonnette.

BABETTE (*sings*).

" *Once at the Angelus*
   (*Ere I was dead*),
Angels all glorious
   Came to my Bed:—
Angels in blue and white
   Crowned on the Head."

M. VIEUXBOIS (*drowsily*).

"She was an Angel" . . . "Once she laughed" . . .
What was I dreaming?

Where's the draught?

BABETTE (*showing the empty cup*).

The draught, M'sieu'?

M. VIEUXBOIS.

How I forget!
I am so old! But sing, Babette!

BABETTE (*sings*).

" One was the Friend I left
Stark in the snow ;
One was the Wife that died
Long,—long ago ;
One was the Love I lost . . .
How could she know ? "

M. VIEUXBOIS (*murmuring*).

Ah, Paul ! . . . old Paul ! . . . Eulalie too !
And Rose . . . and O ! "the sky so blue !"

BABETTE (*sings*).

" One had my Mother's eyes,
Wistful and mild ;
One had my Father's face ;
One was a child :
All of them bent to me—
Bent down and smiled ! "

(He is asleep !)

M. VIEUXBOIS (*almost inaudibly*).

"How I forget !"
"I am so old !" . . . "Good-night, Babette !"

TO LORD DE TABLEY

Still may the Muses foster thee, O Friend,
    Who, while the vacant quidnuncs stand at gaze,
Wond'ring what Prophet next the Fates may send,
    Still tread'st the ancient ways ;

Still climb'st the clear-cold attitudes of Song,
  Or ling'ring "by the shore of Old Romance,"
Heed'st not the vogue, how little or how long,
    Of marvels made in France.

Still to the summits may thy face be set,
  And long may we, that heard thy morning rhyme,
Hang on thy noon-day music, nor forget
    In the hushed even-time?

"IN AFTER DAYS"

In after days when grasses high
O'er-top the stone where I shall lie,
  Though ill or well the world adjust
  My slender claim to honoured dust,
I shall not question nor reply.

I shall not see the morning sky;
I shall not hear the night-wind sigh;
  I shall be mute, as all men must,
    In after days!

But yet, now living, fain were I
That some one then should testify,
  Saying, "He held his pen in trust
  To Art, not serving shame or lust."
Will none?—Then let my memory die
    In after days!

DR. RICHARD GARNETT.

THE BALLAD OF THE BOAT

The stream was smooth as glass, we said: " Arise, and
    let's away ;
The Siren sang beside the boat that in the rushes lay,
And spread the sail, and strong the oar, we gaily took
    our way.
When shall the sandy bar be cross'd ?   When shall we
    find the bay ?

The broadening flood swells slowly out o'er cattle-dotted
    plains ;
The stream is strong and turbulent, and dark with heavy
    rains ;
The labourer looks up to see our shallop speed away.
When shall the sandy bar be cross'd ?   When shall we
    find the bay ?

Now are the clouds like fiery shrouds ; the sun superbly
    large,
Slow as an oak to woodman's stroke sinks flaming at
    their marge ;
The waves are bright with mirror'd light as jacinths on
    our way.
When shall the sandy bar be cross'd ?   When shall we
    find the way ?

The moon is high up in the sky, and now no more we
    see
The spreading river's either bank, and surging distantly
There booms a sullen thunder as of breakers far away,
Now shall the sandy bar be cross'd, now shall we find
    the bay.

The sea-gull shrieks high overhead, and dimly to our
    sight
The moonlit crests of foaming waves gleam towering
    through the night.
We'll steal upon the mermaid soon, and start her from
    her lay,
When once the sandy bar is cross'd, and we are in the
    bay.

What rises white and awful, as a shroud-enfolded ghost?
What roar of rampant tumult bursts in clangour on the
    coast?
Pull back! pull back! The raging flood sweeps every
    oar away.
O stream, is this thy bar of sand? O boat, is this the
    bay?

WILLIAM ALEXANDER, D.D., **Primate of all
Ireland**

OXFORD AND HER CHANCELLOR

Fair as that woman whom the prophet old
In Ardath met, lamenting for her dead,
With sackcloth cast above the tiar of gold,
    And ashes on her head.

Methought I met a lady yestereven ;
A passionless grief, that had nor tear nor wail,
Sat on her pure proud face, that gleam'd to Heaven,
    White as a moon-lit sail.

She spake : "On this pale brow are looks of youth,
Yet angels listening on the Argent floor
Know that these lips have been proclaiming truth
    Nine hundred years and more.

And Isis knows what time-grey towers reared up,
Gardens and groves, and cloister'd halls are mine,
Where quaff my sons from many a myrrhine cup
    Draughts of ambrosial wine.

He knows how night by night my lamps are lit,
How day by day my bells are ringing clear,
Mother of ancient lore and Attic wit,
    And discipline severe.

It may be long ago my dizzied brain
Enchanted swam beneath Rome's master spell,
Till, like light tinctured by the painted pane,
    Thought in her colours fell.

Yet when the great old tongue with strong effect
Woke from its sepulchre across the sea,
The subtle spell of Grecian intellect
    Work'd mightily in me.

Time passed—my groves were full of warlike stirs ;
The student's heart was with the merry spears,
Or keeping measure to the clanking spurs
    Of Rupert's cavaliers.

All these long ages, like a holy mother,
I rear'd my children to a lore sublime,
Picking up fairer shells than any other
    Along the shores of Time.

And must I speak at last of sensual sleep,
The dull forgetfulness of aimless years ?
Oh, let me turn away my head and weep
    Than Rachel's bitterer tears.

Tears for the passionate hearts I might have won,
Tears for the age with which I might have striven,
Tears for a hundred years of work undone,
    Crying like blood to Heaven.

I have repented, and my glorious name
Stands scutcheon'd round with blazonry more bright ;
The wither'd rod, the emblem of my shame,
    Bloom'd blossoms in a night.

And I have led my children on steep mountains,
By fine attraction of my spirit brought
Up to the dark inexplicable fountains
    That are the springs of thought.

Led them where on the old poetic shore
The flowers that change not with the changing moon
Breathe round young hearts, as breathes the sycamore
    About the bees in June.

And I will bear them as on eagles' wings,
To leave them bow'd before the sapphire throne,
High o'er the haunts where dying pleasure sings
    With sweet and swan-like tone.

And I will lead the age's great expansions
Progressive circles toward thought's Sabbath rest;
And point beyond them to the many mansions
    Where Christ is with the blest.

Am I not pledged, who gave my bridal ring
To that old man heroic, strong and true,
Whose grey-haired virtue was a nobler thing
    Than even Waterloo?

Surely that spousal morn my chosen ones
Felt their hearts moving to mysterious calls,
And the old pictures of my sainted sons
    Look'd brighter from the walls.

He sleeps at last—no wind's tempestuous breath
Played a Dead March upon the moaning billow
What time God's Angel visited with death
    The old Field-Marshal's pillow.

There was no omen of a great disaster
Where castled Walmer stands beside the shore;
The evening clouds like pillar'd alabaster
    Hung huge and silent o'er.

The moon in brightness walked the "fleecy rack,"
Walked up and down among the starry fires ;
Heaven's great cathedral was not hung with black
    Up to its topmost spires !

But mine own Isis kept a solemn chiming,
A silver Requiescat all night long,
And mine old trees with all their leaves were timing
    The sorrow of the song.

And through mine angel-haunted aisles of beauty
From grand old organs gush'd a music dim,
Lauds for a champion who had done his duty—
    I knew they were for him.

OXFORD IN 1845

(*Written in* 1885)

A city of young life astir for fame,
    With generations each of three years' date,—
The waters fleeting, yet the fount the same,—
    Where old age hardly enters thro' the gate.

Forty years since ! Thoughts now long overblown
    Had just begun to quicken in the germ,
We sat discussing subjects dimly known
    One pleasant evening of the Summer Term.

So question came of all things new and old,
    And how the movement sped and where should lead ?
Some, peradventure, scorn'd, but more wax'd bold,
    And bravely flaunted their triumphant creed.

Grave grew the talk, and golden grew the gloom ;
  The reason might be weak, the voice was strong ;
Outside by fits and starts, from room to room,
  Boy call'd to boy, like birds, in bursts of song.

Of forms they talked that rose, as if in joy,
  Like magic isles from an enchanted foam ;
They prophesied (no prophet like a boy !)
  Some fairer Oxford and some freer Rome.

An Oxford of a more majestic growth,
  A Rome that sheds no blood, and makes no slave,
The perfect flower and quintessence of both,
  More reverent science, faith by far more brave.

Faith should have broader brow and bolder eye,
  Science sing " Angelus " at close of day ;
Faith have more liberal and lucent sky,
  And science end by learning how to pray.

And " Hail the hour," they cried, " when each high
    morn
  England, at one, shall stand at the church gate,
And vesper bells o'er all the land be borne,
  And Newman mould the Church and Gladstone stamp
    the State."

EPITAPH IN FAHAN CHURCHYARD

Alone with Christ in this sequester'd place
Thy sweet soul learn'd its quietude of grace ;
On sufferers waiting in this vale of ours,
Thy gifted touch was train'd to higher powers.

Therefore when death, O Agnes! came to thee—
Not on the cool breath of our lakelike sea,
But in the workhouse hospital's hot ward,
A gentle helper with the gentle Lord—
Proudly as men heroic ashes claim,
We ask'd to have thy fever-stricken frame,
And lay it in our grass beside our foam,
Till Christ the Healer call His healers home.

EPITAPH IN THE CATHEDRAL OF DERRY

Down through our crowded lanes and closer air,
O friend, how beautiful thy footsteps were;
When through the fever's waves of fire they trod,
A form was with thee like the Son of God.
'Twas but one step for those victorious feet,
From their·day's walk unto the golden street;
And they who watch'd that walk, so bright and brief,
Have mark'd this marble with their hope and grief.

PREFACE TO "THE FINDING OF THE BOOK AND OTHER POEMS"

I never yet heard music, howe'er sweet,
  Never saw flower or light, ocean or hill,
  But a quick thrill of something finer still
Touch'd me with sadness.   Never did I meet
Any completeness but was incomplete;
  Never found shapes half fair enough to fill
  The royal galleries of my boundless will;

Never wrote I one line that I could greet
   A twelvemonth after with a brow of fire.
Thus then I walk my way and find no rest—
   Only the beauty unattain'd, the cry
After the inexpressible unexpressed,
   The unsatiated insatiable desire
Which at once mocks and makes all poesy.

REV. FATHER RYDER.

PHOTOGRAPHIC ALBUM

A book of friends who still are friends,
   With friendship waxing stronger;
A books of friends who once were friends,
   But now are friends no longer.

I wonder as I turn the leaves
   What further changes yet may be,
Or e'er the Master bind the sheaves
   And friends are friends eternally.

EDMUND GOSSE.

THE CHARCOAL-BURNER

He lives within the hollow wood,
 From one clear dell he seldom ranges ;
His daily toil in solitude
 Revolves but never changes.

A still old man, with grizzled beard,
 Grey eye, bent shape, and smoke-tanned features,
His quiet footstep is not feared
 By shyest woodland creatures.

I love to watch the pale blue spire
 His scented labour builds above it ;
I track the woodland by his fire,
 And, seen afar, I love it.

It seems among the serious trees
 The emblem of a living pleasure,
It animates the silences
 As with a tuneful measure.

And dream not that such humdrum ways
 Fold naught of nature's charm around him ;
The mystery of soundless days
 Hath sought for him and found him.

He hides within his simple brain
 An instinct innocent and holy,
The music of a wood-bird's strain—
 Not blithe, nor melancholy,

But hung upon the calm content
 Of wholesome leaf and bough and blossom—
An unecstatic ravishment
 Born in a rustic bosom.

He knows the moods of forest things,
 He holds, in his own speechless fashion,
For helpless forms of fur and wings
 A mild paternal passion.

Within his horny hand he holds
 The warm brood of the ruddy squirrel ;
Their bushy mother storms and scolds,
 But knows no sense of peril.

The dormouse shares his crumb of cheese,
 His homeward trudge the rabbits follow ;
He finds, in angles of the trees,
 The cup-nest of the swallow.

And through this sympathy perchance,
 The beating heart of life he reaches
Far more than we who idly dance
 An hour beneath the beeches.

Our science and our empty pride,
 Our busy dream of introspection,
To God seem vain and poor beside
 This dumb, sincere reflection.

Yet he will die unsought, unknown,
 A nameless headstone stand above him,
And the vast woodland, vague and lone,
 Be all that's left to love him.

MR. JOHNSTONE.

THE GARDENER'S BURIAL

This is the grave prepared; set down the bier:
Mother, a faithful son we bring thee here,
In loving ease to lie beneath thy breast,
Which many a year with loving toil he drest.
His was the eldest craft, the simple skill
That Adam plied, ere good was known by ill;
The throstle's song at noon his spirit tuned;
He set his seeds in hope, he grafted, pruned,
Weeded and mow'd, and with a true son's care
Wrought thee a mantle of embroidery rare.
The snowdrop and the winter aconite
Came at his call ere frosts had ceased to bite:
He bade the crocus flame as with a charm;
The nestling violets bloom'd, and fear'd no harm,
Knowing that for their sakes a champion meek
Did bloodless battle with the weather bleak:
But when the wealthier months with largess came
His blazon'd beds put heraldry to shame,
And on the summer air such perfume cast
As Saba or the Spice Isles ne'er surpassed.
The birds all loved him for he would not shoot
Even the winged thieves that stole his fruit;
And he loved them—the little fearless wren,
The red-breast, curious in the ways of men,
The pilgrim swallow, and the dearer guest
That sets beneath our eaves her plaster'd nest:
The merry whitethroat, bursting with his song,
Fluttered within his reach and fear'd no wrong,
And the mute fly-catcher forgot her dread
And took her prey beside his stooping head.

Receive him, Mother Earth; his work is done;
Blameless he liv'd and did offence to none;
Blameless he died, forbidding us to throw
Flowers in his grave, because he loved them so.
He would not have them stifle underground,
But bloom among the grasses on his mound.
We, that have loved, must leave him: Mother, keep
A faithful watch about him in his sleep.

SAMUEL WADDINGTON.

BEATA BEATRIX

And was it thine, the light whose radiance shed
Love's halo round the gloom of Dante's brow?
Was thine the hand that touched his hand, and thou
The spirit to his inmost spirit wed?
O gentle, O most pure, what shall be said
In praise of thee to whom Love's minstrels bow?
O heart that held his heart, for ever now
Thou with his glory shall be garlanded.
Lo 'mid the twilight of the waning years,
Firenze claims once more our love, our tears:
But thou, triumphant on the throne of song—
By Mary seated in the realm above—
O, give us of that gift than death more strong,
The loving spirit that won Dante's love.

W. H. LECKY.

ON AN OLD SONG

Little snatch of ancient song,
What has made thee live so long?
Flying on thy wings of rhyme
Lightly down the depths of time,
Telling nothing strange or rare,
Scarce a thought or image there,
Nothing but the old, old tale
Of a hapless lover's wail;
Offspring of an idle hour,
Whence has come thy lasting power?
By what turn of rhythm or phrase,
By what subtle careless grace,
Can thy music charm our ears
After full three hundred years?

Little song, since thou wert born,
In the Reformation morn,
How much great has passed away,
Shattered or by slow decay,
Stately piles in ruins crumbled,
Lordly houses lost and humbled,
Thrones and realms in darkness hurled,
Noble flags for ever furled,
Wisest schemes by statesmen spun,
Time has seen them one by one
Like the leaves of Autumn fall—
A little song outlives them all.

There were mighty scholars then,
With the slow, laborious pen,

Piling up their words of learning,
Men of solid, deep discerning,
Widely famous as they taught
Systems of connected thought,
Destined for all future ages;
Now the cobweb binds their pages;
All unread their volumes lie
Mouldering so peaceably,
Coffined thoughts of coffined men,
Never more to stir again.
In the passion and the strife,
In the fleeting forms of life,
All their force and meaning gone
As the stream of thought flows on.

Art thou weary, little song,
Flying through the world so long?
Canst thou on thy fairy pinions,
Cleave the future's dark dominions,
And with music soft and clear
Charm the yet unfashioned ear,
Mingling with the things unborn,
When perchance another morn,
Great as that which gave thee birth,
Dawns upon the changing earth?
It may be so, for all around,
With a heavy crashing sound,
Like the ice of polar seas
Melting in the summer breeze,
Signs of change are gathering fast,
Nations breaking with their past.

The pulse of thought is beating quicker,
The lamp of faith begins to flicker,
The ancient reverence decays
With forms and types of other days,

And old beliefs grow faint and few
As knowledge moulds the world anew,
And scatters far and wide the seeds
Of other hopes and other creeds ;
And all in vain we seek to trace
The fortunes of the coming race,
Some with fear and some with hope—
None can cast its horoscope.
Vap'rous lamp or rising star,
Many a light is seen afar,
And dim shapeless figures loom
All around us in the gloom—
Forces that may rise and reign
As the old ideals wane.

Landmarks of the human mind
One by one are left behind,
And a subtle change is wrought
In the mould and cast of thought ;
Modes of reasoning pass away,
Types of beauty lose their sway ;
Creeds and causes that have made
Many noble lives must fade,
And the words that thrilled of old
Now seem hueless, dead, and cold ;
Fancy's rainbow tints are flying,
Thoughts, like men, are slowly dying ;
All things perish, and the strongest
Often do not last the longest ;
The stately ship is seen no more,
The fragile skiff attains the shore ;
And while the great and wise decay,
And all their trophies pass away,
Some sudden thought, some careless rhyme,
Still floats above the wrecks of Time.

GEORGE MEREDITH.

DIRGE IN WOODS

A wind sways the pines,
     And below
Not a breath of wild air;
Still as the mosses that glow
On the flooring, and over the lines
Of the roots, here and there,
The pine-tree drops its dead;
They are quiet, as under the sea.
Overhead, overhead
Rushes life in a race,
As the clouds the clouds chase;
     And we go
And we drop like the fruits of the tree,
       Even we,
       Even so.

AUBREY DE VERE.

SAD IS OUR YOUTH

Sad is our youth, for it is ever going,
   Crumbling away beneath our very feet;
Sad is our life, for onward it is flowing
   In current unperceived, because so fleet;
Sad are our hopes, for they were sweet in sowing—
   But tares, self-sown, have overtopped the wheat;
Sad are our joys, for they were sweet in blowing—
   And still, oh still, their dying breath is sweet;
And sweet is youth, although it hath bereft us
   Of that which made our childhood sweeter still;
And sweet is middle life, for it hath left us,
   A nearer good to cure an older ill;
And sweet are all things, when we learn to prize them,
Not for their sake, but His, who grants them or denies
    them!

LE RÉCIT D'UNE SŒUR

Whence is the music?   Minstrel, see we none;
Yet soft as waves that, surge succeeding surge,
Roll forward, now subside, anon emerge,
Upheaved in glory o'er a setting sun,
Those beatific harmonies sweep on!
O'er earth they sweep from heaven's remotest verge
Triumphant hymeneal, hymn and dirge,
Blending in everlasting unison.

Whence is the music? Stranger, these were they
That, great in love, by love unvanquished proved :
These were true lovers, for in God they loved :
With God, these Spirits rest in endless day,
Yet still for Love's behoof, on wings outspread
Float on o'er earth, betwixt the Angels and the Dead !

SIR FREDERICK POLLOCK.

THE SIN OF SIR PERTAB SINGH

(From " The Spectator," February 13, 1897)

A king is great, and the gods are high
    Beyond all gods and kings
Is the Veda's timeless rule whose bonds
    Hold all created things.

A king may smite and a god may blast,
    And pardon be to win
A twice-born man who breaks his law
    Hath sinned eternal sin.

Ye may sharpen the sword and point the spear
    Till, whenso war betide,
As friends to her friend, as foes to her foe,
    Ye fight on the White Queen's side.

Ye may hunt the boar with the stranger folk
    And play the polo game :
But strange men's meat and a stranger's corse
    Are ghostly death and shame.

Yet one god is over the Veda's self,
    The soul of the world's deep plan,
And his works are higher than rule and book
    In the faith of man to man.

It was a chieftain of high degree,
    Of the sun-born Rahtore name ;
His guest was an English soldier lad
    Who might not live to fame.

Death fell on the lad by Jodhpur's keep,
   With none of his kin beside :
Fast as that keep on world-old rock
   Stands twice-born Rajputs' pride.

It was Pertab Singh laid hand to the corse
   Like a Rajput giving his best,
Yea, were it his soul, lest aught should lack
   To honour the soldier guest.

The Sun-god sat with his holy scribes
   When an eagle brought the tale :
He said : "Now judge me my children's deed,"
   And the scribes with dread waxed pale.

The holiest spake, and sad was he :
   "For such an one 'tis well
If eightfold penance and ninefold fine
   May save his soul from hell."

The Sun-god spake : "Right well ye judge,
   But the judgment is of earth :
The doom I deem on Pertab Singh
   Shall befit a high god's worth.

"Make ready, my scribe, a pen full fair
   And write a goodly thing,
A charter first among my chiefs
   For my true son Pertab Singh."

C. K. PAUL.

LINES

In the merry hay-time we raked side by side,
In the harvest he whispered—Wilt thou be my bride?
And my girl-heart bounded—Forgive, God, the crime,
If I loved him more than Thee in the merry hay-time.

In the sad hay-time I sit on the grass,
The scythe whistles clear, the merry mowers pass;
But he cometh never, for under the lime
Is a long low hillock since the last hay-time.

HERMAN MERIVALE.

FROM "THE WHITE PILGRIM"

Thordisa in the agony of lost love calls on Death, the White Pilgrim, to appear to her.

THORDISA.

Spirit, I know thee not.   I look on thee
With awe, but not with terror.   All my fears
Fall from me as a garment.   Art thou——

PILGRIM.

Hush!

Miscall me not!   Men have miscalled me much;
Have given harsh names and harsher thoughts to me,
Reviled and evil entreated me,
Built me strange temples as an unknown god,
Then called me idol, devil, unclean thing,
And to rude insult bowed my godhead down.
Miscall me not! for men have marred my form,
And in the earth-born grossness of their thought
Have coldly modelled me of their own clay,
Then fear to look on that themselves have made.
Miscall me not! ye know not what I am,
But ye shall see me face to face, and know.
I take all sorrows from the sorrowful,
And teach the joyful what it is to joy.
I gather in my land-locked harbour's clasp,
The shattered vessels of a vexèd world,
And even the tiniest ripple upon life
Is to my calm sublime as tropic storm.
When other leech-craft fails the breaking brain,
I, only, own the anodyne to still

Its eddies into visionless repose.
The face, distorted with life's latest pang,
I smooth, in passing, with an angel wing;
And from beneath the quiet eyelids steal
The hidden glory of the eyes, to give
A new and nobler beauty to the rest.
Belie me not; the plagues that walk the Earth,
The wasting pain, the sudden agony,
Famine, and War, and Pestilence and all
The terrors that have darkened round my name—
These are the works of Life, they are not mine;
Vex when I tarry, vanish when I come,
Instantly melting into perfect peace,
As at His word, whose master spirit I am,
The troubled waters slept on Galilee.
Tender I am, not cruel: when I take
The shape most hard to human eyes, and pluck
The little baby-blossom yet unblown,
'Tis but to graft it on a kindlier stem,
And leaping o'er the perilous years of growth,
Unswept of sorrow, and unscathed of wrong,
Clothe it at once with rich maturity.
'Tis I that give a soul to memory;
For round the follies of the bad I throw
The mantle of a kind forgetfulness;
But, canonised in dear Love's calendar,
I sanctify the good for evermore.
Miscall me not! my generous fulness lends
Home to the homeless, to the friendless, friends;
To the starved babe, the mother's tender breast;
Wealth to the poor, and to the restless, rest!
Shall I unveil, Thordisa? If I do,
Then shall I melt at once the iron bonds
Of this mortality that fetters thee.
Gently, so gently like a tired child,

Will I enfold thee.   But thou mayst not look
Upon my face and stay.   In the busy haunts
Of human life, in the temple and the street,
And when the blood runs fullest in the veins,
Unseen, undreamed of, I am often by,
Divided from the giant in his strength
But by the thickness of this mighty veil,
But none can look behind that veil, and stay
Shall I withdraw it now?

THORDISA.

A little while
Give me a little yet!   Spirit, I love him,
And would not go till I have heard once more
In accents, whose rich music was the tune
To which my life was set, not that he loves me,
But that he loved me once.   Spirit, not yet!
I am all too earthly in my thoughts of him;
I am not fit for——

PILGRIM.

Hush! Miscall me not!

FROM "OLD AND NEW ROME"

.   .   .   .   .

Still, as we saunter down the crowded street,
    On our own thoughts intent, and plans, and pleasures,
For miles and miles beneath our idle feet,
    Rome buries from the day yet unknown treasures.

The whole world's alphabet, in every line
  Some stirring page of history she recalls,
Her Alpha is the Prison Mamertine,
  Her Omega, St. Paul's, without the walls.

Above, beneath, around, she weaves her spells,
  And ruder hands unweave them all in vain:
Who once within her fascination dwells,
  Leaves her with but one thought—to come again.

So cast thine obol into Trevi's fountain—
  Drink of its waters, and, returning home,
Pray that by land or sea, by lake or mountain,
  "All roads alike may lead at last to Rome."

J. W. COURTHOPE.

THE CHANCELLOR'S GARDEN

.   .   .   .   .   .

And when with joyous heart they 'gan prepare
Renewe their pilgrimage, then one by one,
This Clerk would have them to his garden fair:
So swete a pleasaunce in that land was none:
Secure it lay towards the setting sun;
And right from ende to ende a velvett way
Of verdaunt turfe did to a river run,
Whose crystall face shott back the dazzling day,
And 'neath the gliding streme you saw the green reeds
    sway.
Ah! how the pleasures of that path to sing!
Whose close soft grass might hide no uglie weed;
But, on each side, through all the months of Spring
He bade the race of passing flowers succeed,
Most rare of scent or sight, from bulb or seed;
The crocus coming when the March winds call;
Jonquils that after hyacinths make speed;
Narcissus fair, snow-white and swete withal;
And tulips gay, and eke Saint Bruno's lilie tall.

Beneath the northern wall, in happie nook
Warmed with the sun and sheltered from the wind,
Where he might easie come from bed or book,
He had of mountayn plantes all manner kind;
Such as with paines the curious searchers find,
Remote, on beetling crag, in deep ravine,
In clifts of western Andes some enshryned,
And some on heights of Himalaya green,
Or Jura's pine-clad rockes, or valley Engadine.

There noble Edelweiss was seen to drink
From alien airs her hues of fadeless white ;
With saxifrage, whose blossomes to the brink
Of parlous cliffs oft tempt botanic wight ;
Sundew, to whom the sunlesse noon is night ;
The bearded harebell, and the Alpine rose,
Adventurous climber of the rockie height ;
And soldanella, hardie nymph, who shows
Her modest bosom first above the melting snows.

And there was seen the blue forget-me-not,
Flashing through all her flowers Lake Leman's blue ;
Matched with her peer androsace, who shot
From many clustered blooms a rosie hue :
Fair alchemilla peeped her mantle through ;
And dryas fair, with modest shining gem
In eight white petals sett, yet lowlie grew ;
And gentian of the snow, whose single stem
Gleams through the circling grass with sapphire diadem.

To rear these plantes the Clerk with mickle craft
Congeniale soils would oft from distance bring,
And mix with buried sherd and broken shaft
Of antique niche, whereto their roots might cling
Rock-like, and watered from the coldest spring :
Alsoe, when winds blew soure or winter froze ;
Boughs would he fetch to be their covering ;
Well so he deemed his nurselings might suppose
Their heads were safe and warm beneath their mountain
        snows.

Then, too, would he his tender children call,
And in their lot full many an emblem see
Of human life and types angelicale :
" For lo ! as with a father's hand," sayde he,
" I guard these flowers from Mutabilitie,

And rear them in strange soil and foreign air,
Ev'n soe than grasse of field what more are we,
Who must through mortall world full briefly fare?
Yet is each planted Soul our Heavenlie Father's care.

Thrice happie they, yea happier they alone,[1]
Who in Religion's breast fair haven find!
To whom the rurall Deities are known,
And Nature's heart, and all the lawes of kynd!
They fear not Change nor greedie Death behind;
No lust of power or perishable reign
To mad Ambition moves their quiet mind:
Though customs die, tongues vanish, empires wane,
For them the Throne of God, the changelesse Heav'ns
    remain.

[1] Virgil, *Georg.* ii. 490–99.

ANONYMOUS.

A NIGHT IN THE MEDITERRANEAN
(1877)

As he leans over the vessel's side,
  Watching her track of sapphire and snow,
Does he muse and wonder what might betide,
  If he sought for peace in the depths below?
After that plunge comes a Saviour's breast,
Or the depths of hell, or unconscious rest?

Holy man, who from ages past
  Your heritage proud of faith have gained,
Have you no spell to hold him fast,
  To bid Christ reign where the devil has reigned?
Cannot the sign of the Cross control
And save the tortured and maddened soul?

Faith, above all things, spoke the priest,
  Implicit faith in the Church is needed;
Without it no hope for the greatest or least,
  Their most fervent prayers will pass unheeded.
Doubt of itself implies damnation,
And suicide is but an aggravation.

Thus far the Priest; now for the man
  Who has left his teaching far behind:
No God and no future, his accents ran,
  But a form of words is the soul and mind.
Only some fibre and tissue grey,
Which in seventy years will have had its day.

But seventy years is a mighty gift,
  Not to be lightly flung away,
And of future hope for himself bereft,
  A man may hope for his race alway,
And deem that each struggle of body and mind
Enhances the weal of all human kind.

The line of light in the West grew low,
  The Priest and Philosopher went to dinner,
Over them sounded to and fro
  The weary tramp of the restless sinner,
And the sapphire waves to ink had turned,
And the foam-flakes white with sea-fire burned.

The ship drove on; through the bitter night
  Whistled the wind in each creaking shroud;
Underneath her till morning light
  The water kept up a grinding loud,
Like some monster with cruel teeth alway
Crunching and crushing the bones of its prey.

Morning at last on the weary din—
  The sun shed a wild white light ahead,
And the vessel that stood Marseilles to win
  Was beating off Puerto Mahon instead;
While the steward who had counted the numbers failed,
To make them the same as when he sailed.

Just by one had he counted higher;
  He noticed one berth was, still and neat,
Unslept in amid the confusion dire,
  And drew his conclusion just and meet,
Duly reporting a man overboard;
No wonder when waves so wildly roared.

An accident—the Priest was kind,
  And masses said for the stricken soul ;
The Philosopher talked of an unstrung mind,
  And a spirit beyond its own control :
To neither perhaps occurred the thought
Of a wearied child who the Father sought.

Worn with sorrow and stained by sin,
  Was he not wise to seek that shore,
Where alone a new life might begin,
  Where alone the past would be really o'er ?
Who knows ?   Like a child in the night he cried,
And the storm and the darkness alone replied.

ANONYMOUS.

FROM THE "ETON MAGAZINE," 1848

O were I a cross on thy snowy breast,
  Or were I a gem in thy raven hair;
O were I the soft-blowing wind of the west,
  To play round thy bosom with cooling air.

O were I a bracelet upon thy arm,
  Or a ring on thy taper hand to shine,
How blythe would I view each rising charm,
  And grow bright in thy brightness, Caroline.

In vain! I may never see thee more,
  Save through the dark glass of memory;
Yet my vows for thy welfare I still must pour,
  And unburden my foolish heart to thee.

Fair offspring to stay thee when thou art old,
  And a happy lot in life be thine;
And a grave with thy sires in the churchyard mould,
  And a home in the heavens, Caroline.

Mr. SIMCOX.

IN THE JACQUERIE

Anstice and Amalie watching late,
Sat over Sir Raoul's castle gate,
And saw the rabble foam up in hate:
Raoul would fight and Amalie fly,
But Anstice sat quietly waiting to die.

Raoul was beaten down to his knee,
They tore from his girdle the silver key
Of the postern where Amalie meant to flee;
He cast to the tower a warning cry,
Where Anstice sat quietly waiting to die.

They bound his hands and they bound his feet,
They left him his shirt for winding-sheet;
They hung up Sir Raoul against the sky,
But Anstice sat quietly waiting to die.

Amalie covered her golden head,
Hid her face from the noble dead,
But looking out with a tearless eye,
Anstice sat quietly waiting to die.

Amalie slunk through the gate to flee,
She stumbled over the caitiff's knee
Who had taken Sir Raoul's silver key.
She swooned to earth, and no help was nigh,
But Anstice sat quietly waiting to die.

The rabble sat drinking the wine and the mead,
And Amalie served them in Beggar's weed;
But she cast up a torch to avenge her shame,
And the roof fell down on their heads in flame,
And the beams of the tower fell down from high,
Where Anstice sat quietly waiting to die.

The tower has sunk in the castle moat,
And the cushat warbles her one clear note
In the elms that grow into the brooding sky,
Where Anstice sat long ago waiting to die.

SIR A. LYALL.

THEOLOGY IN EXTREMIS

Oft in the pleasant summer years,
   Reading the tales of days bygone,
I have mused on the story of human tears,
   All that man unto man has done—
Massacre, torture, and black despair;
Reading it all in my easy-chair.

Passionate prayer for a minute's life;
   Tortured, crying for death as rest;
Husband pleading for child or wife;
   Pitiless stroke upon tender breast.
Was it all real as that I lay there
Lazily stretched on my easy-chair?

Could I believe in those hard old times
   Here in this safe luxurious age?
Were the horrors invented to season rhymes,
   Or truly is man so fierce in his rage?
What could I suffer, and what could I dare?
I who was bred to that easy-chair.

They were my fathers, the men of yore,
   Little they recked of a cruel death;
They would dip their hands in a heretic's gore;
   They stood and burnt for a rule of faith.
What would I burn for, and whom not spare?
I who had faith in an easy-chair.

Now do I see old tales are true,
  Here in the clutch of a savage foe;
Now shall I know what my fathers knew,
  Bodily anguish and bitter woe;
Naked and bound in the strong sun's glare,
Far from my civilised easy-chair.

Now have I tasted and understood
  That old-world feeling of mortal hate;
For the eyes all round us are hot with blood;
  They will kill us coolly—they do but wait:
While I, I would sell ten lives at least,
For one fair stroke at that devilish priest,

Just in return for the kick he gave,
  Bidding me call on the prophet's name;
Even a dog by this may save
  Skin from the knife, and soul from the flame.
My soul! if he can let the prophet burn it,
But life is sweet if a word may earn it.

A bullock's death, and at thirty years!
  Just one phrase, and a man gets off it;
Look at that mongrel clerk in his tears,
  Whining aloud the name of the prophet;
Only a formula easy to patter,
And, God Almighty, what can it matter?

" Matter enough," will my comrade say,
  Praying aloud here close at my side,
" Whether you mourn in despair alway,
  Cursed for ever by Christ denied;
Or whether you suffer a minute's pain
All the reward of Heaven to gain."

Not for a moment faltereth he,
    Sure of the promise and pardon of sin ;
Thus did the martyrs die, I see,
    Little to lose and muckle to win ;
Death means Heaven, he longs to receive it ;
But what shall I do if I don't believe it ?

Life is pleasant, and friends may be nigh,
    Fain would I speak one word and be spared ;
Yet I could be silent and cheerfully die,
    If I were only sure God cared ;
If I had faith, and were only certain
That light is behind that terrible curtain.

But what if He listeth nothing at all
    Of words a poor wretch in his terror may say ?
That mighty God who created all
    To labour and live their appointed day ;
Who stoops not either to bless or ban,
Weaving the woof of an endless plan.

He is the Reaper, and binds the sheaf ;
    Shall not the season its order keep ?
Can it be changed by a man's belief ?
    Millions of harvests still to reap.
Will God reward, if I die for a creed,
Or will He but pity, and sow more seed ?

Surely He pities, who made the brain,
    When breaks that mirror of memories sweet,
When the hard blow falleth, and never again
    Nerve shall quiver nor pulse shall beat ;
Bitter the vision of vanishing joys ;
Surely He pities when man destroys.

Here stand I on the ocean's brink.
   Who hath brought news of the further shore?
How shall I cross it? Sail or sink,
   One thing is sure, I return no more;
Shall I find haven, or aye shall I be
Tossed in the depths of a shoreless sea?

They tell fair tales of a far-off land,
   Of love rekindled, of forms renewed;
There may I only touch one hand,
   Here life's ruin will little be rued;
But the hand I have pressed and the voice I have
    heard,
To lose them for ever, and all for a word!

Now do I feel that my heart must break,
   All for one glimpse of a woman's face;
Swiftly the slumbering memories wake
   Odour and shadow of hour and place;
One bright ray through the darkening past
Leaps from the lamp as it brightens last,

Showing me summer in western land,
   Now as the cool breeze murmureth
In leaf and flower—and here I stand
   In this plain all bare save the shadow of death;
Leaving my life in its full noonday,
And no one to know why I flung it away.

Why? Am I bidding for glory's roll?
   I shall be murdered and clean forgot;
Is it a bargain to save my soul?
   God, whom I trust in, bargains not;
Yet for the honour of English race,
May I not live or endure disgrace?

Ay, but the word, if I could have said it,
   I by no terrors of hell perplext;
Hard to be silent and have no credit
   From man in this world, or reward in the next;
None to bear witness, and reckon the cost
Of the name that is saved by the life that is lost.

I must be gone to the crowd untold
   Of men by the cause which they served unknown,
Who moulder in myriad graves of old;
   Never a story and never a stone
Tells of the martyrs who die like me,
Just for the pride of the old countrie.

A NIGHT IN THE RED SEA

The strong hot breath of the land is lashing
   The wild sea-horses, they rear and race;
The plunging bows of our ship are dashing
   Full in the fiery South Wind's face.

She rends the water, it foams and follows,
   And the silvery jet of the towering spray,
And the phosphor sparks in the deep wave hollows,
   Lighten the line of our midnight way.

The moon above with its full-orbed lustre,
   Lifting the veil of the slumberous land,
Gleams o'er a desolate island cluster,
   And the breakers white on the lonely sand.

And a bare hill range in the distance frowning,
  Dim wrapt in haze like a shrouded ghost,
With its jagged peaks the horizon crowning,
  Broods o'er the stark Arabian coast.

See, on the edge of the waters leaping,
  The lamp, far flashing, of Perim's Strait
Glitters and grows, as the ship goes sweeping
  Fast on its course for the Exile's gate.

And onward still to the broadening ocean,
  Out of the narrow and perilous seas,
Till we rock with a large and listless motion
  In the moist soft air of the Indian breeze.

And the Southern Cross, like a standard flying,
  Hangs in the front of the tropic night,
But the Great Bear sinks, like a hero dying,
  And the Pole Star lowers its signal light;

And the round earth rushes toward the morning,
  And the waves grow paler and wan the foam,
Misty and dim, with a glance of warning,
  Vanish the stars of my northern home.

Let the wide waste sea for a space divide me,
  Till the close-coiled circles of time unfold,
Till the stars rise westward to greet and guide me,
  When the Exile ends, and the years are told.

MEDITATIONS OF A HINDU PRINCE

All the world over, I wonder, in lands that I never have
    trod,
Are the people eternally seeking for the signs and steps
    of a God?
Westward across the ocean, and Northward ayont the
    snow,
Do they all stand gazing, as ever, and what do the wisest
    know?

Here, in this mystical India, the deities hover and swarm,
Like the wild bees heard in the tree-tops, or the gusts of
    a gathering storm;
In the air men hear their voices, their feet on the rocks
    are seen,
Yet we all say, " Whence is the message, and what may
    the wonders mean?"

A million shrines stand open, and ever the censer swings,
As they bow to a mystic symbol, or the figures of ancient
    kings;
And the incense rises ever, and rises the endless cry
Of those who are heavy laden, and of cowards loth to die.

For the Destiny drives us together, like deer in a pass of
    the hills,
Above is the sky, and around us the sound of the shot
    that kills;
Pushed by a power we see not, and struck by a hand
    unknown,
We pray to the trees for shelter, and press our lips to a
    stone.

2 K

The trees wave a shadowy answer, and the rock frowns
    hollow and grim,
And the form and the nod of the demon are caught in
    the twilight dim ;
And we look to the sunlight falling afar on the mountain
    crest,
Is there never a path runs upward to a refuge there and
    a rest ?

The path, ah ! who has shown it, and which is the faithful
    guide ?
The haven, ah ! who has known it ? for steep is the
    mountain side,
For ever the shot strikes surely, and ever the wasted
    breath
Of the praying multitude rises, whose answer is only
    death.

Here are the tombs of my kinsfolk, the fruit of an
    ancient name,
Chiefs who were slain on the war-field, and women who
    died in flame ;
They are gods, these kings of the foretime, they are
    spirits who guard our race,
Ever I watch and worship ; they sit with a marble face.

And the myriad idols around me, and the legion of
    muttering priests,
The revels and rites unholy, the dark unspeakable feasts !
What have they wrung from the Silence ?   Hath even a
    whisper come
Of the Secret, whence and whither ?   Alas, for the gods
    are dumb.

Shall I list to the word of the English, who come from
    the uttermost sea?
" The Secret, hath it been told you, and what is your
    message to me?"
It is nought but the wide-world story how the earth and
    the heavens began,
How the gods are glad and angry, and a Deity once was
    man.

I had thought, " Perchance in the cities where the rulers
    of India dwell,
Whose orders flash from the far land, who girdle the
    earth with a spell,
They have fathomed the depths we float on, or measured
    the unknown main "—
Sadly they turn from the venture and say that the quest
    is vain.

Is life, then, a dream and delusion, and where shall the
    dreamer awake?
Is the world seen like shadows on water, and what if the
    mirror break?
Shall it pass as a camp that is struck, as a tent that is
    gathered and gone
From the sands that were lamp-lit at eve, and at morning
    are level and lone?

Is there nought in the heaven above, whence the hail
    and the levin are hurled,
But the wind that is swept around us by the rush of the
    rolling world;
The wind that shall scatter my ashes, and bear me to
    silence and sleep
With the dirge, and the sounds of lamenting, and voices
    of women who weep?

AFTER THE SKIRMISH

ROHILCUND, 1858

'Mid the broken grass of a trampled glade,
    Where the bayonets met and the fight was sorest,
We had found him lying; and there we laid
    Our friend in the depth of an Indian forest;

Just as the evening shadow's pall
    Over his grave from the hills came streaming,
By the rippled fret and the eddying fall
    Of a snow-fed river, cool and creaming,

With the funeral march still echoing round,
    We had spread the mould o'er his tartan gory;
But as we turned from the shapeless mound
    Sweet rose the music of "Annie Laurie"—

Full and clear from the pacing band,
    Passionate strain of a love-lorn story.
How can they breathe it in strangers' land,
    Air of our northern "Annie Laurie"?

For he whom we leave in the lonely brake,
    Watched by the Himalay Mountains hoary,
Will not his brain from the death-sleep wake,
    Touched by the magic of "Annie Laurie"?

Heaven forfend!   May the earth lie dense
    O'er the heart that beat and the eyes that glistened;
What if a motionless nerve has sense?
    What if an upturned face had listened?

Listened! as over his prison close
    Floated that rich, voluptuous cadence,
Faint with the scent, like an autumn rose,
    Of youth, and beauty, and soft-hued maidens;

Of a long late eve, and the falling dew;
  Never again shall the dewdrop wet him;
Of a woman's hand, and a promise true—
  Will not the kindliest now forget him?

Chaining his spirit's upward flight,
  Staying his soul, though at heaven's own portal,
With the soft refrain of a lost delight,
  With the shadowy charm of a fairy mortal.

Lured by the sensuous melody's spell,
  Little he recks of the angel's glory;
Piercing sad is the earth's farewell
  Sighed in the music of " Annie Laurie."

MRS. EARL.

ON THE DEATH OF MRS. HOLLAND

Carve no stone above her head,
Rather let her praise be read
In the shining eyes of youth,
Taught by her to gaze at Truth;
Let her honour be approved
In the deeds of those she loved,
And each life inspired by her
Be her worthy chronicler.

Never soul more chastely wise
Watched the world through deeper eyes;
Hardly shall the future tell
What the influence of her spell;
How her speech's virgin gold
Took the grace of antique mould;
How her heart like altar fire
Burned with flame of high desire;
How divine Philosophy,
Handmaid of the Lord, stood nigh
Prompting her the Truths that wrought
In her every look and thought—
All has fled; no written scroll
Holds the story of her Soul;
In Time's archives is set forth
No escutcheon of her worth,—
Naught remains save memory!
Nay, such sweetness cannot die,
Though her name be never set
In Fame's tarnished Coronet.

As within a garden green
Shall that dearest name be seen,
Showing as in lilies writ,
And with roses framing it.
We who hung upon her words
Caught the throb of heavenly chords,
Touching harmonies of earth
Into a diviner birth;
Felt the Stoics rigid School
Soften into Christian rule;
Learnt what hidden virtue lies
In the life which fools despise;
Longed to play the nobler part
With the right chivalric heart;
Honeyed lore of poet and sage,
Simples of the golden age—
These, as into sweets distilled,
All her days with fragrance filled;
These, as garlands wreathed and fair,
Guard her solemn sepulchre.

All Love's herald could proclaim
Lies within her twofold name,
Mary, hers, whose home was blest
By the living Lord as guest;
Sibyl, her majestic eyes
Rapt in lofty mysteries,
But, if childhood met her sight,
Melted into loving light.
Precious as her counsel's store,
Yet her comforting was more;
When she stood by misery
With divining sympathy,
When her every grace and power
Found in Love its crowning dower.

Where the hallowed sunshine fills
That lone vale 'mid Kentish hills,
Where her stainless child has rest
'Neath her native earth's kind breast,
Let her sleep, while April rain
Calls the blossoms forth again,
While the nightingales rejoice,
And the wild bees' murmurous voice
Hums the sombre trees among,
Like an echo of old song.
While the fading leaves shall fall
To one lonely thrush's call,
While the snow shall drift and pass
Like a shadow on life's glass,
While the world shall onward roll
Nearer its mysterious goal.

Strew with violets dim the sod,
Leave her Epitaph with God.

W. WATSON.

IN LALEHAM CHURCHYARD

'Twas at this season, year by year,
The singer who lies songless here
Was wont to woo a less austere,
    Less deep repose,
Where Rotha to Winandermere
    Unresting flows,—

Flows through a land where torrents call
To far-off torrents as they fall,
And mountains in their cloudy pall
    Keep ghostly state,
And Nature makes majestical
    Man's lowliest fate.

There, 'mid the August glow, still came
He of the twice illustrious name,
The loud impertinence of fame
    Not loth to flee—
Not loth with brooks and fells to claim
    Fraternity.

Linked with his happy youthful lot,
Is Loughrigg, then, at last forgot?
Nor silent peak nor dalesman's cot
    Looks on his grave.
Lulled by the Thames he sleeps, and not
    By Rotha's wave.

'Tis fittest thus! for though with skill
He sang of beck and tarn and ghyll,
The deep, authentic mountain-thrill
    Ne'er shook his page!
Somewhat of worldling mingled still
    With bard and sage.

And 'twere less meet for him to lie
Guarded by summits lone and high
That traffic with the eternal sky
    And hear, unawed,
The everlasting fingers ply
    The loom of God,

Than in this hamlet of the plain
A less sublime repose to gain,
Where Nature, genial and urbane,
    To man defers,
Yielding to us the right to reign,
    Which yet is hers.

And nigh to where his bones abide,
The Thames with its unruffled tide
Seems like his genius typified—
    Its strength, its grace,
Its lucid gleam, its sober pride,
    Its tranquil face.

But ah! not his the eventual fate
Which doth the journeying wave await—
Doomed to resign its limpid state
    And quickly grow
Turbid as passion, dark as hate,
    And wide as woe.

Rather, it may be over much
He shunned the common stain and smutch,
From soilure of ignoble touch
        Too grandly free,
Too loftily secure in such
        Cold purity.

But he preserved from chance control
The fortress of his 'stablisht soul;
In all things sought to see the whole;
        Brooked no disguise;
And set his heart upon the goal,
        Not on the prize.

With those Elect he shall survive
Who seem not to compete or strive,
Yet with the foremost still arrive,
        Prevailing still:
Spirits with whom the stars connive
        To work their will.

And ye, the baffled many, who,
Dejected, from afar off view
The easily victorious few
        Of calm renown,—
Have ye not your sad glory too,
        And mournful crown?

Great is the facile conqueror;
Yet haply he, who wounded sore,
Breathless, unhorsed, all covered o'er
        With blood and sweat
Sinks foiled, but fighting evermore,
        Is greater yet.

T. HERBERT WARREN.

IN MEMORIAM—ALFRED, LORD TENNYSON

Last left of the mortal Immortals, art thou too taken at
   last,
Loved part so long of the present, must thou too pass
   to the past?
Thou hast lain in the moonlight and lapsed in a glory
   from rest into rest,
And still is the teeming brain, and the warm heart cold
   in the breast,
And frozen the exquisite fancy, and mute the magical
   tongue,
From our century's tuneful morn to its hushing eve that
   had sung.
Crowned poet and crown of poets, whose wealth and
   whose wit could combine
Great echoes of old-world Homer, the grandeur of
   Milton's line,
The sad sweet glamour of Virgil, the touch of Horace
   divine,
Theocritus' musical sigh, and Catullus daintily fine!

Poet of Art and of Nature, of sympathies old and new,
Who read in the earth and the heavens, the fair and the
   good and the true,
And who wrote no line and no word that the world will
   ever rue!
Singer of God and of men, the stars were touched by
   thy brow,
But thy feet were on English meadows, true singer of
   England thou!
We lose thee from sight, but thy brothers with honour
   receive thee now,

From earliest Chaucer and Spenser to those who were
    nearer allied,
The rainbow radiance of Shelley, and Byron's furious
    pride,
Rich Keats and austere Wordsworth, and Browning who
    yesterday died
By sunny channels of Venice, and Arnold from Thames'
    green side.

Knells be rung, and wreaths be strung, and dirges be
    sung for the laurelled hearse,
Our tears and our flowers fade scarce more fast than our
    transient verse,
For even as the refluent crowds from the glorious Abbey
    disperse,
They are all forgotten, and we go back to our fleeting
    lives ;
But we are the dying, and thou the living, whose work
    survives,
The sum and the brief of our time, to report to the
    after years
Its thoughts and its loves and its hopes and its doubts
    and its faiths and its fears ;
They live in thy lines for ever, and well may our era
    rejoice
To speak to the ages to come with so sweet and so
    noble a voice.

EMILY M. P. HICKEY.

"EMPEROR EVERMORE"

Who bad thee do and suffer bids thee rest:
Sleep, greatest Hohenzollern, on His breast.

He gave thee strength of body and soul, and then
He gave thee will to do and think for men.

He taught thee to possess thy soul and wait:
He called thee to the ruler's high estate,

Soldier and statesman, great in field and rede,
Strong in thy thought and glorious in thy deed;

Yet mightier strength and brighter glory shed,
Kaiser, on thee, by suffering perfected:

For more than Empire welded, battle won,
Is to have learnt to say *Thy Will be done.*

So, on thy life of life He wrote it plain,
All the divine significance of pain.

Thee, when the great death-angel came, he found
King unanointed, emperor uncrowned.

Better than gold and oil of sovranty,
His patience crowned thee and anointed thee;

Thee by His grace who loved and did and bore,
King over pain and suffering's emperor.

HAREBELLS

Blue bells, on blue hills, where the sky is blue,
Here's a little blue-gowned maid come to look at you;
Here's a little child would fain, at the vesper time,
Catch the music of your hearts, hear the harebells
 chime,
  "Little hares, little hares," softly prayeth she,
  "Come, come across the hills, and ring the bells
   for me."

When do hares ring the bells, does my lady say?
Is it when the sky is rosed with the coming day?
Is it in the strength of noon, all the earth aglow?
Is it when at eventide sweet dew falleth slow?
Any time the bells may ring, morn, or noon, or even;
Lovebells, joybells, earthbells heard in heaven.
Any time the happy hills may be lightly swept
By the ringers' little feet; any time, except
When by horse and hound and man, chased and frighted
 sore,
Weak and panting, little hares care to ring no more.
It must be upon the hills where the hunt comes ne'er,
Chimes of bells ring out to greet touch of little hare.
  Harebells, blue bells, ring, ring again!
  Set a-going, little hares, the joyaunce of the strain.

Not a hare to ring the bells on the whole hillside?
Could she make the harebells ring, if my darling tried?
Harebells, harebells, a little child blue-gowned
Stands and listens longingly; little hands embrowned
Touch you; rose mouth kisses you; ring out!
Is a little child a thing any flower should flout?
Child's hand on poet's heart makes it bloom in song:
Let her hear your fairy chimes, delicate ding-dong.

Let her hear what poet's voice never caught nor sung :
Let a child ring the bells little hares have rung !
Soft she whispers to the flowers, bending o'er them
      there—
    Let me ring your bonny bells ! I'm a little hare !
    No, I'm only a little child, but I love you so !
    Let me ring your little bells, just to say, you know.
    Harebells, blue bells, ring, ring again !
    Set a-going, little child, the joyaunce of the strain.

Oh, the look upon her face for the music heard !
Is it wind in fairy soughs ?   Is it far-off bird ?
Does the child hear melody grown folk cannot hear ?
Is the harebells' music now chiming on her ear ?
Father, give this little child, as she goeth on,
Evermore to keep the gift by this music won ;
Gift which makes this earth of ours very Paradise
For delight of opened ears, joy of opened eyes.
    Harebells, joy bells, love bells, dear and blest,
    Ring in the sacredness of her happy breast.

MRS. MEYNELL.

THE SHEPHERDESS

She walks—the lady of my delight—
 A shepherdess of sheep.
Her flocks are thoughts. She keeps them white;
 She guards them from the steep.
She feeds them on the fragrant height,
 And folds them in for sleep.

She roams maternal hills and bright,
 Dark valleys safe and deep.
Into her tender breast at night
 The chastest stars may peep.
She walks—the lady of my delight—
 A shepherdess of sheep.

She holds her little thoughts in sight,
 Though gay they run and leap.
She is so circumspect and right;
 She has her soul to keep.
She walks—the lady of my delight—
 A shepherdess of sheep.

MISS MAY PROBYN.

CHRISTMAS CAROL

Lacking samite and sable,
   Lacking silver and gold,
The Prince Jesus in the poor stable
   Slept, and was three hours old.

As doves by the fair water,
   Mary, not touched of sin,
Sat by Him,—the King's daughter,
   All glorious within.

A lily without one stain, a
   Star where no spot hath room.
Ave, gratia plena—
   Virgo Virginum.

Clad not in pearl-sewn vesture,
   Clad not in cramoisie,
She hath hushed, she hath cradled to rest, her
   God the first time on her knee.

Where is one to adore Him?
   The ox hath dumbly confessed,
With the ass, meek kneeling before Him,
   Et homo factus est.

Not throned on ivory or cedar,
   Not crowned with a Queen's crown,
At her breast it is Mary shall feed her
   Maker, from Heaven come down.

The trees in Paradise blossom
  Sudden, and its bells chime—
She giveth Him, held to her bosom,
  Her immaculate milk the first time.

The night with wings of angels
  Was alight, and its snow-packed ways
Sweet made (say the Evangels)
  With the noise of their virelays.

Quem vidistis, pastores?
  Why go ye feet unshod?
Wot ye within yon door is
  Mary, the Mother of God?

No smoke of spice is ascending
  There—no roses are piled—
But, choicer than all balms blending,
  There Mary hath kissed her child.

Dilectus meus mihi
  Et ego Illi—cold
Small cheek against her cheek, He
  Sleepeth, three hours old.

VIOLET FANE (LADY CURRIE).

AFTERWARD

I know that these poor rags of womanhood—
   This oaten pipe, whereon the wild winds play'd,
   Making sad music,—tatter'd and outfray'd,
Cast off, play'd out,—can hold no more of good,
   Of love, or song, or sense of sun and shade.

What homely neighbours elbow me (hard by
   'Neath the black yews) I know I shall not know,
   Nor take account of changing winds that blow,
Shifting the golden arrow, set on high
   On the grey spire, nor mark who come and go.

Yet would I lie in some familiar place,
   Nor share my rest with uncongenial dead,—
   Somewhere may be, where friendly feet will tread,—
As if from out some little chink of space
   Mine eyes might see them tripping overhead.

And though too sweet to deck a sepulchre
   Seem twinkling daisy-buds and meadow-grass;
   And so would more than serve me, lest they pass
Who fain would know what woman rested there,
   What her demeanour, or her story was,—

For these I would that on a sculptured stone
   (Fenced round with ironwork to keep secure),
   Should sleep a form with folded palms demure,
In aspect like the dreamer that was gone,
   With these words carved, *I hoped, but was not sure.*

F. BOURDILLON.

THE NIGHT HAS A THOUSAND EYES

The Night has a thousand eyes
    And the day but one ;
Yet the light of a whole world dies
    With the setting sun.

The Mind has a thousand eyes
    And the heart but one ;
Yet the light of a whole life dies
    When love is done.

WHERE RUNS THE RIVER

Where runs the river?   Who can say
Who hath not followed all the way
By alders green and sedges grey
    And blossoms blue?

Where runs the river?   Hill and wood
Curve round to hem the eager flood ;
It cannot straightly as it would
    Its path pursue.

Yet this we know: O'er whatso plains
Or rocks or waterfalls it strains,
At last the Vast the stream attains ;
    And I, and you.

ANONYMOUS.

ONCE

(From " The Child World," 1870)

Sing to me, nightingale, that sweet tune
You sang last night to the waning moon !
It filled the shadow, it pierced the light,
It made a day in the midst of night.
I want to hear it before I die ;
Sing till the moon comes out of the sky !
" No, no !" the nightingale sings ;
" Once is enough for all best things !
I shall trill many a lovely strain ;
But I never shall sing that song again !"

Make for me, sky, that tender hue
You made last night ere the sun dropped through !—
Colour melted in burning air,
Flowing we know not whence nor where.
Before I die I want to see—
Make that colour again for me !
" No, no ! I paint all day
Rose and amethyst, gold and grey,
Purple precipice, silver rain ;
But I never shall paint that hue again."

Breathe to me, friend, that deep love-tone
You breathed last night when we were alone
It told a life which I never guessed,
It covered sorrow with floods of rest.

Before I die I want to know
Whether you always love me so.
" No, no!   The moment came
Once, but never again the same :
Once, deep Love finds utterance clear ;
Often silent, 'tis always here."

W. B. YEATS.

THE STOLEN CHILD

Where dips the rocky highland
    Of Slewth Wood in the lake,
There lies a leafy island
    Where flapping herons wake
The drowsy water rats;
There we've hid our fairy vats
Full of berries
And of reddest stolen cherries.
Come away, O human child!
To the woods and waters wild
With a fairy, hand in hand,
For the world's more full of weeping than
    you can understand.

Where the wave of moonlight glosses
    The dim grey sands with light,
Far off by furthest Rosses
    We foot it all the night,
Weaving olden dances,
Mingling hands and mingling glances
Till the moon has taken flight;
To and fro we leap
And chase the frothy bubbles
While the world is full of troubles,
And is anxious in its sleep.
Come away, O human child!
To the woods and waters wild
With a fairy, hand in hand,
For the world's more full of weeping than
    you can understand.

Where the wandering water gushes
   From the hills above Glen-Car,
In pools among the rushes
   That scarce could bathe a star,
We seek for slumbering trout,
And whispering in their ears
We give them evil dreams,
Leaning softly out
From ferns that drop their tears
Of dew on the young streams.
Come, O human child!
To the woods and waters wild
With a fairy, hand in hand,
For the world's more full of weeping than
     you can understand.

Away with us he's going,
   The solemn-eyed—
He'll hear no more the lowing
   Of the calves on the warm hill-side,
Or the kettle on the hob
   Sing peace into his breast,
Or see the brown mice bob
   Round and round the oatmeal chest.
For he comes, the human child,
To the woods and waters wild
With a fairy, hand in hand,
For the world's more full of weeping than
     he can understand.

ALFRED PERCEVAL GRAVES.

THE WRECK OF THE *AIDEEN*

Is it cure me, docthor, darlin'? an ould boy of siventy-
   four,
Afther soakin' off Berehaven three and thirty hour and
   more,
Wid no other navigation underneath me but an oar.

God incrase ye, but it's only half myself is livin' still,
An' there's mountin' slow but surely to my heart the
   dying' chill;
God incrase ye for your goodness, but I'm past all
   mortial skill.

But ye'll surely let them lift me, won't you, dochtor,
   from below?
Ye'll let them lift me surely—very soft and very slow—
To see my ould ship, *Aideen*, wanst agin before I go?

Lay my head upon your shoulder; thank ye kindly,
   dochtor dear,
Take me now; God bless ye, Cap'n! now together!
   sorra fear!
Have no dread that ye'll distress me—now, agin,
   ochone! I see her.

Ologone! my Aideen's *Aideen*, christened by her
   laughin' lips,
Wid a sprinkle from her finger as ye started from the
   slips,
Thirty years ago come Shrovetide, like a swan among
   the ships.

And we both were constant to ye till the bitter, bitter
day,
Whin the typhus took my darlin', and she pined and
pined away,
Till yourself's the only sweetheart that was left me on
the say.

So through fair and foul we'd travel, you and I thin—
usen't we?
The same ould coorse from Galway Bay, by Limerick
and Tralee,
Till this storm it shook me overboard, and murthered
you, machree.

But now, agra, the unruly wind has flown into the west,
And the silver moon is shinin' soft upon the ocean's
breast,
Like Aideen's smilin' spirit come to call us to our rest.

Still the sight is growin' darker, and I cannot rightly
hear;
The says too cold for one so old; O, save me, Cap'n,
dear!
Now it's growin' bright and warm agin, and Aideen,
Aideen's here.

MOIRA O'NEILL.

LOOKIN' BACK

Wathers o' Moyle an' the white gulls flying,
 Since I was near ye what have I seen?
Deep great seas, an' a sthrong wind sighin'
 Night an' day where the waves are green.
Struth na Moile, the wind goes sighin'
 Over a waste o' wathers green.

Slemish an' Trostan, dark wi' heather,
 High are the Rockies, airy-blue ;
Sure ye have snows in the winter weather,
 Here they're lyin' the long year through.
Snows are fair in the summer weather,
 Och, an' the shadows between are blue !

Lone Glen Dun an' the wild glen flowers,
 Little ye know if the prairie is sweet.
Roses for miles, an' redder than ours,
 Spring here undher the horses' feet.
Ay, an' the black-eyed gold sunflowers,—
 Not as the glen flowers small an' sweet.

Wathers o' Moyle, I hear ye callin'
 Clearer for half o' the world between,
Antrim hills an' the wet rain fallin'
 Whiles ye are nearer than snow-tops keen :
Dreams o' the night an' a night-wind callin'—
 What is the half o' the world between?

H. NEWBOLT.

THE *FIGHTING TÉMÉRAIRE*

It was eight bells ringing,
  For the morning watch was done,
And the gunner's lads were singing
  As they polished every gun.
It was eight bells ringing,
And the gunner's lads were singing,
For the ship she rode a-swinging,
  As they polished every gun.

Oh ! to see the linstock lighting,
  Téméraire ! Téméraire !
Oh ! to hear the round shot biting,
  Téméraire ! Téméraire !
Oh ! to see the linstock lighting,
And to hear the round shot biting,
For we're all in love with fighting
  On the Fighting Téméraire.

It was noontide ringing,
  And the battle just begun,
When the ship her way was winging,
  As they loaded every gun.
It was noontide ringing,
When the ship her way was winging,
And the gunner's lads were singing
  As they loaded every gun.

There'll be many grim and gory,
  Téméraire ! Téméraire !
There'll be few to tell the story,
  Téméraire ! Téméraire !

There'll be many grim and gory,
There'll be few to tell the story,
But we'll all be one in glory
    With the Fighting Téméraire.

There's a far bell ringing
    At the setting of the sun,
And a phantom voice is singing
    Of the great days done,
There's a far bell ringing,
And a phantom voice is singing
Of renown for ever clinging
    To the great days done.

Now the sunset breezes shiver,
    Téméraire ! Téméraire !
And she's fading down the river,
    Téméraire ! Téméraire !
Now the sunset breezes shiver,
And she's fading down the river,
But in England's song for ever
    She's the *Fighting Téméraire.*

RUDYARD KIPLING.

"WHAT HAPPENED"

Hari Chunder Mukerji, pride of Bow-Bazar,
Owner of a native press, Barrister at Lar,
Waited on the Government with a claim to wear
Sabres by the bucketful, rifles by the pair.

Then the Indian Government, winked a wicked wink,
Said to Chunder Mukerji :—"Stick to pen and ink,
They're the safest implements :—but if you insist,
We will let you carry arms wheresoe'er you list."

Hari Chunder Mukerji went to Rodda's, and
Bought the tubes of Lancaster, Ballard, Deane and
    Bland,
Bought a shiny bowie-knife, bought a town-made sword,
Jingled like an ekka-horse when he went abroad.

But the Indian Government, always keen to please,
Also gave parwanas to horrid men like these ;
Yar Mahomed, Yusufzai, down to kill or steal,
Chimbu Singh from Bikanir, Tantia the Bhil.

Killa Khan the Marri Chief, Jowar Singh the Sikh,
Nabbi Baksh, Punjabi Jât, Abdul Huq Rafiq—
(He was a Wahábi) lastly little Boh Hla-Oo
Took advantage of the Act and . . . a Snider too.

They were unenlightened men, Rodda's knew them not,
They procured their swords and guns mostly on the
    spot ;
And the lore of centuries, plus a hundred fights,
Made them slow to disregard one another's rights.

Nabbi Baksh, Punjabi Jât, found a hide-bound flail,
Chimbu Singh from Bikanir, oiled his Tonk Jezail,
Yar Mahomed, Yusufzai, spat and smiled with glee,
As he ground the butcher-knife of the Khyberee.

Jowar Singh the Sikh secured tulwar, quoit and mace,
Abdul Huq, Wahábi, took his peshkalz [1] from its place
And amid the jungle-grass, danced and grinned and
jabbered,
Little Boh Hla-Oo and jerked his dah-blade from the
scabbard.

With a unanimity dear to patriot hearts,
All these hairy gentlemen out of foreign parts,
Said :—" The good old days are back ! Let us go to
war ! "
Swaggered down the Grand Trunk Road into Bow
Bazar.

Did they meet with Mukerji ? Soothly who can say ?
Yar Mahomed only grins in a nasty way,
Jowar Singh is reticent, Chimbu follows suit,
But the belts of all of them simply bulge with loot !

What became of Rodda's guns ? Afghans, black and
grubby,
Sell them for their silver weight to the men of Pubbie,
And the shiny bowie-knife and the town-made sword are
Hanging in a Marri hut just across the Border !

What became of Mukerji ? Ask Mahomed Yar,
Prodding Shiva's sacred bull down the Bow Bazar,
Speak to bovine Nabbi Baksh. Question land and sea,
Ask the Indian Delegates—only don't ask me.

---

[1] Knuckledusters.

MANDALAY

By the old Moulmein Pagoda, lookin' eastward to the
 sea
There's a Burmah girl a-settin', and I know she thinks
 o' me ;
For the wind is in the palm-trees, and the temple bells
 they say :
"Come you back, you British soldier ; come you back
 to Mandalay ! "
   Come you back to Mandalay,
   Where the old Flotilla lay :
   Can't you 'ear their paddles chunkin' from
    Rangoon to Mandalay ?

   On the road to Mandalay,
   Where the flyin' fishes play,
   An' the dawn comes up like thunder outer
    China 'crost the Bay !

'Er petticoat was yaller an' 'er little cap was green,
An' 'er name was Supi-yaw-lat—jes' the same as Theebaw's
 Queen.
An' I seed her just a-smokin' of a whackin' white cheroot
An' a-wastin' Christian kisses on a 'eathen idol's foot :
   Bloomin' idol made o' mud—
   Wot they called the Great Gawd Budd—
   Plucky lot she cared for idols when I kissed 'er
    where she stud !
   On the road to Mandalay . . .

When the mist was on the rice-fields an' the sun was
 droppin' slow,
She'd git her little banjo an' she'd sing *Kulla-lo-lo !*

        2 M

With her arm upon my shoulder an' her cheek agin' my
    cheek
We useter watch the steamers an' the *hathis* pilin' teak.
        Elephints a-pilin' teak
        In the sludgy, squdgy creek,
        Where the silence 'ung that 'eavy you was 'arf
           afraid to speak!
        On the road to Mandalay . . .

But that's all shove be'ind me—long ago an' fur away,
An' there aint no busses running from the Bank to
    Mandalay ;
An' I'm learnin' 'ere in London what the ten-year soldier
    tells,
" If you've 'eard the East a-callin', you won't never 'eed
    naught else."
        No ! you won't 'eed nothin' else
        But them spicy garlic smells,
        An' the sunshine an' the palm-trees an' the
           tinkly temple-bells;
        On the road to Mandalay . . .

I am sick o' wasting leather on these gritty pavin'-stones,
An' the blasted Henglish drizzle wakes the fever in my
    bones ;
Tho' I walks with fifty 'ousemaids outer Chelsea to the
    Strand,
An' they talks a lot o' lovin', but wot do they under-
    stand?
        Beefy face an' grubby 'and—
        Law ! what do they understand?
        I've a neater, sweeter maiden in a cleaner,
           greener land !
        On the road to Mandalay . . .

Ship me somewheres east of Suez, where the best is like
    the worst,
Where there aren't no Ten Commandments an' a man
    can raise a thirst;
For the temple-bells are callin'; and it's there that I
    would be—
By the old Moulmein Pagoda, looking lazy at the sea;
      On the road to Mandalay,
      Where the old Flotilla lay,
      With our sick beneath the awnings when we
        went to Mandalay!

      O the road to Mandalay,
      Where the flyin'-fishes play,
      An' the dawn comes up like thunder outer
        China 'crost the Bay!

RICHARD LE GALLIENNE.

TO MY WIFE, MILDRED
(*October* 22, 1891)

Dear wife, there is no word in all my songs
But unto thee belongs :
Though I indeed before our true day came
Mistook thy star in many a wandering flame,
Singing to thee in many a fair disguise,
Calling to thee in many another's name
Before I knew thine everlasting eyes.

Faces that fled me like a hunted fawn
I followed singing, deeming it was Thou,
Seeking this face that on our pillow now
Glimmers behind thy golden hair like dawn,
And, like a setting moon, within my breast
Sinks down each night to rest.
Moon follows moon before the great moon flowers,
Moon of the wild, wild honey that is ours ;
Long must the tree strive up in leaf and root
Before it bear the golden-hearted fruit :
And shall great Love at once perfected spring,
Nor grow by steps like any other thing ?
The lawless love that would not be denied,
The love that waited, and in waiting died,
The love that met and mated, satisfied.

Ah, love, 'twas good to climb forbidden walls,
Who would not follow where his Juliet calls ?
'Twas good to try and love the angel's way,
With starry souls untainted of the clay ;
But best the love where earth and heaven meet
The God made flesh and dwelling in us, Sweet.

STEPHEN PHILLIPS.

FROM "MARPESSA"

[Marpessa, wooed by Apollo and Idas, determines to accept her
mortal lover.]

. . . .

"But if I live with Idas, then we two
On the low earth shall prosper, hand in hand,
In odours of the open field, and live
In peaceful noises of the farm, and watch
The pastoral fields burned by the setting sun.
And he shall give me passionate children, not
Some radiant god that will despise me quite,
But clambering limbs and little hearts that err.
And I shall sleep beside him in the night,
And, fearful from some dream, shall touch his hand,
Secure; or at some festival we two
Will wander through the lighted city streets;
And in the crowd I'll take his arm and feel
Him closer for the press.   So shall we live.
And though the first sweet sting of love be past
The sweet that almost venom is, though youth,
With tender and extravagant delight,
The first and secret kiss by twilight hedge,
The insane farewell repeated o'er and o'er,
Pass off; there shall succeed a faithful peace;
Beautiful friendship tried by sun and wind,
Durable from the daily dust of life.
And though with sadder, still with kinder eyes,
We shall behold all frailties, we shall haste
To pardon, and with mellowing minds to bless.
Then though we must grow old, we shall grow old
Together, and he shall not greatly miss
My faded bloom, and waning light of eyes,

Too deeply gazed in ever to seem dim ;
Nor shall we murmur at, nor much regret
The years that gently bend us to the ground,
And gradually incline our face ; that we
Leisurely stooping, and with each slow step,
May curiously inspect our lasting home.
But we shall sit with luminous holy smiles,
Endeared by many griefs, by many a jest,
And custom sweet of living side by side ;
And full of memories not unkindly glance
Upon each other.   Last, we shall descend
Into the natural ground—not without tears—
One must go first, ah God ! one must go first ;
After so long one blow for both were good ;
Still, like old friends, glad to have met, and leave
Behind a wholesome memory on the earth.
And thou, beautiful God, in that far time,
When in thy setting sweet thou gazest down
On this grey head, wilt thou remember then
That once I pleased thee, that I once was young ? "
When she had spoken, Idas with one cry
Held her, and there was silence ; while the God
In anger disappeared.   Then slowly they,
He looking downward, and she gazing up,
Into the evening green wandered away.

FROM "PAOLO AND FRANCESCA"

PAOLO.

I have fled from her ; have refused the rose,
Although my brain was reeling at the scent.
I have come hither as through pains of death ;
I have died, and I am gazing back at life.

Yet now it were so easy to return,
And run down the white road to Rimini!
And might I not return?

(*He starts up and looks at the towers, red with sunset.*)

Those battlements
Are burning! they catch fire, those parapets!
And through the blaze doth her white face look out
Like one forgot, yet possible to save.
Might I not then return? Ah, no! no! no!
For I should tremble to be touched by her,
And dread the music of her mere good-night
Howe'er I sentinelled my bosom, yet
That moment would arrive when instantly
Our souls would flash together in one flame,
And I should pour this torrent in her ear
And suddenly catch her to my heart.

FROM "HEROD"

GADIAS (*Interrupting*).

Lo! the chief builders, masons, engineers,
Who made at thy command the sea-coast ring
From Gaza northward unto Cæsarea.

CHIEF BUILDER.

O King, since thou wast sick all idle stands
In scaffolded and roofless interruption,
An unborn desolation of blank stone,
Bird-haunted as a dead metropolis.

HEROD.

I will create a city of my own ;
And therefore with sea-thwarting bastions
And mighty moles will make impregnable
That beach where Cæsarea shall arise.

(*He passes his hand over his brow.*)

How easy this ! Yet against flooding thoughts—

(*Turns to the Court.*)

Well, well, a harbour then for every nation,
Whereon shall ride the navies of the world.
There vessels from the sunset shall unlade ;
The harbour one vast bosom shall become
For towering galleons of the ocean weary ;
For driven things a place of rest. Rest—rest—
How easy this. Yet for the driven mind !

(*Suddenly.*)

Go, tell the queen that I would speak to her.

ALGERNON CHARLES SWINBURNE.

FROM "THE CASQUETTES"

All shores about and afar lie lonely,
  But lonelier are these than the heart of grief,
These loose-linked rivets of rock, whence only
  Looks one low tower from the sheer main reef,
With a blind wan face in the wild wan morning,
  With a live-lit flame on its brows by night,
That the lost may lose not its word's mute warning,
  And the blind by its grace have sight.

Here, walled in with the wide waste water,
  Grew the grace of a girl's lone life,
The sea's and the sea-wind's foster-daughter,
  And peace was hers in the main mid strife.
For her were the rocks clothed round with thunder
  And the crests of them carved by the storm-smith's
    craft :
For her was the mid-storm rent in sunder
  As with passion that wailed and laughed.

For her the sunrise kindled and scattered
  The red rose-leaflets of countless cloud :
It heard all round it the strong storms wrangle,
  Watched far past it the waste wrecks float.
But her soul was stilled by the sky's endurance,
  And her heart made glad with the sea's content,
And her faith waxed more in the sun's assurance
  For the winds that came and went.

Sweetness was brought for her forth of the bitter
    Sea's strength, and light of the deep sea's dark.
From where green lawns on Alderney glitter
    To the bastioned crags of the steeps of Sark.
These she knew from afar beholden,
    And marvelled haply what life would be
On moors that sunset and dawn leave golden,
    In dells that smile on the sea.

And forth she fared as a stout-souled rover,
    For a league-long raid on the bounding brine;
And light winds ferried her light bark over
    To the lone soft island of fair-limbed kine.
And her heart within her was vexed, and dizzy
    The sense of her soul, as a wheel that whirled:
She might not endure for a space that busy
    Loud coil of the troublous world.

Too full, she said, was the world of trouble,
    Too dense with noise of the things of earth;
And she turned her again to replenish with double
    Delight her desire of the things of her birth.
For joy grows loftier in air more lonely,
    Where only the sea's brood fain would be;
Where only the heart may receive in it only
    The love of the heart of the sea.

Time lay bound as in painless prison
    There, closed in with a strait small space:
Never thereon, as a strange light risen,
    Change had unveiled for her grief's far face.
Three white walls, flung out from the basement,
    Girt the width of the world, whereon,
Gazing at night from her frame-lit casement,
    She saw where the dark sea shone.

Hardly the breadth of a few brief paces,
   Hardly the length of a strong man's stride,
The small court, flower-lit with children's faces,
   Scarce held scope for a bird to hide.
Yet here was a man's brood reared and hidden
   Between the rocks and the tower and the foam,
Where peril and pity and peace were bidden
   As guests to the same sure home.

Here would pity keep watch for peril,
   And surety comfort his heart with peace,
No flower save one, where the reefs lie sterile,
   Gave of the seed of its heart's increase.
Pity and surety and peace most lowly
   Were the root and the stem and the bloom of the
      flower,
And the light and the breath of the buds kept holy
   That maid's else blossomless bower.

With never a leaf but the seaweed's tangle,
   Never a bird's but the sea-mew's note,
For her the blasts of the spring-tide shattered
   The strengths reluctant of waves back-bowed.
For her would winds in the mid-sky levy
   Bright wars that hardly the night bade cease :
At noon, when sleep on the sea lies heavy,
   For her would the sun make peace.

Peace rose crowned with the dawn on golden
   Lit leagues of triumph that flamed and smiled :
Peace lay lulled in the moon-beholden
   Warm darkness, making the world's heart mild.
For all the wide waves' troubles and treasons,
   One word only her soul's ear heard
Speak from stormless and storm-rent seasons,
   And nought save peace was the word.

All her life waxed large with the light of it,
    All her heart fed full on the sound :
Spirit and sense were exalted in sight of it,
    Compassed and girdled and clothed with it round.
Sense was none but a strong still rapture,
    Spirit was none but a joy sublime,
Of strength to curb and of craft to capture
    The craft and the strength of Time.

THE GARDEN OF PROSERPINE

Here, where the world is quiet ;
    Here, where all trouble seems
Dead winds' and spent waves' riot
    In doubtful dreams of dreams ;
I watch the green field growing
For reaping folk and sowing,
For harvest-time and mowing,
    A sleepy world of streams.

I am tired of tears and laughter,
    And men that laugh and weep ;
Of what may come hereafter,
    For men that sow to reap :
I am weary of days and hours,
Blown buds of barren flowers,
Desires and dreams and powers,
    And everything but sleep.

Here life has death for neighbour,
    And far from eye or ear
Wan waves and wet winds labour,
    Weak ships and spirits steer ;

They drive adrift and whither
They wot not who make thither;
But no such winds blow hither,
    And no such things grow here.

No growth of moor or coppice,
    No heather-flower or vine,
But bloomless buds of poppies,
    Green grapes of Proserpine,
Pale beds of blowing rushes,
Where no leaf blooms or blushes
Save this whereout she crushes
    For dead men deadly wine.

Pale, without name or number,
    In fruitless fields of corn,
They bow themselves and slumber
    All night till light is born;
And like a soul belated,
In hell and heaven unmated,
By cloud and mist abated
    Comes out of darkness morn.

Though one were strong as seven,
    He too with death shall dwell,
Nor wake with wings in heaven,
    Nor weep for pains in hell;
Though one were fair as roses,
His beauty clouds and closes
And well though love reposes,
    In the end it is not well.

Pale, beyond porch and portal,
    Crowned with calm leaves she stands,
Who gathers all things mortal
    With cold immortal hands;

Her languid lips are sweeter
Than love's who fears to greet her,
To men that mix and meet her
    From many times and lands.

She waits for each and other,
    She waits for all men born;
Forgets the earth her mother,
    The life of fruits and corn;
And spring and seed and swallow
Take wing for her and follow
Where summer song rings hollow,
    And flowers are put to scorn.

There go the loves that wither,
    The old loves with wearier wings;
And all dead years draw thither,
    And all disastrous things;
Dead dreams of days forsaken,
Blind buds that snows have shaken,
Wild leaves that winds have taken,
    Red strays of ruined springs.

We are not sure of sorrow,
    And joy was never sure;
To-day will die to-morrow:
    Time stoops to no man's lure;
And love, grown faint and fretful,
With lips but half regretful,
Sighs, and with eyes forgetful,
    Weeps that no loves endure.

From too much love of living,
    From hope and fear set free,
We thank with brief thanksgiving
    Whatever gods may be

That no life lives for ever;
That dead men rise up never;
That even the weariest river
    Winds somewhere safe to the sea.

There star nor sun shall waken,
    Nor any change of light:
Nor sound of waters shaken,
    Nor any sound or sight:
Nor wintry leaves nor vernal,
Nor days nor things diurnal;
Only the sleep eternal,
    In an eternal night.

THE MAKING OF MAN

Before the beginning of years
    There came to the making of man,
Time, with a gift of tears;
    Grief, with a glass that ran;
Pleasure, with pain for leaven;
    Summer, with flowers that fell;
Remembrance fallen from heaven,
    And madness risen from hell;
Strength without hands to smite;
    Love that endures for a breath;
Night, the shadow of light,
    And life, the shadow of death.

And the high gods took in hand
    Fire and the falling of tears;
And a measure of sliding sand
    From under the feet of the years;

And froth and drift from the sea ;
　　And dust of the labouring earth ;
And bodies of things to be
　　In the houses of death and birth ;
And wrought with weeping and laughter,
　　And fashioned with loathing and love,
With life before and after,
　　And death beneath and above,
For a day, and a night, and a morrow,
　　That his strength might endure for a span
With travail and heavy sorrow,
　　The holy spirit of man.

From the winds of the North and the South,
　　They gathered as unto strife ;
They breathed upon his mouth,
　　They filled his body with life ;
Eye-sight and speech they wrought
　　For the veils of the soul therein ;
A time for labour and thought,
　　A time to serve and to sin.
They gave him light in his ways,
　　And love, and a space for delight,
And beauty, and length of days,
　　And night, and sleep in the night.

His speech is a burning fire ;
　　With his lips he travaileth ;
In his heart is a blank desire ;
　　In his eyes foreknowledge of death.
He weaves and is clothed with derision ;
　　Sows, and he shall not reap ;
His life is a watch or a vision
　　Between a sleep and a sleep.

THE EARL OF CREWE.

"MILLET AND ZOLA"

("L'Angélus" and "La Terre")

Against the sunset glow they stand,
Two humblest toilers of the land,
Rugged of speech and rough of hand,
    Bowed down with tillage;
No grace of garb or circumstance
Invests them with a high romance,
Ten thousand such through fruitful France,
    In field and village.

The day's slow path from dawn to west
Has left them soil-bestained, distrest,
No thought beyond the nightly rest—
    New toil to-morrow;
Till solemnly the " Ave " bell
Rings out the sun's departing knell,
Borne by the breeze's rhythmic swell
    O'er swathe and furrow.

O lowly pair ! you dream it not,
Yet on your hard unlovely lot
That evening gleam of light has shot
    A glorious presage;
For prophets oft have yearned and kings
Have yearned in vain to know the things
Which to your simple spirits brings
    That curfew message.

.   .   .   .   .

Turn to the written page and read
In other strain the peasant's creed,
With satyr love and vampire greed,
      How hearts are tainted ;
Read to the end unmoved who can,
Read how the primal curse on man
May shape a fouler Caliban
      Than poet painted.

And this is Nature !   Be it so :
It needs a Master's hand to show
How through the man the brute may grow
      By Hell's own leaven :
We blame you not ; enough for us
Those two lone figures bending thus,
For whom that far-off Angelus
      Speaks Hope and Heaven.

ARTHUR E. J. LEGGE.

THE LOSING SIDE

Helmet and plume and sabre, banner and lance and
    shield,
Scattered in sad confusion over the trampled field ;
And a band of broken soldiers, with a weary, hopeless
    air,
With heads in silence drooping, and eyes of grim despair.
      Like foam-flakes left on the shifting sand
        In the track of the falling tide,
        On the ground where their cause has failed they
          stand,
          The last of the losing side.

Wisdom of age is vanquished, and generous hopes of
    youth,
Passion of faith and honour, fire of love and truth ;
And the plans that seemed the fairest in the fight have
    not prevailed,
The keenest blades are broken, and the strongest arms
    have failed.
      But souls that know not the breath of shame,
        And tongues that have never lied,
      And the truest hearts, and the fairest fame,
        Are here,—on the losing side.

The conqueror's crown of glory is set with many a gem,
But I join not in their triumph—there are plenty to
    shout for *them ;*

The cause is the most applauded whose warriors gain
    the day,
And the world's best smiles are given to the victors in
    the fray.
        But dearer to me is the darkened plain,
           Where the noblest dreams have died,
        Where hopes have been shattered and heroes slain
           In the ranks of the losing side.

WALTER WILSON GREG.

ON THE TOMB OF GUIDARELLO GUIDARELLI
AT RAVENNA

With peace at last and silent of all moan
   Far from the busy crowd that laughs and weeps,
In darkness and in stillness and alone,
   Here Guidarello Braccioforte sleeps ;
The secret tale, the polished marble stone
   Eloquently impenetrable keeps.

LAURENCE BINYON.

TRAFALGAR SQUARE

Slowly the dawn a magic paleness drew
    From windows dim; the Pillar, high in air,
Over dark statues and dumb fountains threw
    A shadow on the solitary square.

They that all night, dozing disquieted,
    Huddled together on the benches cold,
Now shrank apart, distrustful and unfed,
    And by the growing radiance unconsoled.

Then one, a woman, silently arose,
    And came to the broad fountain, brimming cool,
And over the stone margin leaning close,
    Dipped hands and bathed her forehead in the pool.

Now as the fresh drops ran upon her brow
    And her hands knotted up her hair, the ways
Of old lost mornings came to her, and how
    Into her mirror she would smile and gaze.

Then she was troubled; and looked down once more
    Into the glimmering water; and she seemed
The very depth of darkness to explore,
    If it might yield all that she feared and dreamed.

But that kind clouding mirror answered her
    With a soft answer, liquid mysteries
Of shadow, with a pale breeze just astir,
    Yielded only the brightness of her eyes.

It was herself; but O what magic wrought
  A presage round her, tender and obscure?
The water without stain refused her not:
  In that deep vision she rejoined the pure.

The dawn stole on, and from its buried place
  Rose in her bosom the sweet strength of youth;
She, the rejected, had no more disgrace:
  Her opening heart drew in a different truth.

She that had come past her last hope, and found
  Nothing beyond, and had shed no more tears,
But closing with dull ashes her first wound,
  Had trodden into the daily dust all fears;

She now began to wonder and to thrill
  Upon a new horizon; and the pain
Of hope began to quicken and to fill
  The world with strangeness and desire again.

O then I am not come quite to the end,
  She murmured, and life holds more than I knew,
Somewhere by seeking I may find a friend
  Perhaps, and something in this world be true.

Alone in this bright battle, whose fierce din
  Even now awakes round her defenceless lot,
Without home, friend, comfort or peace within,
  The very stones might weep her.   She weeps not;

But as a plant, that under parching drought
  Thirsted and drooped and daily heavier grew,
Rises afresh to the soft showering south,
  She lifts her forehead to the sun anew.

And in her spirit a still fountain springs
  Deeper than hunger, faith crying for life,
That to her eyes an inward clearness brings,
  And to her heart courage for any strife.

DOUGLAS AINSLIE.

LINES PREFIXED TO "ST. JOHN OF DAMASCUS"

" Worshipper of the Sun and Moon
and the Evening Star this people was,
before we brought the priceless boon
and held before its eyes the Cross."

Thus speak the priests of every creed
and the Old God's perish as is due,
and the New triumph, till indeed
these new are old and men make new.
But always as the old creed wanes
her votaries will linger yet,
and though Lord Christ in Heaven reigns,
Queen Venus they will not forget.
See them steal forth at still of eve,
alert while all the world is sleeping ;
see the stained altar, see them weave
her mystic wreaths while she is peeping
through the pale cloud.   Just so one day
the tale of Christ a tale of Fairy
to the new men will seem when they
to Venus shall have added Mary
among the myths of old : they smile
handling the crown of thorns ; for them
the Christian legend will beguile
an idle hour, the azure hem
of Mary's robe, the Cherubim,
the glistening glories of the sainted
are but old fancies growing dim
as fade the marvels Vinci painted.

2 O

Thus of the world in man's first youth ;
he wanders on until arrested
he stands before the temple Truth
built on the hill-top olive-crested.
He kneels, and glowing there between
the white slim columns of her shrine ;
perfect, implacable, serene,
dawns upon him the queen divine.
Then says the world : "An empty shell
for the true goddess you have taken ;
long ages past the old faith fell
and the marble temple was forsaken ;
you are a man now and behold
these things are really worth the scheming :
science and power and art and gold
and women fairer than your dreaming."
And as the pagan with the priest,
so manhood spurns his boyhood's god
vowing he cares nor knows the least
where winds the hilly path he trod.
But when the field of youth is mown
and earlier his evening closes,
lo ! he steals trembling forth alone
to deck the scornèd shrine with roses,
and weeping in the sacred place,
see him recant his blasphemies :
iron-grey his hair and in his face
engraven the world's miseries.

O Goddess, grant him kneeling here,
pilgrim and penitent of youth,
vision ineffable to appear—
that art religion, love and truth.